The Amish

IN THEIR OWN WORDS

The Amish

IN THEIR OWN WORDS

Amish writings
from 25 years of
Family Life magazine

Compiled by
Brad Igou

Herald
Press

Scottdale, Pennsylvania
Waterloo, Ontario

Library of Congress Cataloging-in-Publication Data
The Amish in their own words : Amish writings from 25 years of Family life
  magazine / compiled by Brad Igou.
     p. cm.
  Includes bibliographical references.
  ISBN 0-8361-9123-4 (alk. paper)
  1. Amish—Social life and customs. 2. Mennonite Church.
I. Igou, Brad, 1951- .
BX8129.A5A43 1999
289.7'3—dc21   99-22217

Unless otherwise noted, Scripture is adapted from the *King James Version of
the Holy Bible* or Luther's *Bibel*. Some is from the *Good News Bible*—Old
Testament: copyright © American Bible Society 1976; New Testament: copyright © American Bible Society 1966, 1971, 1976.

These excerpts from *Family Life* magazine, Pathway Publishers, Route 4,
Aylmer, Ontario, are gratefully used and adapted by permission.

To my parents and Abner

Contents

Foreword

BACK IN 1967 the coming of a new magazine called *Family Life* was announced in *The Budget* (a weekly newspaper read by the Amish). The ads sounded interesting, so I decided to be among the charter subscribers. I was not disappointed when I received the first issue of *Family Life* in January 1968. In the thirty years since then, I have kept, preserved, and organized every issue.

I initially subscribed to *Family Life* to learn more about the Amish. Certainly one can get an in-depth, inside look at the Amish from this magazine in a way that cannot be realized by reading an Amish-related novel or a sociological study on the Amish. Indeed, *Family Life* portrays the Amish "in their own words." On history, theology, and church practices, it publishes material from the perspective of the Amish themselves, not a reinterpretation. We hear "right from the horse's mouth" why the Old Order people drive buggies, not cars; why they wear plain clothing, not the fashions of the world; why they do not pose for photographs; and why they sing traditional slow hymn tunes.

Family Life articles demonstrate the unique approach the Amish have taken to keep themselves "unspotted from the world" (James 1:27). Unlike much literature written about the Amish by outsiders, *Family Life* does not put the Amish on a pedestal or on a dissecting table, nor does it present them as a mission field. "In their own words," they come through as real, down-to-earth people, with both strengths and weaknesses.

The Amish have proscribed television, radio, and other electronic media, to limit the corrupting influences coming into the home. They enjoy the simple pleasures of reading and writing as primary pastimes. The art of letter writing is still much alive among the Old Order Plain People. Community news is shared in *The Budget* or *Die Botschaft*, weekly newspapers sharing letters from the various Old Order communities.

Family Life and the other two publications from Pathway Publishers, *Young Companion* and *Blackboard Bulletin*, are immensely popular among the Amish and other Plain People. They fill a need for wholesome literature reflecting their own values. The appearance of these magazines is characteristic of their makers and readers—plain and simple. There are no glossy color photos, no fancy graphics, just straightforward text and simple line drawings, but without human faces, in accord with Amish teachings.

Although the target audience of *Family Life* is the Old Order Plain People (both Amish and Mennonites), many of the articles speak to any human, especially those who are trying to sincerely follow God. Inspirational articles, stories of physical and emotional struggles, and discussions about marriage and child rearing—they all reflect an Amish perspective. Yet these insights can be appreciated by anyone not confined by modern theological and psychological trends.

Family Life is an appropriate title for an Amish magazine. Amish life certainly does revolve around the family, and daily life is as consequential to one's faith as intangible beliefs. The church and the family are inseparable. The family abode is the house of worship, and daily living is an expression of doctrine. The size of an Amish community is measured by the number of families, not the number of individual members.

Over the years, it has been my privilege to get to know quite well the producers of *Family Life* at Pathway Publishers. They are solidly Old Order Amish and are dedicated to promoting true biblical discipleship. To these devout Christians, the Amish faith is not bound to dead traditions. Instead, it is a living faith that meets the challenges of contemporary society and is equipped with the godly traditions of their forebears to stabilize and guide them. They do not blindly accept the old ways. Rather, they scrutinize "the way we always did it" to discern if time-honored customs and practices are truly ancient church traditions or comparatively recent departures from the faith.

Family Life does not try to hide the fact that the Amish have some real problems, some quite serious in anyone's book. The magazine has met these problems head-on, in an effort to bring about moral reforms in Amish communities. Such efforts have been much appreciated in many communities where changes for the better have been made in recent years.

I have often referred to *Family Life* and referred others to its articles for information about a variety of different topics. Since there is no cumulative topical index, finding the right article in one of over three hundred issues can be quite difficult. *The Amish in Their Own Words* makes the rich material that has appeared in *Family Life* accessible both to those already familiar with the publication and those who will be introduced to it through this book.

In every issue, the pages of *Family Life* carry something for every member of the family, covering topics on many facets of life. The same is true of this compilation. Brad Igou has done a fine job in selecting a wide range of material from the first twenty-five years of *Family Life*.

—*Stephen Scott, Author of books on the Old Order Plain People
   Young Center, Elizabethtown College*

Preface

"I JUST SAW my first horse and buggy!" So exclaimed a visitor from Australia while walking along the street in the village of Intercourse, Lancaster County, Pennsylvania.

The Amish may sometimes wonder what causes that special fascination visitors seem to have for them. At first, it is the physical and tangible indicators of their faith—the horse and carriage, the plain way of dress, farming with horses, and so on. Some visitors still think the Amish are really locals paid to dress up and live this way to attract tourists.

The Amish are real, of course, and visitors are naturally fascinated that any group of people living in America would choose to live so differently, without the cars, computers, televisions, and other trappings of our technologically advanced society. Amish children walking home from the one-room school, or farmers plowing the fields with horses—these scenes seem to come from another time and place. On a misty morning, the landscape takes on a dreamy, otherworldly atmosphere.

After the excitement of "seeing my first buggy," sensitive visitors start to ponder exactly *who* the Amish are and *why* they live as they do. Some are surprised to discover that "Amish" is the name of a religion, and that they are Christians and not members of some commune or cult. Others want to visit an Amish farm, walk through an Amish home, or stop and talk to the people themselves. Few ever have the chance to do so. With millions of visitors coming every year and about twenty thousand Amish in Lancaster County, each Amish person would need to "entertain" several hundred guests a year!

Other visitors come mainly to look at the Amish and take photographs. Few of us would care to be photographed and stared at while going about our daily lives. But the Amish do live in a fishbowl. They do not seek the attention of the world around them. Yet the world seems endlessly fascinated and drawn to their way of life.

Even the local newspapers often put the word *Amish* in their headlines, such as "Amish Boys Cited for Underage Drinking." I can imagine the public outcry if the word *Catholic* or *Jewish* were put in similar headlines! Photographs of the Amish frequently appear on the front pages of the paper. How many of us would stand up to such scrutiny? Yet most of the Amish understand the curiosity visitors have for their way of life.

Many books have been written about the Amish, and no year goes by without several new ones being published. The Amish continue to be the subject of Hollywood movies, from *Witness* to *Kingpin* and *For Richer or Poorer*. They are often the subject of TV shows, from *Picket Fences* to *Harvest of Fire* (Hallmark Hall of Fame) and *Murder She Wrote*.

With the exception of the occasional documentary, these portrayals of the Amish tend to range from fairly accurate to ridiculous, offensive, or sensational. The media have spread many false ideas about the Amish. They suffer from being portrayed as ignorant country bumpkins or as saintly people living in utopia. They are, of course, neither.

The problem then is to see the Amish as they are, as real people, as our friends and neighbors. Like other church members, there are good and not-so-good Amish. Like other Americans and Canadians, they sometimes make mistakes, fail to live up to their faith, suffer criticism and ridicule, worry about how to raise their children, and have doubts about themselves. Yet, for anyone who has spent a few hours sitting and talking with the Amish, there is also something special about the experience.

After observing and talking to many visitors, I wondered if there were a way to give people a better idea of what the Amish are like as people. I wanted readers to see them not as a monolithic group, but as individuals, families, and communities, living in various settlements in the USA and Canada. Certainly the last thing the world needs is another book about the Amish, or the personal writings of non-Amish people whose lives were changed because of their Amish friends.

While living on an Amish farm, I began to read some publications from a place called Pathway Publishers in Ontario, Canada. This Amish publishing house produces three monthly magazines and many books. The Amish do the writing and manage the company, something unusual. These publications solicit articles and letters from Old Order Amish and Old Order Mennonites all over the United States and Canada.

The Pathway periodicals are unlike *The Budget* (Sugarcreek, Ohio) or *Die Botschaft* (Lancaster, Pa.), newspapers that mainly give short news reports from local communities. Instead, Pathway has tackled areas such as religious interpretation, social issues, and problems of readers. There are articles on church history, church controversies, and even personal problems. Through these three magazines, I discovered a way to "meet" hundreds of Amish and hear their thoughts.

The *Blackboard Bulletin* centers on schools and advice for teachers and parents. The *Young Companion* is for young people and offers stories and advice relevant to them as they move toward deciding to join the Amish faith.

Family Life, however, is the magazine that appealed to me the most. In its pages I came to see the Amish as they are, trying to deal with daily problems, applying their faith in a difficult modern world, and sometimes disagreeing with each other on how to do it. I relished the humor revealed in some of the articles, and other times the touching stories moved me to tears.

From this, an idea hatched. I decided to read through the first twenty-five years of this monthly magazine, select a broad range of articles, pull them together in an organized fashion, and make a book. Thus, rather than some outsider writing *about* the Amish, the Amish at last speak *for themselves*. You, the reader, can hear these Amish voices, not from hundreds of years ago, but from today, as we move with them into the twenty-first century.

Here, then, is a book about the Amish, written by the Amish. Though I have selected the material, I have tried to keep myself out of it as much as possible, so that the Amish may emerge with their own character rather than as "odd" or "saintly."

To include more selections, I have edited many longer articles and condensed some stories, always trying not to destroy the style and message of the writer. I have given the Pathway editorial staff an opportunity to check the results and make sure meanings are not altered. Sometimes articles are so compelling, informative, or well-written that I included them whole.

In the following pages, sensitive readers will learn many details of Amish life and religious customs. They also will hear the very human and deep thoughts these people have in their daily lives. Many excerpts are anonymously written or signed only with initials. Most Amish are not likely to engage in intense self-analysis or bare their souls to others. As they wrote their feelings, I believe many found a wonderful outlet for their personal concerns. Some people think the Amish are rather stoic; these writings, however, are filled with emotion, joy, and sorrow.

I thank all of these known and unknown contributors whose writings I chose to be part of this project. I trust their words may be educational and inspirational. Certain writers on the editorial staff contributed articles on a monthly basis from the magazine's inception. About 75 percent of this book consists of their thoughtful, distinctive writing. They include David Wagler, Joseph Stoll, David Luthy, and Elmo Stoll.

One friend (who happens to be Amish) must be singled out. He let me visit him once a week and read through back issues of *Family Life*. I worked the Amish way, writing things down by hand and only occasionally taking longer articles to be photocopied. He offered encouragement, friendship, and snacks to keep me going. His spoken words and the words from *Family Life* helped me continue the long process of reading through thousands of pages and then typing everything into the computer. More important, during all this, we became great friends, and I try to continue my weekly visits. Thank you, Abner!

Pathway publisher David Luthy wrote me from time to time to ask how the project was going. I went through long dry spells when nothing seemed to be happening. The words of Elmo Stoll helped to push me and became a personal motto: "A person's devotion to an idea is not tested until the newness has worn off, until the challenge has lost its initial excitement, and the fun and glamour have faded. Then, when only hard work remains—the daily tasks, the mundane labor—that is when a person's commitment to a project is truly tested."

To David Garber and everyone at Herald Press, thank you for believing that the book has an audience. My sincere appreciation for all the personal care, help, and professionalism with which the entire publishing process was carried out.

There are many other people with whom I shared bits and pieces of this book as it developed. Their greatly appreciated comments and interest encouraged me and helped convince me to keep going.

Finally, in a book gleaned from a magazine called *Family Life*, special thanks go to my mother and father, who have always encouraged and supported me, even when not always agreeing with me. They have taught me in human terms what unconditional love is all about.

Now I hope that you, the reader, will come to see beneath the surface, into the lives and thoughts of the Amish. Some of them have challenged me with their silence, shown their affection through simple acts, and shared their problems and laughter. By accepting me as I am, they have taught me the dangers of judging those who are different or imposing my values on others. They have unwittingly guided me down many of life's paths, not just by words, but also by their actions and their example.

In these pages you will understand, think, laugh, cry, and be touched in a personal way by these individuals, a people at once ordinary and extraordinary, a people focused not so much on this world but on the next. I hope that you, too, will come to call them friends.

—*Brad Igou*
Lancaster, Pennsylvania

About the Selections

I have grouped the hundreds of selections into chapters by topics. They are not in chronological order, but arranged by subject matter to flow logically from one to another. My own brief introductory remarks precede each chapter and some selections, in distinctive type. When words of explanation or summary are needed within the quoted articles, they appear in square brackets [like this].

Titles have been copied or supplied from ideas in the articles. A pen name, like a signature, appears at the end of a piece, such as "Puzzled." In parentheses following each selection, the reader will see any column title ("Letter" means "Letters to the Editor"), author's name if known (first initial and last name for writers-editors: David Wagler, Joseph Stoll, David Luthy, and Elmo Stoll [who died on Sept. 2, 1998]), where the writer lives if known, and the magazine month and year. For example, 7-83 means the July 1983 issue. A writer who asks for name and address to be withheld will be shown as anonymous (Anon.).

Almost all the writers are Old Order Amish, who sometimes use the term "English" to refer to the non-Amish. About a dozen shorter pieces are by Old Order Mennonites. Nevertheless, their writings would not be in *Family Life* if they were not in keeping with Amish values.

Family Life continues to be published. You may wish to subscribe for your own family and friends or even to write a letter or article for it.

To obtain subscription rates or information about periodicals, write to Pathway Publishers, Route 4, Aylmer, ON N5H 2R3, Canada.

To obtain a Pathway Book Catalog or to order books favored by the Amish, write to Pathway Bookstore, 2580N 250W, LaGrange, IN 46761, USA.

1
What Is *Family Life?*

The year 1992 marked the 25th year of the Amish publication *Family Life*. It started in 1968 as a monthly magazine "dedicated to the promotion of Christian living among the plain people, with special emphasis on the appreciation of our heritage." At that time, the staff of writers-editors consisted of David Wagler, assisted by Joseph Stoll, David Luthy, Elmo Stoll, and Sarah Weaver. They estimated they would need 4,000 subscribers for a 40-page magazine, or 5,000 for 50 pages. The subscription price then was $4.00 a year.

The April 1969 issue was mailed to 8,149 homes, and to 113 bookstores for resale, in 38 states, four Canadian provinces, and nine foreign countries, including Germany, Australia, and Japan. The states of Pennsylvania, Ohio, and Indiana received the most.

By March 1982, *Family Life* was being sent to over 13,000 homes in 45 states, eight Canadian provinces, and 13 foreign countries, including India as well as Central and South America. In 1992, paid circulation was 19,000, and by 1998 more than 23,000.

In January 1968, the editors at Pathway Publishing in Aylmer, Ontario, began the first issue of their new magazine with this question:

What Is *Family Life*?

Family Life is the name of the magazine you are holding in your hands. But it is much more. The family is the heart of the community and the church. Even a nation is made up of families. If there is a strong family life, then the church, the community, and the nation will be likewise. If family life degenerates, then all will suffer.

Family life must be translated into terms of everyday living. What can we do to the community? Do we realize that our everyday work should be a God-given opportunity to serve him? Can we appreciate and make the most of the everyday blessings we receive? Do we stop to enjoy God's creation all around us, and the works of his fingers?

This is the goal of *Family Life*—to be an instrument through which thoughts and ideas can be transmitted.

Do not feel that the *Family Life* writers or editors pretend to be experts in this field. Indeed, we often need the helps and inspirations offered in these pages as much as anyone. We hope that by sharing our cupful of oil, it will be increased even as that of the poor widow of Zarephath (see 1 Kings 17:10-16).   (1-68)

Across the Editor's Desk

There is no way of accurately telling the sources of material contributed for *Family Life*. Regarding material arriving from outside the Pathway office, we estimate that it has come from the following writers: 60 percent from Old Order Amish, 30 percent from Old Order Mennonites, and 10 percent from selected or other sources. The Old Order Mennonites, with about 10 percent of the subscribers, are contributing about 30 percent of the material sent in. We appreciate this but can't help wondering what would happen if our Amish readers would send in as much material per subscriber as do the Old Order Mennonites.   (5-76)

We [the editors] are all Old Order Amish, and most of our contributors are either Amish or from related "horse and buggy" groups of plain people.   (10-88)

Practically everything that goes into *Family Life* is checked carefully by a minister. If it is a doctrinal article or one that is controversial, we like to have several ministers or bishops look it over. After it is published, it goes into nearly every community of plain folks in the United States and Canada. Anyone who finds anything misleading has the privilege and the responsibility to inform us of it. We have this confidence in our readers that they will let us know if there is anything that will be a hindrance to anyone. Of course, there is often a difference of opinion on some matters due to the fact that no person has a full understanding of any subject.

First Corinthians 13:9 says that we know only in part, but that the time shall come when our knowledge is perfect, but not in this life.

                    (7-72)

The stories in *Family Life* are either true stories or true-to-life stories. Sometimes a writer takes incidents from the lives of different people and puts them together in one story. The characters in true-to-life stories often make us say, "That's just like someone I used to know."   (1-72)

We once received a story from a man. It sounded so true-to-life that we thought it probably was a true happening. How surprised we

were when the man added at the end of the story, "As far as I know, none of this story is true." We wondered for a moment how he could have written a story that was so real, so true-to-life, if he got it all from his imagination. But then we saw that he had added, "Please do not sign my name, or my relatives will think I wrote this story about them." The story may not have been true in details, but was true in the ways that really mattered. In attitudes, problems, failures, and habits portrayed, it was true, *too* true.   (1-74)

I wonder how many of our readers realize how much time and effort goes into each of the historical articles that appear in Family Life. The historical editor is constantly working on many different projects at the same time and corresponding with hundreds of people. In this way, bits of information are being discovered and assembled on the various topics until there is enough for a whole article on one subject.   (8/9-75)

In November 1968, a subscriber wrote to say that there were too many "pat-your-own-back" articles, letters from readers saying how much they like the magazine. The editors agreed and decided not to print letters saying nice things about the magazine, but only comments on particular articles.

In March 1968, a reader wrote to say that because of all his farmwork, he didn't have time to read everything in *Family Life*. There simply was too much. The editors answered by saying, "If you are too busy to read it, then you're too busy."

Yet another lady explained that she feared she might be neglecting her Bible reading because of the publication. This prompted the editors to respond, "If reading our papers makes you neglect the Bible, we hope you will cancel your subscription."

2
The Amish Story
Turbulent Beginnings

The story of the Amish religion begins in Zurich, Switzerland, following Martin Luther's historic Reformation. The emergence in 1525 of the Swiss Brethren or Anabaptists, forebears of the Mennonites and the Amish, is a history as compelling and inspiring as can be found anywhere. Beliefs in adult baptism and separation of church and state were viewed as a threat both to Zwingli's Reformed Church and to the local government, with which it was allied. Thousands of these "radicals" were put to death in the following years.

Accounts of their individual stories are found in books like the *Martyrs Mirror* (in print from 1660) and the *Ausbund* (songs from 1535, in print from 1564), the hymnal used in Amish worship services. These are stories of pacifism and persecution, love and peace amidst hatred and violence, a testimony to faith and survival at horrible costs. Upon arriving in America, the Amish faith grew and prospered, with each generation finding new and different challenges forced upon them by the times.

Four Centuries with the *Ausbund*

Felix Manz was born in 1498 in Zurich, Switzerland. He received a very good education, and when Zwingli founded his Reformed Church, Felix joined him. But it was not long before Felix felt Zwingli had not broken far enough away from the Catholic Church, especially concerning baptism. Because Zwingli continued to baptize babies, Felix and some others broke away and founded a church in which only adults were baptized. He was the first of the Swiss Brethren to give his life for the faith [in a Reformed area. Bolt Eberli was burned at the stake in a Catholic canton, May 29, 1525].

Felix was drowned in January 5, 1527, by order of the Zurich city authorities. He and Conrad Grebel are considered the founders of the Anabaptist movement in Switzerland, and our Amish churches today can count him a forefather in faith.

Georg Blaurock's life could fill a book, as it was very eventful. It should suffice to say that he was a Catholic monk who joined the Anabaptists in the early years of the movement. He was baptized by Conrad Grebel and was a fellow worker with him and Felix Manz. Georg was a forceful and eloquent preacher, and very zealous. Many times he was cast into prison, punished, and banished, yet he remained true to the faith. He died a martyr's death in 1529, being burned at the stake.   ("Yesterdays and Years," D. Luthy, 6-71)

Children of Martyrs

We plain people often refer to our ancestors, the Anabaptists. Willingly, they offered up their lives and accepted death. Hardly a sermon is preached in our churches today without some mention being made of our forebears and what they suffered.

Many of our homes have a copy of the *Martyrs Mirror*, well over a thousand pages, telling us about our ancestors in the faith, how they suffered, what they believed, and why they died. Yet we are so busy with our daily work that we seldom find time or interest to read this monumental book.

Take Michael Sattler, for instance. His story is only one of the hundreds in the *Martyrs Mirror*. His sentence has been recorded for us, preserved down through the years: "Judgment is passed that Michael Sattler shall be delivered to the executioner, who shall cut out his tongue, then throw him upon a wagon, and tear his body twice with red-hot tongs; and after he has been brought without the gate, he shall be pinched five times in the same manner."

Notice that they took out his tongue at the outset. The martyrs were famous for letting their tongues be heard during their last moments. They would shout aloud to their fellow believers, or they would entreat their persecutors to think seriously about what they were doing.

So the first thing the judges decreed was that Michael Sattler be relieved of his tongue. Then, bring on the hot tongs.

With these preliminaries taken care of, Michael was sentenced to be burned alive. They tied him to a wooden stake, binding him hand and foot.

However, Michael's testimony was not to be hindered by the loss of his tongue. He had told fellow believers beforehand that if he still remained faithful to God, he would lift two fingers aloft for a sign.

As the flames leapt around him, as the heat scorched his body and the pain seared him mercilessly, Michael must have struggled with almost superhuman strength to retain consciousness. At last the ropes that bound his wrists were severed. Mustering his faltering strength, he lifted his arm aloft, two fingers outstretched toward heaven. There can be no doubt: the final act of Michael Sattler inspired and breathed courage and renewed boldness into more onlookers than any mere words his tongue could have uttered.

("Views and Values," E. Stoll, 8/9-87)

Four Centuries with the *Ausbund*

By 1535, the religious awakening in Europe had for more than a decade been affecting Moravia [later part of Czechoslovakia; since 1992 part of the Czech Republic]. Living in Moravia were some Anabaptist refugees from Bavaria [a part of South Germany] who had fled there to escape death because of their religious views. But during the summer, a decision was made to attempt returning to their homes in Bavaria. So a group of sixty Anabaptists left Moravia in August and traveled along the Danube River. They had barely set foot inside Bavarian territory when they were captured by the Catholic authorities from the city of Passau. They were taken to the bishop's castle in Passau and imprisoned in the castle's dungeons.

Hans Betz was born in Eger, Bavaria, and was a weaver by trade. He was a gifted man with words, as can be seen in the twelve songs he wrote. Little is known about his life except that he was an Anabaptist minister and that he died while held captive in the Passau castle. He was not sentenced to death, but he likely died as a result of torture, in 1537.

Michael Schneider was a fellow prisoner with Hans Betz. He was the leader of the prisoners, serving as their bishop. Not much is known of his life, except that he was born in Bruchsal, Baden [the state next to Bavaria], and that his wife was also a prisoner in the Passau castle dungeons. His initials are found after eleven songs in the *Ausbund*. The records do not show that Michael died in prison, so he likely was released with fellow prisoners in 1540.

None of the Anabaptist prisoners in the Passau castle were condemned to death. But many were tortured and died as a result of this and their miserable living conditions in the dungeons. A few gave up their faith entirely, but most remained steadfast. In 1540, five years after their capture, the prisoners who were yet alive were released.

("Yesterdays and Years," D. Luthy, 6-71)

Children of Martyrs

We are children of martyrs! That phrase sets us apart from other people. There's only one problem. If we do not have the spirit of the martyrs, but shrink from hardships, from self-denial, from sacrifice, from a life of discipline and restraint—then the martyrs were not our forebears at all, and we are not their children.

If we have the spirit of this world, loving ease and pleasure and luxury and leisure, we are the children of the prince of this world [John 12:31]. We are only deceiving ourselves if we then talk of the martyrs as being our ancestors. The simple truth is, unless we follow in their footsteps, we are not their children.

("Views and Values," E. Stoll, 8/9-87)

The Amish Division of 1693

Nearly every Amish person can likely tell you that the Mennonites got their name from Menno Simons, but fewer realize where their own name, *Amish*, comes from. The explanation for this is quite simple: Menno Simons was a writer and his writings are still used in Amish homes, but Jacob (Jakob) Ammann wasn't a writer, and thus his name is seldom seen in print. Today he might be called a silent figure in history. But in 1693, his name was a common word in Mennonite homes in Europe.

In Europe during the 1600s, there were five areas where most of the Mennonites lived: Switzerland, Alsace, northern Germany, southern Germany, and Holland. [Alsace is a region between France, Germany, and Switzerland; it passed between French and German control several times.] Holland was the first to experience a serious church division. This occurred in 1557 and again in 1567, and somewhat affected the Mennonites living in North Germany.

By 1632, serious attempts were made to heal the breach in the Mennonite churches of Holland. A number of ministers came together in the city of Dort, Holland, and drew up a confession of faith upon which they could all agree. This is what we today call the "Dordrecht Confession of Faith," the "18 Articles of Faith," or the "Glaubensbekenntnis." Before baptism, everyone asking to be an Amish church member must be in agreement with this confession of faith.

(D. Luthy, 10-71)

The Decisions We Make

In 1632, the Dutch Mennonites gathered at Dordrecht [Dordt, Dort] in Holland and reached agreement on eighteen basic articles of doctrine, which we know as the Dordrecht Confession of Faith. These Mennonites, we believe, still held and practiced the doctrines of the earlier Anabaptists of the preceding century, when Menno Simons and Dirk Philips were living. These were Dutch Mennonites and not the group of [Swiss Brethren Anabaptist] churches that later came to be known as Amish.

At the time the Dordrecht Confession was drawn up, many of the Dutch Mennonites were already becoming wealthy and adapting themselves to the ways and wisdom of the world. During the next sixty years, the Dutch Mennonites rapidly changed their thought and practices. In the end, it was the churches of Alsace and southern Germany who were best able to retain the original faith of the Anabaptists as summarized in the eighteen articles of the Dordrecht Confession. [These churches in Alsace and southern Germany were composed largely of Swiss Brethren Anabaptists who had fled persecution in Switzerland.]   ("Now That I Think of It," D. Wagler, 4-92)

The Amish Division of 1693

Thirty-three years later in Alsace (1693), the Amish division took place largely because the Dordrecht Confession of Faith was accepted in 1660. It is a strange but true fact that the confession which was meant to unify Mennonites in Holland proved to be a wedge for division in other parts of Europe. Why the situation came to a crisis in 1693 centers on two Mennonite bishops, Hans Reist (in the Emmental, Switzerland] and Jacob Ammann [in the Alsace].

(D. Luthy, 10-71)

Lost Names Among the Amish

Only a few facts are known about Jacob Ammann's family. He had at least two children: a daughter, whose name is unknown, left the Amish in 1730 and joined the state church; and a son, Baltz, who in 1741 inherited his father's *Psalmenbuch*. What became of Jacob Ammann's descendants is not known. The name *Ammann* means "a bailiff, an officer having custody of prisoners brought into court."

[Jacob Ammann likely migrated from Switzerland to Alsace around 1690 because of new government mandates against the Swiss Brethren. He was a resident in Upper Alsace from about 1694 and signed petitions or lists there in 1696, 1704, and 1708 (*Mennonite Encyclopedia*, 1:98).]

(D. Luthy, 4-84)

The Amish Division of 1693

The first difference between the two bishops [elders Jacob Ammann and Hans Reist] seems to have been on the holding of communion. Traditionally, the Mennonites had held communion once a year, but Jacob Ammann began holding it twice a year [frequency not specified in Dordrecht Confession]. Hans Reist did not feel this was necessary. Bishop Reist had to call in "strange [outside] ministers" to settle the matter [the innovation was permitted].

When Jacob Ammann heard that two ministers were going to the Reist congregation on "church business," he asked them to talk with Reist concerning the subject of shunning [as in Dordrecht Confession, art. 17]. From this time on, no mention was made of the communion question; attention was now focused on the question of shunning.

Hans Reist was a bishop of Switzerland. Jacob Ammann had been born in Switzerland, but by 1693 was residing in Alsace. The Swiss ministers had never agreed to the 1632 Dordrecht Confession of Faith as had their brethren in Alsace in 1660. Why Jacob Ammann felt it was his duty to force the issue with the Swiss ministry is a hard question to answer. Modern Mennonite historians have repeatedly tried to put the blame on Jacob Ammann's shoulders. Although much of it belongs there, behind him stood a united Alsace ministry of nineteen men. Without their support, he would never have been able to seriously oppose the Swiss ministry.

There were other issues which had made the Alsace ministers lose confidence in their Swiss Brethren. Certain Swiss ministers were preaching that the "true-hearted" people, who did not join the Mennonites but were sympathetic to them, would be saved. Also, there was the question of banning people who lied. The Alsace ministers felt this was very serious. Involved, too, was plain and uniform dress—the Swiss being liberal and the people in Alsace strict. The Swiss allowed the trimming of the beard, and the ministers from Alsace did not. Finally, there was the matter of members attending services in the state church. The Swiss were allowing it, and their brethren in Alsace thought this was a serious mistake.

[Ammann called two meetings of the ministers on both sides, but Hans Reist did not come to either. The second time he said he was too busy with the harvest.]

This seemingly indifferent attitude of Bishop Reist was too much for Jacob Ammann. After stating six charges against Reist, he excommunicated him. Then, turning to the Swiss ministers present, he asked them how they stood on the shunning question. Those who said they agreed with Hans Reist were excommunicated.

[In fall 1693, Mennonite ministers in the Palatinate of Germany supported the Swiss ministers. Ammann said the Palatine ministers also would be excommunicated and put under the ban if they did not confess the disputed article of faith (Dordrecht, art. 17).]

The division was now complete. Out of 22 ministers in Alsace, 20 sided with Jacob Ammann. In southern Germany, he had but six out of 25 ministers on his side, and in Switzerland only one out of 20. Jacob Ammann's followers then became known as the ["Amish Mennonites," shortened to] "Amish."

[There were three attempts to get the two sides back together—fall 1693; spring 1694; and 1700, when Ammann and several other Amish ministers humbly "offered to excommunicate themselves temporarily from the fellowship as a sign of their repentance" if the Reist group would accept shunning (J. D. Roth in Letters of the Amish Division, Goshen, Ind.: Mennonite Historical Society, 1993). The Reist group kept their distance and also did not agree to foot washing at communion, as taught by the Dordrecht Confession, art. 11.]

After 1700, no attempts were made to reunite the two groups. It wasn't long before the Swiss Mennonites were emigrating to America, and the Amish [Mennonites] were leaving Alsace for the same destination. Even in this new frontier, the two groups remained separate. [Yet in the late 1800s, Amish "progressive" elements were on a path toward uniting with the Mennonites, and did so by 1927; see below.]   (D. Luthy, 10-71)

The Decisions We Make

Although a church division resulted, Ammann was successful in getting the majority of the churches in that region to join him in a move toward greater discipline and strictness, and in a closer adherence to the Dordrecht Confession.

We can sum up the beliefs and concerns of the Amish group as follows:

1. Adherence to the eighteen articles of the Dordrecht Confession of 1632.

2. Additional standards and restrictions were needed in dress and modes of living, to keep worldly trends out of the church.

3. Resistance to change, not only in church administration, but also in everyday living. It is essential that the church be resistant to change, and consent to it only when there is a clear and definite need (and then only if it is the right direction).

4. A solid foundation to ensure the continuity of the church without depending upon any certain person or persons. If our bishop or ministers are called away in death tomorrow, we should have the confidence that others will fill the empty places and the church will be able to continue.   ("Now That I Think of It," D. Wagler, 4-92)

Nine Points of Difference

In studying the letters and other history of the Amish division, it becomes clear there were nine points on which Jacob Ammann and his followers differed from the other Mennonites of his day:

1. Ammann believed in the literal shunning of those who are excommunicated.

2. Ammann did not believe the true-hearted (those who gave food and shelter to the Anabaptists) should be considered as Christians.

3. Ammann felt the need for stronger discipline in dress and everyday living.

4. He felt that men should cut their hair fairly short and let their beards grow; the others followed the prevailing fashions of letting the hair grow very long and shaving the beard.

5. He believed the body of believers who followed the teachings of Menno Simons were the one true church, and he excommunicated those who opposed him.

6. He re-introduced foot washing into the communion service, as this had been neglected for some time.

7. He introduced the practice of observing communion twice a year.

8. He thought it was wrong to attend the state church services, even at a funeral.

9. It is quite clear that the party of Jacob Ammann did not tolerate the teaching of premillennialism [the belief that Christ's return will usher in a thousand years of messianic rule]. As late as 1900, people were banned who believed this.

It is interesting to note that of all the different Mennonite branches, only the Old Order Amish and the Holdeman Mennonites still adhere to all the nine points mentioned here.   (Noah Keim, 4-72)

Two Waves of Amish Migration to America

So far no historian has been able to pinpoint the exact date the first Amish settler arrived in America. Without a doubt, Amish immigrants had settled in Pennsylvania before 1737, which year marks the definite coming of the largest group of Amish settlers in that century. What the Mayflower is to the Puritans, the ship Charming Nancy is to the Amish. When it docked at Philadelphia on October 8, 1737, it had on board some twenty-one Amish immigrants.

Amish pioneers continued to arrive in America every few years until nearly the beginning of the Revolutionary War, in 1775. During the last quarter of that century, no Amish are known to have reached America's shores. Many more, however, came during the following century. Since so much time elapsed between the Amish who immigrated in the 1700s and those who came during the 1800s, historians speak of the "first and second waves" of Amish migration.

No accurate count of the Amish immigrants and their families can be made, but historians estimate that fewer than five hundred men, women, and children came during the "first wave" of migration in the 1700s. In sharp contrast to that number are the estimated three thousand who arrived during the 1800s. The majority of the Amish today descend from the "first wave" of immigrants.

It must be pointed out that during each century descendants of non-Amish immigrants have added their surnames to Amish society. Some entered as orphans and joined the Amish church when they grew to maturity. Others seemingly joined in order to marry, choosing though to remain the rest of their lives. And some were converts who joined because of religious convictions.

Of the many such surnames present today among the Amish, only five entered during the 1700s: Headings, Glick, Keim, Renno, and Riehl. On the other hand, thirty-two entered during the 1800s.

The descendants of the "second wave" immigrants, added to converts, form a more-significant portion of Amish society today than historians have previously thought.

Records show that some Amish immigrants from Europe were on the ocean for as little as 54 days to as long as 120 days.

("Yesterdays and Years," D. Luthy, 3-88)

A fascinating series of articles give the stories behind many common Amish names. Here are two of the many stories, which are also a wealth of information about early Amish history. Note how names often underwent changes in spelling.

Amish and Mennonite Family Names

Treyer/Troyer

One of the first Swiss Anabaptist martyrs was Hans Drier, who was drowned in Bern on July 8, 1529, along with two other Anabaptists. When he was questioned before the court, he explained the points of his faith: he held fast to believers baptism, did not think it right to swear oaths, and did not believe true Christians would let others suffer want.

Jakob Treyer was an Anabaptist of Laufen, Switzerland. In 1529, he was put in neck irons and brought to the marketplace of Basel. A crowd of spectators soon gathered. Jakob boldly spoke to them concerning repentance and the new life. However, when some time later he was sentenced to death by beheading, he cast himself at the feet of the judges and begged for mercy. Because he wanted to recant, he was pardoned.

Beginning about 1733, some Treyers from Bern moved to Pennsylvania, settling in Berks County. They were all Amish. By 1752, the brothers Michael and Andreas Troyer were listed as members of the Northkill Amish congregation in Berks County.

In later years the Troyers spread westward, and today they are one of the numerous Amish families. Bishop David A. Treyer of Holmes County was an influential Amish bishop during the last half of the nineteenth century. He wrote the booklet *Hinterlassene Schriften* (Writings bequeathed to children), first published in 1920.

John Troyer, who lived near Kokomo, Indiana, had an unusually large family, perhaps the largest of all time among Amish or Mennonites. John was first married to Catherine Schrock, who bore him twelve children. Following her death, he married her cousin Caroline (Schrock) Kendall, a young widow with two children. John and Caroline in turn had seventeen additional children. This made a total of thirty-one children.

Zug/Zook

The Zook family was originally from Signau in the Swiss canton of Bern. Hans Zoug was a noted Anabaptist minister in Switzerland who endured much persecution. Three of his grandsons, the brothers

Christian, Moritz, and Johannes Zug, arrived in Philadelphia in 1742, and became the ancestors of the many Zooks in our churches today. By 1942, two hundred years after their arrival in Philadelphia, these brothers were believed to have had about twenty-five thousand descendants. Many of these are Quakers, or belong to some religious belief other than Amish or Mennonite.   (J. Stoll, 3-69)

The Northkill Amish

Because of its size and early founding, the Lancaster Amish settlement in Pennsylvania was often thought to have been the first Amish settlement in America. But it wasn't. In 1740, an Amish settlement was flourishing in Berks County, Pennsylvania. Known as the Northkill settlement, it was located near the present town of Hamburg, Pennsylvania.

In the 1730s, Northkill began receiving settlers from the Amish settlement in Switzerland. By 1749, the settlement had received its first minister, Jacob Hertzler, who was later ordained bishop through a letter sent from bishops in Switzerland. The French in Canada stirred up the Indians to attack various settlements in Pennsylvania, for they did not like the Germans and English settling there. Because of the Indian raids, the Amish left the Northkill settlement less than twenty years after its establishment. They moved to other parts of Berks County, and sometime later to Lancaster County.

On June 27, 1959, a state historical marker was erected commemorating the Northkill settlement:

NORTHKILL AMISH

The first organized Amish Mennonite congregation in America. Established by 1740. Disbanded following Indian attack, September 29, 1757, in which a Provincial soldier and three members of the Jacob Hochstetler family were killed near this point.

("Yesterdays and Years," D. Luthy, 11-71)

Following is an account, in story form, of the famous Indian attack
on the Hochstetler family. It was reprinted in an issue of *Family Life*
as it appears in *Our Heritage,* a book for the eighth grade in the
Pathway Reading Series for Amish schools.

One Dark Night

The Northkill settlement was established in 1739 close to what is
now Harrisburg, Pennsylvania. Indians roamed the area. While William
Penn governed the territory, they were peaceful and friendly. But after his death in 1718, misunderstandings arose, caused at least in part
by Thomas Penn's cheating the Indians.

When the French and Indian War broke out in 1754, conditions
were ripe in Pennsylvania for conflict between the red men and white.
The once quiet and peaceable frontier became the scene of violent
raids, bloodshed, death, and terror.

All summer at Northkill, there had been reports of Indian raids
and unrest. The Amish families did not risk having many gatherings.
But as fall came, tension seemed to have lessened, and the Jacob Hochstetler family invited the young people to their home for an apple-
schnitzing and an evening of fellowship. It was a pleasant evening.

As the Hochstetlers said good-bye to their friends, little did they
know that tragedy and death stalked the woods about them.

Attacked

"Jacob, Jacob. Wake up!"

Jacob Hochstetler groaned sleepily, and then with a start he was
wide awake. In the dim light that found its way through the narrow
window in the log cabin, he could see his wife bending over him. Jacob could not see the fear in her eyes, but cold shivers went up his
back as he caught the alarm in her voice. "Jacob, there's something,
. . . there's something going on outside."

Instantly Jacob remembered the reports of Indian raids they had
heard all summer. Could anything like that happen to them? "What
was it? What did you hear?" he asked in a low voice, swinging his
feet out and sitting on the bed.

"The dog barked, barked so suddenly, so strangely, as if something surprised him. There was something about it that I just couldn't help thinking . . ."

"I heard it too, Mom," someone spoke from the adjoining room. It was young Jake, their third son. His voice was calm and reassuring in the quietness of the cabin. "It is probably nothing," he said. "I'll go to the door and look out." The lad jumped from his bunk along the wall.

His father started to speak, started to say, "Wait, let me go," but did not.

Slowly young Jake unbolted the heavy door and stood there, straining to see in the dim light of the waning moon. The night seemed so quiet, so friendly and peaceful.

Without warning, the night was shattered by a bloodcurdling whoop. A shot rang out. With a sharp cry of pain, the unsuspecting boy half fell, half leaped back into the protecting shelter of the cabin. His father sprang to the door and with trembling fingers slipped the bolt into position.

"Jacob, my son, are you hurt?" gasped the anxious father.

"I don't think it's serious," the brave boy replied. "The shot struck me in the leg."

"Shall I light a lamp?" shuddered Mrs. Hochstetler.

"No, no," answered her husband. "What we do must be done in the dark. They could see us too clearly if we had a light."

The two oldest boys, Joseph and Christian, and their only sister were awakened by the commotion. They joined the group huddled together in the center of the cabin.

"Maybe they have left," Christian ventured after they waited in silence a few minutes. "Let me go to the window and look out." Stealthily he crept to the window and peeped into the darkness. "There they are," he whispered, pointing with his finger. His father and Joseph stood close behind him, following his gaze. "Right there by the outdoor oven. Can you see them?"

A half dozen tall dusky figures moved in the shadowy darkness. They appeared to be counseling.

"Quickly, now's our chance," Joseph said, grabbing his rifle from the wall and directing Christian to do likewise. "I'll wait until you're ready, and we'll shoot together."

Joseph felt a restraining hand on his shoulder. "No, boys," Mr. Hochstetler said. "It's wrong to kill. We cannot do that."

"But if we don't shoot, they will kill us. Jacob is already wounded."

"No, no," replied the older man firmly. "You know it is not right to harm another, even to protect ourselves."

"But think, Father, we have plenty of powder and shot here. We could hold them off until daylight, and then they will leave."

"No, we will not shoot. We will trust in God, boys." There was a note in Jacob Hochstetler's voice that told his sons further begging was useless; the decision was final.

Was something moving outside? The family could not be certain. They thought they heard a stone click. The dog barked, but he was not at the house. The bark seemed to come from the top of a nearby hill. At one corner of the cabin sounded the grate of something rubbing. Breathlessly, the Hochstetlers waited. All was quiet except for their breathing—loud and rasping with tenseness. A rustling noise, a crackling sound, and the Hochstetlers knew without speaking that the thing they had feared was upon them: the redskins had set fire to their house.

Through the chinks in the wall, they could see the eerie glow of the leaping flames. Smoke stung their nostrils.

After the warm summer, the logs of the cabin were dry and caught like tinder. The trapped family could feel the warmth of the blaze as they crouched low on the floor to escape the choking fumes of the thickening smoke.

To go out would be suicide. That was exactly what the waiting savages expected and were prepared for. There would not be the slightest chance of escape.

"Let's go to the cellar," the younger Jacob suggested. They closed the door tightly behind them to keep the smoke from following. The damp cellar was crowded and even darker than the smoke-filled cabin had been, but at least they could breathe.

Silently they prayed and waited while the fire raged above them. They had fled its punishing heat for a moment, but they knew that like a relentless monster cheated of its prey, it would follow them, and there would be nowhere else to go. With a splintering crash, one section of the roof collapsed, shaking the beams in the cabin floor and sending a shower of fine dust upon them.

Christian choked and then sneezed, but it was only a stifled faint little sound drowned out by the growing roar of the fierce fire raging above their heads.

As the fire burned on, the strangling heat engulfed them in the shallow cellar. At one end the floor above burned through, just a tiny red eye glaring at them in the inky blackness. Then like a glowing cancer, it spread and grew.

Stumbling against a large wooden barrel, Jacob Hochstetler was struck with an idea. With the desperateness of a drowning man, he seized upon it. Fumbling with the tight-fitting cover, he exclaimed, "Why don't we splash this apple juice on the fire? It might slow it down."

Carefully he splashed a dipper of the liquid on the angry hole of fire. It sizzled and spat back like an angry cat, but its rage was noticeably dampened. They did it again and again; for a moment the fire was checked. The family began to hope. Then the dipper scraped the bottom of the barrel, and they knew it was empty.

A wall fell in, and a shower of sparks shot through the flame-eaten boards at a dozen places. Smoke poured down, and the heat was unbearably intense.

"Couldn't we escape through the window?" Joseph asked. "Maybe the Indians have left by now." With strong arms he wrenched the sturdy window frame loose and looked outside. The gray dawn was breaking over the wooded hills of Pennsylvania.

With a glad cry of joy he turned and exclaimed, "It's beginning to be daylight outside, and I see no one around."

"Wait a minute," the father said. "Here is something that may come in useful." He held up a small basket of peaches from the cellar floor. "Stuff these in your pockets, boys, in case we have to hide in the woods a few days." Quickly the boys grabbed a few of the firmer fruits, and then one by one the family squeezed through the narrow opening and gathered in a thankful circle beside the smoldering ruins of their home.

Captives

With the coming of dawn, the wary redskins had melted farther and farther into the comforting protection of the nearby forest. When they saw no sign of life from the cabin, they were at last satisfied that the inhabitants had perished. Silently they turned to follow unmarked trails through the wilderness to their teepee homes.

Then they heard a shout and halted in their tracks. One young Indian boy had lingered behind to eat peaches in the Hochstetler's fine hillside orchard. Thoroughly enjoying his feast on the white man's fruit, he was astonished to see the entire family emerge, alive and well, from the burned building. It took only a shout and a moment to recall his departing companions. For the Hochstetler family, just escaped from the cabin furnace, the shrill call of the Indian lad resounded with tragedy.

Immediately the small group was surrounded. As the Indians closed in, Joseph sprang and broke through, running with incredible fleetness. Two braves followed him in close pursuit, but Joseph was an able runner and finally shook them off. Then he lay hiding behind a large log, resting while his breath came in great tearing gasps and his heart throbbed with fear.

The father and two husky sons offered no resistance as the maddened savages struck dead three of their number—the mother, young Jake, and the only daughter. One stalwart brave swung back his deadly tomahawk over Christian, then changed his mind and took him captive along with his father.

Dazed and in shock, the two grief-stricken survivors were marched away. Later they were joined by Joseph. The warriors had stumbled upon his hiding place and, before he could flee, had captured him. The outlook was dark for the unhappy captives. They were constantly guarded so there was no possibility of escape.

"Why was I saved instead of my wife?" the sorrowing father wondered as they tramped through the wilderness. He remembered how she had told him earlier in the summer that a band of hungry Indians had come to their cabin one day, while he and the boys were absent. They had asked for food, but for some reason his wife had refused to give them any. They had left disappointed, scowling and muttering angrily. Did the incident have any connection with the fatal nightmare only a few hours behind him? Jacob could only wonder as he walked numbly on and on.

After marching weary miles, the tired party reached an Indian village. The first thing in store for the prisoners was the gauntlet. This was a brutal form of torture to which Indians often put their captives. Standing in two long rows and armed with clubs and whips, the Indians forced the unfortunate victims to run between the two lines. This was a hideous experience, and many fell beneath the cruel blows, unable to make it to the end of the gauntlet.

Jacob and his sons watched in horror as the tribesmen dashed about, picking out whips and stout sticks to be used in beating them.

"My God," half prayed and half groaned the weary father, "have we not suffered enough?" Limply his hands dropped to his side. Then he remembered the peaches they had guarded so carefully since their capture.

"The peaches," he whispered hoarsely to his sons. The Indians were already beginning to line up. The entire village could be seen gathering to watch the sport, curious to know how the weak palefaces would fare. Standing slightly aloof from the rest with his hands folded solemnly across his chest stood the majestic figure of the chief.

Joseph held out the two peaches he had left. Jacob looked at them. "Hardly good enough," the father muttered. They were both badly bruised. Joseph had crushed them when he lay behind the log to hide from his pursuers.

Reaching into his pocket, Christian produced three peaches. They were in much better condition. Taking them quickly from his son, Jacob walked toward the forbidding figure of the great chief.

The chief stared with unblinking eyes at the man before him, his dark handsome face expressionless.

"Here, a gift for you." Jacob smiled and held out the peaches. "For the great chief." Jacob smiled again.

The leader's face changed, and his eyes beamed with pleasure; he was immensely pleased. Jabbering excitedly to his followers, he forbade them to go on with the gauntlet. With a sigh of relief, Jacob turned and joined his waiting sons.

A few days later they were aware of some unusual activity in the camp. "I fear they are going to separate us," Jacob told the boys. His soft eyes filled with sudden tears at the painful thought of parting with the only two sons he had left. He sensed that their time to talk was short. "No matter what happens," he admonished them, "be kind to the Indians. Don't try to resist them. They have used us well since we are at the camp. Act as if you were content, but never give up that you may someday escape. Even if you forget everything else, try to remember your name and the Lord's Prayer."

The anxious father had guessed correctly. With a heavy heart, he was led away to another village. The boys were parted, too, but they were frequently allowed to see each other. They were young and soon grew accustomed to Indian ways.

The cold winter passed. One warm thawing morning in early spring, the boys were united after not seeing each other for a while.

"What's up?" Christian asked, looking at his brother standing in front of him, dressed exactly like an Indian.

"I'm not sure," Joseph replied, "but something is." The Indians were glancing at them and talking excitedly. Finally they seemed to have made up their minds. As they approached the boys, the one who could speak English the best said, "Paleface become brother to Indian."

The entire group stood around the boys, smiling pleasantly at them. "We like you," the spokesman went on. "We brothers. But redskin no have this." He pointed to Joseph's beard and then to Christian's. "No have this." He rubbed his own smooth skin.

The boys understood what was happening. They were to be adopted into the tribe. Having their beards plucked out one hair at a time was a painful process, and most of the hair on their heads received the same treatment. The only hair the Indians left untouched was a small tuft at the top of their heads.

Having their hair plucked was not the only thing connected with adoption. There were various ceremonies and Indian rites to be endured. Once they were taken to the river and scrubbed with a stiff brush to wash the white blood from their veins.

Escape

Every day Jacob watched for his chance, but it seemed as if it would never come. The lonesome man wondered if he would ever see his two sons again.

His captors were careful never to tell Jacob where he was, and this made escape even more impossible. If he could escape, which way should he travel? The situation was discouraging.

Slowly the days turned into weeks and the weeks into months. One year passed. Another year came and went. Through three long years of weary days, Jacob Hochstetler waited and prayed and watched and hoped.

"What was that old man doing by his tent?" Jacob wondered as he went quietly about his usual work one morning. His job was to provide food for the camp while the rest of the men were on the warpath.

Without drawing attention to his presence, Jacob worked his way closer to the old man. Several husky warriors were grouped around him, and with a short stick he was making marks on the ground.

"A map!" Jacob gasped under his breath. "If I could only get close enough to see, perhaps I might discover something of where we are. With God's help, I'll escape yet," he resolved.

Pretending to be busy working, Jacob edged closer and closer. It was hard to see clearly, but in the loose dust the old man seemed to be sketching mountains and rivers and forest trails. Jacob caught the words "paleface camp here," and he saw where the stick pointed. Finally, he had a hazy idea of what he longed so much to know. He watched for a chance more closely than ever before.

Under cover of darkness, he slipped away one night while most of the men were away fighting. He knew the Indians would try their best to trail him and bring him back. Carefully he destroyed all signs of his passing, so no one could track him. Constantly he feared he would meet some of the warriors returning from battle.

He traveled miles on foot, mostly by night, taking his directions the best he could from the stars. He had to find his food without shooting, for he did not dare risk being betrayed by the sound of his gun. When he crossed creeks, he would wade upstream to break his scent.

His years with the Indians had taught him wood lore, and now he needed all he had.

Coming upon a river, he fashioned a crude raft with his bare hands, tying the logs together with grapevine ropes.

Day after day he sat on the raft, floating down river. Uncertainty and doubt plagued him. "Am I getting closer to friends and loved ones?" he would wonder. Often a worried look would cross his face, and he would talk to himself. "What if the current is only daily taking me farther into the depth of a trackless wilderness?"

Constantly there was the problem of food. Now and then he chanced upon a few bites of something he could eat, but generally he became hungrier and thinner and weaker. At last his tired body became too starved and weakened to get up, and he could only lie helplessly, staring at the unbroken line of trees as he drifted by.

Suddenly Jacob's dim eyes, clouded with fatigue, opened wide in surprise and disbelief. "Are those really buildings?" He tried to raise his head. "Have I reached a fort at last?" he whispered in near delirium. "Or is it only the feverish working of my mind?"

Jacob struggled desperately to get to his feet, to shout or wave. He was persuaded now that it was a fort. "Have I come this far only to drift by unnoticed, and on to my fate?" With his last bit of feeble strength, he fought to rise, but all he could do was hold one thin hand up. Slowly the dying man floated past the fort, a lonely speck on a wide river. He hoped in vain. There was no shout of recognition. He had not been seen.

Just below the fort at a shallow place in the river, a man stood watering his horse. He looked up and saw the frail raft.

"Whoa," the man exclaimed in surprise. "What do I see?" He stood squinting his eyes, gazing curiously at the drifting object.

"Sure looks like a raft," he observed idly. "But it can't be. I see nothing moving. Probably just an odd-shaped log."

Just then Jacob's arm grew tired. Exhausted with the effort, his hand dropped to his side.

The watching man caught the slight movement. "The thing is alive," he declared to his horse. "It looks like a man, too." Mounting his horse, he galloped to the fort to report what he had just witnessed.

Jacob was rescued and given food and kind care. That night in the soft bed at the fort, Jacob closed his eyes and slept the slumber of a grateful man. While others stood in awe and marveled at the hardships he had endured, the worn man quietly rested, secure in the knowledge that his faith in God had brought him back.

Some time later, a cool summer breeze was blowing as Jacob sat in his cabin, eating his noon meal. He glanced up, slightly startled as a shadow darkened the open doorway.

A tall Indian stood there, silent and straight. He didn't say a word. His glance went all around the cabin, resting briefly on Jacob. Then turning, he made his way to a stump in the small clearing and sat down. All the while Jacob was eating, he sat there, patiently waiting.

"I wonder what he wants?" Jacob mused, finishing his meal and rising from the table. "I guess I had better go out and see."

The tall Indian arose as Jacob approached him. He stood there, eyeing the man before him for a long moment. He stepped closer, searching every line in Jacob's wrinkled face. Then he stepped back. Slowly he said in broken German, "Ich bin der Christli Hochstetler (I am Christian Hochstetler)."

("Yesterdays and Years," E. Stoll, 8-68)

Division Between the Old Orders and the Progressives

The Amish in America lived in unity for many generations. But by the 1850s, there was tension between different settlements and within settlements. New things were creeping in. The camera had been invented, and some Amish were having family photographs taken. Young men were beginning to wear neckties, and other customs in dress were changing. The ban was not strictly enforced in some congregations. Some ministers were discarding prayer books. Insurance was catching on among the "English," and some Amish were interested and subscribed to the plan. A few congregations wondered if it wouldn't be better to baptize in running water.

In 1851, David Beiler, a well-known and strict bishop of Lancaster County, Pennsylvania, wrote a letter to Moses B. Miller, the bishop at Johnstown, Pennsylvania:

"I have often been thinking that a general ministers' meeting is needed, so we could admonish each other orally with love, in a humble spirit, with Christian simplicity, so that nobody would insist on his own opinion, but take the Word of the Lord as a guide."

A general ministers' meeting (*Diener-Versammlung*) was not held until eleven years after David Beiler made his suggestion. Meanwhile, another problem arose among the Amish churches—the question of meetinghouses. A small log meetinghouse had been built in 1830 by the Amish in Stark County, Ohio, and a small frame one in 1848 in the Clinton district in Elkhart County, Indiana.

Actually, the first Amish meetinghouse in America had been erected as early as 1795 in Chester County, Pennsylvania, but the settlement had become extinct within a generation. No other eastern Amish settlement followed the example of the Chester County Amish.

The first general ministers' meeting was held in June of 1862 in Wayne County, Ohio. Some strict Amish bishops attended the sessions. But from studying in which communities the meetings were held and who the chairmen were, it is obvious that from the beginning the meetings were under the control of the progressive Amish bishops, not the stricter ones. Instead of the ministers' meetings being an aid in stopping drift in the Amish church, it opened the door and let the changes in.

A year later, in May of 1863, the second general ministers' meeting was held. For the next fifteen years, they continued to be held annually, except in 1877.

The final general ministers' meeting was held in 1878 in Woodford County, Illinois. After that session, the ministers decided to discontinue holding the meetings. They saw that the meetings were failing to restore unity among the Amish in America. By this time, the stricter bishops had given up hope of holding the progressive ones back. And the progressive bishops had grown tired of being reminded of "the old way."

The meetings had begun in 1862 with the hope of arriving at new unity, but the only new unity reached was among the progressive bishops. They soon formed three regional conferences of their own. Altogether, there were approximately seventy congregations. They no longer referred to themselves simply as "Amish," but adopted the term "Amish-Mennonite," which was very fitting, for they were a church between the Amish and the Mennonites.

It has been estimated that two-thirds of the Amish in America went with this liberal movement, the other third remaining Amish and calling themselves "Old Order Amish." The Amish-Mennonites continued to change, and by 1927 nearly all the congregations had dropped the term "Amish" and had united with the Mennonite church.

("Yesterdays and Years," D. Luthy, 1-73)

Settlements and Migrations

• The most settlements: Pennsylvania with 40, Ohio with 23, Michigan with 18

• The most congregations: Ohio with 188, Pennsylvania with 165, Indiana with 133

• Largest settlements:
Holmes/Wayne Counties, Ohio, with 111 congregations
Lancaster/Chester Counties, Pennsylvania, with 77
LaGrange/Elkhart Counties, Indiana, with 54

• The three oldest settlements (all in Pennsylvania):
Lancaster County, founded 1760
Somerset County, founded 1772
Mifflin County, founded 1791

[Ben J. Raber lists current Amish districts and ministers in his annual *Almanac,* from Raber's Book Store, Baltic, OH 43804.]

Besides the search for cheaper farmland, which is always a prime motive for Amish migration, other factors enter in. People move for a variety of reasons and sometimes even for the opposite reasons:

1. To establish a plainer church discipline

2. To establish a more modern church discipline

3. To escape church problems

4. To improve youth problems

5. To avoid urban crowding and the regulations it imposes on rural people

6. To better oneself financially   (12-84)

Fireside Chats

Up to 1966, no permanent Amish settlement had been established in any of the Latin American countries. But in the fall of that year, almost an entire membership of the small Amish church at St. Joe, Arkansas, decided to move to British Honduras [Belize]. Several families from Pennsylvania joined the group. This colony of ten families is now in its third year, located near Cayo, only a few miles from the Guatemalan border.

During 1967, the first Amish families moved to Paraguay, a South American country five thousand air miles south of New York City. The distance here is greater than that covered by our ancestors, who came to America from Europe, but the advances in transportation make it seem closer.

The Paraguay Amish moved from Orange County, Indiana, to their new homes south of the equator. Some of them settled in the Chaco region, and others have located in southeastern Paraguay.

In the past few months, four families from Ontario have also moved to Paraguay, a land where summer comes in wintertime, and winter never comes.

The motive for moving should certainly not be a selfish one, or the venture will be doomed to failure. The motive should be religious—a desire to worship God in freedom, and to present a true Christian witness. (J. Stoll, 1-69)

Settlements

Fifteen settlements founded after 1974 were extinct by 1984, including those in Virginia, Nebraska, Honduras, and Paraguay [described above]. As of 1984, Amish were found in twenty states and one province of Canada: Arkansas, Delaware, Florida, Illinois, Indiana, Iowa, Kansas, Kentucky, Maryland, Michigan, Minnesota, Missouri, Montana, New York, Ohio, Oklahoma, Pennsylvania, Tennessee, Texas, Wisconsin, and Ontario.

[By 1999, North Carolina, Virginia, and West Virginia were added; and Arkansas subtracted. Ben J. Raber's *Almanac* of 1999 lists 1,151 districts (congregations). There are on average about 150 adults and children in an Amish district.]   (12-84)

New Settlements

We asked our readers to write what they consider the most common pitfalls a family can expect to meet when they become part of a new settlement venture. [People mentioned climate and weather, financial difficulties, and power struggles.] *Here are some answers:*

"One of the biggest problems is the power struggle that often results when people from different locations move together. So when moving to a new settlement, be prepared to give in on the little issues that don't mean much anyway. The main trouble is too many chiefs and not enough Indians."

[Comment by the editors:] Sometimes people pretend to be moving for spiritual betterment, but all they really want is more liberty to do as they please. This is a motive upon which no blessing can follow, and a foundation upon which no church can prosper.

"To avoid another pitfall, get the electricity and telephone out as soon as possible, or better yet, before you move. Experience has taught us the longer you use it, the harder it is to put away."

"Some people use a new settlement like a reformatory. They leave their children in a bad influence for sixteen years, then when things get out of control, they take them and dump them into a new settlement, expecting the new settlement to instantly undo the harm of the old. But it never has worked to throw a bad apple into a bushel with good ones and then expect the good will change the bad. Usually it goes the other way. If parents wait too long, they have a problem getting their children out of the old settlement, and even more of a problem to get the old settlement out of their children!"

[Comment:] I have noticed that if there are mostly young people in a new settlement, some things may gradually become accepted in the church that older people might see a danger in, and give a warning.

[Other pitfalls include gossip, different backgrounds, and lack of leadership.]

"Why have new settlements so often failed? Is it not usually a lack of planning, a lack of support, a lack of true leadership? A sprinkling of families come haphazardly from the four winds and decide to give the new settlement a try. If it doesn't work, it is easy to pull up stakes and move again. It seems to me it is time our older, established churches took the lead in starting daughter settlements under their supervision and with their support. Perhaps then both the old and new settlements could prosper spiritually with God's full blessings." (4-77)

Amish Life in the Great Depression, 1930-40

Nappanee, Indiana, by Joni D. Gingerich

[Summary:] Joni was married in 1929. He worked in a lamp and chair shop until it went out of business in 1930. Joni had no job the rest of the 1930 winter. March 1931 brought a child, and no income from the summer. In May, he worked on a farm nine miles away for a dollar a day, house and garden rentfree, and pasture for driving horse and cow.

The next year he rented this farm. He followed sales and eventually bought some farm implements, a team of horses, seven milk cows, a few breed sows, some hay and grain. Joni had no manure spreader, so he hauled it in a wagon and spread it by hand twice a week. He planted thirty acres of corn and twelve of soybeans. Non-Amish and Amish helped with some work.

Joni had no money or income that summer, so he couldn't buy groceries. He took a bushel of shelled corn to the milling company to be ground into cornmeal. Thirty-five cents or half the corn was the price. He paid half the corn. Then he bought a bushel of wheat and had half of it ground coarse for cereal, and half of it fine for bread. "That was the main diet around our place for a number of years— whole-wheat cereal, whole-wheat pudding, mush and milk, fried mush, corn bread, and potatoes. We ate that for three meals a day, seven days a week."

He hired a Mennonite man who needed money for his family for a week. The man asked for $1.25 a day, besides food that the Amishman had sent him. The man said another man offered him that much, but it turned out it was a trick to get more money.

Joni feels that lessons were learned and that some young people could benefit from a taste of such hard times. He also asks, "Could it be that we are in a greater depression spiritual-wise than we were back there money-wise?"   ("Yesterdays and Years," 7-71)

Belleville, Pennsylvania, by Jonathan R. Byler Sr.

"As for myself and family, the Depression taught lessons not soon forgotten. It was sometimes hard to tell one's life companion how little money was at hand, especially when clothing and so forth were needed. But being farmers, we usually had plenty to eat. Faith in God and honesty were a great help. I doubt if anyone can know the mercy God has bestowed upon mankind since the beginning of time."

Lancaster, Pennsylvania, by Jonathan Zook

"We were married December 5, 1918, and started farming and housekeeping in the spring of 1919. We had good years until the year of 1930. Around May or June, as nearly as I can tell, the bottom seemed to drop out of everything.

"That spring we had torn down our old barn (116 years old) and were building a new one. The carpenters had charged 65 cents an hour, which was a good wage then. But that fall when we built a chicken house, their price had dropped to 35 cents an hour. By 1931, most building stopped altogether. Carpenters were glad if they could find work at 25 cents. Many contractors went broke because they had new houses on hand at high prices and could not sell them.

"Farmers also had a tough job of making ends meet. If we broke even till the end of the year, we were well satisfied. Hogs sold for 2 cents a pound, steers 4.5 cents a pound, potatoes 25 cents a bushel, and milk 80 cents a hundred. In 1934, it got better. About 1936 things leveled off, and supply and demand took care of themselves. In 1939-40, when Hitler in Germany started to invade countries, prices started to rise and have risen ever since.

"During the Depression, church members needed one another, and church affairs went along nicely. But now things have changed because there is so much money that comes easily and buys so many worldly things." ("Yesterdays and Years," 8-71)

Do You Know Your Amish History?

Quiz

1. The most common Amish family name:
     a. Yoder   b. Miller   c. Bontrager   d. Stoltzfus
2. The *Martyrs Mirror* was first printed in German in—
     a. 1660   b. 1748   c. 1849   d. 1915
3. The Amish settlement at _____ is the only one with a state's capital as a mailing address.
4. Which county has the largest number of Amish residents?
     a. Holmes County, Ohio   b. Lancaster County,
         Pennsylvania   c. LaGrange County, Indiana
5. The most northern Amish settlement:
     a. Milverton, Ontario   b. Norfolk, New York
     c. Wadena, Minnesota
6. In 1940, the Geauga County, Ohio, settlement, had eight church districts. In 1977, it had—
     a. 17   b. 25   c. 34   d. 54
7. *The Budget* has been published since—
     a. 1860   b. 1890   c. 1920   d. 1940
8. When did the Amish first settle in Canada?
     a. 1795   b. 1824   c. 1880   d. 1925
9. Amish bishop who traveled furthest on church matters:
     a. Eli J. Bontrager   b. Andrew Mast   c. Ira Nissley
     d. John Renno
10. All the Amish families bearing the Stoltzfus name descend from one immigrant and his sons. True or False?
11. Why the Amish did not settle in the New England states:
     a. religious intolerance   b. high-priced land
     c. cold climate   d. Indians
12. Many Amish left Reno County, Kansas, in 1936 because oil was discovered on their farms and they did not want to become rich. True or False?

13. Which of these states never had an Amish settlement?

    a. New Mexico b. North Carolina c. Nebraska
    d. Idaho

14. The prayer book *Lustgartlein*, commonly found in Amish homes, is of Anabaptist origin in Europe. True or False?

15. One Amish settlement has white, yellow, and black-top buggies. True or False?

Answers

1. Miller (b). Yoder is the second most common surname.

2. 1748 (b). The first printing of the *Martyrs Mirror* in the German language was done in Ephrata, Pennsylvania, in 1748-49. The original printing in the Dutch language was published in 1660. The first English edition was made in 1836.

3. Dover, Delaware.

4. Holmes County, Ohio (a).

5. Wadena, Minnesota (c).

6. 34 (c).

7. 1890 (b). The first issue was published on May 15, 1890.

8. 1824 (b). Mennonites settled in Canada before 1800, coming from Pennsylvania. The Amish migrated directly from Europe, beginning in 1824.

9. Eli J. Bontrager (a) of Shipshewana, Indiana, had bishop oversight of churches in North Dakota, Oregon, and other western states. He traveled further on church matters than any other known Amish bishop. Eli also visited many CPS [Civilian Public Service] camps during World War II. His autobiography shows that he traveled 466,000 miles by train and nearly 60,000 by bus and car.

10. True. All the Amish bearing the Stoltzfus name descend from Nicholas Stoltzfus, who landed in Philadelphia on October 18, 1766.

11. Religious intolerance (a). Pennsylvania was the first of the original thirteen colonies to grant religious freedom, so the Amish went there. They would not have been allowed to practice their faith in the other colonies.

12. False. Even though some newspapers reported that the Amish left Reno County because of the discovery of oil, it was not true.

They left because they did not agree with the introduction of tractor farming.

13. Idaho (d).

14. False. It is of Lutheran origin, not Anabaptist.

15. True for the Mifflin County, Pennsylvania, settlement.

Score

13-15, Excellent   10-12, Good   6-9, Fair   (8/9-77)

Pennsylvania Dutch: "Kannscht du Deitsch schwetze?" ["Can You Speak Dutch?"]

"What is Pennsylvania Dutch, anyway, and where does it come from?"

Sometimes people refer to Pennsylvania Dutch as "poor German with English words mixed into it." Others refer to it as "Low German." High German is called "high" because it is spoken in the mountainous or higher regions of Germany, whereas Low German is spoken in the lower parts.

Pennsylvania Dutch may be an inaccurate label since it isn't "Dutch" at all [the term "*Deitsch*/Dutch" came from "*Deutsch*," meaning "German"]. But the word "Pennsylvania" is accurate since the dialect is deeply rooted in that state. When William Penn offered his colony of Pennsylvania as a haven for persecuted religious minorities, many people moved there. The Mennonites, Amish, and Brethren Dunkards were early settlers.

They emigrated from the Palatinate, a region in southern Germany. They also came from Baden, Württemberg, Hesse, and Bavaria—also regions in southern Germany. Some came from Alsace and Switzerland. They were known as the Plain People because of their unadorned dress and simple lives.

At the same time that the Plain People moved to Pennsylvania, other emigrants from the exact same areas moved there, too. They came more for financial reasons than because of persecution. They belonged to Lutheran, Catholic, and Reformed churches. They became known as the "gay" Dutch, as opposed to the "plain" Dutch.

One thing which the settlers shared in common, whether "gay" or "plain," was the German language. They all spoke a German dialect, but not the same dialect. As they lived side by side in the southeastern counties of Pennsylvania, their dialects gradually blended to form what we today call Pennsylvania Dutch.

Since the largest number of settlers had come from the Palatinate, the (*pfälzisch*) German dialect of that region became the foundation upon which the Pennsylvania Dutch dialect was built. Nevertheless, the Pennsylvania Dutch dialect does not match 100 percent any dialect in Germany. It is a true German dialect that developed in America rather than Germany.

The Amish immigrants to Pennsylvania made up less than 1 percent of the settlers who spoke a German dialect. Today [1975] the Amish make up about 5 percent of the people who speak Pennsylvania Dutch. Another 5 percent is made up of Mennonites and Dunkards. This means that 90 percent are the descendants of the "gay" Dutch. They are located primarily in fourteen counties of southeastern Pennsylvania.

Since the Amish trace back to the Swiss Brethren in Canton Bern, Switzerland, the dialect of their forebears was *Berndeutsch*. Today, it is commonly referred to in Amish circles as *Schweizer Deitsch* (Swiss German). The Amish who live in Adams and Allen Counties, Indiana, have rather well retained this native Amish dialect. But they are so in the minority today that their speech is looked upon by other Amish as odd.

Professor Albert Buffington of Lancaster County, Pennsylvania, has studied the Pennsylvania Dutch dialect more than anyone else. He estimates that the dialect is made up of from 2 to 8 percent English words. Since the national language in America is English, and Amish are educated in that language, it is only natural that new words that enter Pennsylvania Dutch will be English. Words differ from one settlement to the next, and so does the tone of voice and the accent. It has been estimated that there are half a million people in North America who can converse freely in the dialect, and another half a million who can understand it.

("Yesterdays and Years," D. Luthy, 7-75)

What Is in a Language?

English is the language of our country. But we, the descendants of immigrants from German-speaking parts of Europe, have clung to a language that has become largely our own. Over the years that our people have lived alongside English-speaking neighbors, we have naturally and gradually accepted numerous English words into our German dialect. The Pennsylvania Dutch we speak is really a slowly changing language. It is somewhat different now than it was a hundred years ago, and it is not even exactly the same in different parts of the country. Our case is much like that of the Jews in New Testament times.

The Old Testament was first written almost entirely in the old Hebrew language. It was the language of the Jews until the time of their captivity in the far-off land of Babylon. In that land [a faithful remnant] kept the faith better than the Israelites had during any other time in their history. But by the time they returned to their homeland, most of the people talked a different dialect called Aramaic. Then later, by the time the books were written that now make up the New Testament, roughly between the years A.D. 50-100, another language had worked its way up to become the chief language of commerce in the land of the Jews, and in most of the lands of that part of the world. That language was [Koine] Greek.

Thus, the case of the people at that time was much like ours today. They had the traditional Hebrew for their worship just like we use the German Bible in our homes and churches. They had the Aramaic, a language spoken in their homes, but hardly popular as a written language at that time, much like we use our everyday Pennsylvania Dutch. Then for their writings and correspondence, they had the common Greek, the easy-to-write language of world commerce and business, somewhat similar to the way we use the English language in our day.

Knowing two languages is a privilege God has provided for us, and we can put them to good use. Although we have a knowledge of two languages, it would be wrong not to make an effort to express ourselves better in the English language. But it would be just as wrong to fail to keep and pass on the German to our children—that rich language our forebears left for us. It is a well-known fact that losing our mother tongue and drifting into the world usually go together.

Any time we speak English around the home when just family members are around, or while working or visiting with others who know Pennsylvania Dutch, we put in a vote to drop a rich heritage that will never again be brought back if we lose it.

The value of that heritage is so great that we can't afford to lose it.

("The Scriptures Have the Answers," 2-86)

3
Living in the Present

Many of us see the Amish religion and lifestyle merely as a complex series of rules to be followed. We have difficulty understanding why certain things are allowed, while others are not. As outsiders, we have questions about why photographs are forbidden, why there are so many particulars on how to dress, and so on.

Many Amish themselves cannot answer these questions, beyond a simple "we've always done it that way." Yet little that the Amish practice is done simply by whim. In the pages of *Family Life*, there are many attempts to explore, explain, and even debate the reasons behind practices that have or may become Amish customs and traditions.

The Heritage of Our Church Decisions

Our Amish churches everywhere use rules of conduct or *Ordnung* to maintain uniformity in the church, and to keep unwanted practices out of the church. There are people who label all such as man-made rules, and say they are wrong and detrimental to the church. But we believe one of the points that has enabled the Amish to hold to non-conformity is discipline. To have discipline, we must have standards. If we rebel against the standards decided by the church, it is evident that something is wrong in our heart.

Each restriction we have is the result of some problem or misuse the church faced at one time. When we face new problems, we must make decisions whether we want to act on them or not. When I was a boy, there was no rule against watching or owning a television set, for the simple reason that there was no television. A hundred years ago the church needed no *Ordnung* against short dresses because at that time it was the practice among all women to wear them floor length.

For myself, I prefer to go by the collective decisions that have been made and handed down to us over many generations. Is there not a real danger that if we throw out what we have inherited from our forebears, we may be missing something we will not be able to re-place? ("Now That I Think of It," D. Wagler, 4-91)

Convicting the Hearers

Many members know the church rules better than the scriptural basis for them. I firmly believe fewer young people would be lost to the alluring world if their parents and ministers made sure they knew the biblical foundation of their beliefs, instead of merely telling them that is how the church teaches. It is harder to turn your back on "thus saith the Lord" than on "thus saith the church."

("Letter," Concerned in Pa., 6-92)

What It Means to Be Amish

We dress differently and our lifestyle is different, but is that the only difference between the Amish and all these other churches?

Well, let me tell you a story. Some years ago a group of fifty-two people chartered a bus and came to Holmes County to see the Amish. They had arranged to have an Amishman meet them and answer some of their questions.

For their first question, they began, "We all go to church," and named some churches. "So we know about Jesus. But what does it mean to be Amish?"

The Amishman thought a bit and then he asked a question of his own. "How many of you have TV in your homes?" Fifty-two hands went up. "Now, how many of you feel that perhaps you would be better off without TV in your homes?" Again, fifty-two hands went up. "All right. Now, how many of you are going to go home and get rid of your TV?" Not one hand went up!

Now that is what it means to be Amish. As a church, if we see or experience something that is not good for us spiritually, we will dis-cipline ourselves to do without.

The world in general does not know what it is to do without!

(Monroe L. Beachy, Sugarcreek, Ohio, 8/9-92)

Scriptural Living

My father was never one to deny that the plain church had faults. But he always said that he still feels there is more scriptural living, more New Testament doctrine, more Anabaptist application of the principles of the Bible [with the Amish] than anywhere that he knows of.

("Views and Values," E. Stoll, 8/9-82)

The Ten Commandments in the New Testament

We feel the Ten Commandments are all brought over into the New Testament:

1. Thou shalt have no other gods before me. 1 Corinthians 8:6.

2. Thou shalt not make unto thee any graven image or likeness. Romans 1:23.

3. Thou shalt not take the name of the Lord thy God in vain. Matthew 5:24; James 5:12.

4. Remember the Sabbath day to keep it holy. Matthew 12:8; Mark 2:28.

5. Honor thy father and thy mother. Matthew 15:3-7; Ephesians 6:2-3.

6. Thou shalt not kill. James 2:11; Revelations 13:10.

7. Thou shalt not commit adultery. Ephesians 5:3-5; 4:19.

8. Thou shalt not steal. Ephesians 4:28.

9. Thou shalt not bear false witness. Ephesians 4:25.

10. Thou shalt not covet. Romans 7:7; 13:9.

Jesus said, "I am not come to destroy, but to fulfill the law." Matthew 5:17. (Jesse D. Spicher, Belleville, Pa.)

Going About Doing Good

We are to be witnesses or good examples to others right in our own homes, communities, and churches. That is the place to start. If we are not Christians there, we will not be Christians anywhere else.

Being a witness "unto the uttermost part of the earth" could well mean to the evil and materialistic world around us. There are many around us who see godless pleasure, wealth, and comfort as the only goals in this life. Some of those see only our failings and are hostile to us. But then there are also others who look upon our ideals and have a secret longing for something better than only the empty values that the people of the world have a craving for.

There was once a tourist who, after seeing the plain people, remarked, "I feel that is the way life should be lived, but I know few of us on the outside could stay contented to live that way long because we are now so used to our affluent way of life."

We are to be a witness to the world, but at the same time, we are to be separate from it (2 Cor. 6:17). How could we better be the "salt of the earth" and "a light to the world" than by contentedly living a plain life and by giving up the idols that the world holds so dear?

("The Scriptures Have the Answers," 12-84)

Is Our Light Consistent?

Three oft-quoted passages of Scripture follow each other naturally:

First Peter 2:9: "But you are a chosen generation, a royal priesthood, an holy nation, a peculiar people."

Matthew 5:16: "Let your light so shine before men, that they may see your good works, and glorify your Father which is in heaven."

First Corinthians 2:14: "But the natural man receives not the things of the Spirit of God, for they are foolishness unto him; neither can he know them, because they are spiritually discerned."

We believe the first passage applies to us. If we didn't, there would be something wrong, and it would be time to look at ourselves for improvement.

We consider the second passage as directed at us. To a certain extent, we apply this principle, and there is evidence that it works. Our plain clothes draw attention. If we are honest, generous, helpful; if we are pious and God-fearing; and if we are quiet, peaceful, and law-abiding—people will see our good works.

We like to believe that the last passage (1 Cor. 2:14) is the reason why more people do not follow our way of life. Our customs seem like foolishness to many.

It is easy for us to look down on others and feel they are too proud to humble themselves like we do. They couldn't do without their luxuries! It's easy to assume our way of living is foolishness to them because they receive not the things of the Spirit.

Perhaps. On the other hand, could it be that our light is so smoky, smudged, and sooty that they cannot see our good works?

(Isaac R. Horst, Mt. Forest, Ont., 5-71)

The Gods of This World

Where are our Christian churches today? A look at the main body of the Mennonite Church reveals that as late as the early 1900s, the women wore plain stockings, a modest-length dress of plain material complete with cape and apron, and an appropriate prayer covering tied at the chin. The men wore suspenders and a straight-collar coat.

As the years passed, changes came one by one. The dresses became shorter, flesh-colored stockings appeared, the cape and apron gave way to the skirt and blouse, and then finally to the miniskirt. The prayer covering lost the strings and became smaller and smaller until today it has been completely lost or remains a remnant of what it once was. The wearing of the straight-collar coat gave way among men to the lay-down collar and necktie.

The coming of radio and later television introduced youth heroes like Johnny Cash and Elvis Presley. Many of the Mennonite youth carried pictures of these singing stars in their billfolds, and therefore idolized them.

Within the past twenty years, women in the main body of the Mennonite Church, who traditionally wore long and uncut hair, began wearing cut hair. Many Mennonites deplored these changes, yet nevertheless they came. The question is, Why did these changes come? The answers seem to point to a trend within the church to look and live like the rest of the world.

It is not our purpose to degrade the Mennonite Church. We have used this example only to show what can and did happen in a short span of fifty or sixty years. The question is, Do the plainer Mennonite groups, including the Amish, have anything to boast of? The answer is *no*. The very same spirit which ate into the core and majority of the Mennonite Church is much alive and working away within the Amish churches today. Perhaps the changes come much more slowly or over a longer period of time; yet the same spirit is there, slowly working away.

If you talk to older people, from an older settlement, they will likely admit that their settlement has changed from what it was fifty years ago. The dresses may be shorter, the prayer coverings on the women smaller or more fancy to please the eye. The houses are finer and have more decorations. The church has adopted more of a trend toward modernization, and so forth. When undesired practices enter and become rooted into the church, it becomes almost impossible to root them out, or to bring the church back to what it has lost.

Perhaps you ask, "What can I do to better the conditions in my church?" The place to start is to take a look at your own heart.

(D. B., 6-79)

The World Is Changing

No longer do people want to stay at home and live a quiet and godly life. They must be going, going, going, running after pleasure. The automobile opens the way.

Some think that doing missionary work is the answer. They must go and help people in foreign countries. They do not stop to think that staying at home and being a good example to the neighbors is also doing missionary work. Too often those who go to foreign lands must hear the words, "Physician, heal thyself."

I don't mean that missionary work is wrong, but it seems our first responsibility is to our family. We can also witness to the people around us. But it seems the people in the world today want to have the church salve their conscience, and they still want to keep the things they crave.

Many will probably say, "Someone is always crying wolf." But the truth is that the wolf of worldliness is at our door and ready to devour the sheep.   (L. S., Md., 7-68)

Prayers and Publicans

There are at least two ways we can get into the mistake of being self-righteous—through insincere prayer, and through bragging about our goodness. If these were the only two ways that self-righteousness showed itself, most of us would be pretty safe. As Amish, we don't have prayer meetings or testimony services, two places where these types of self-righteousness seem especially likely to be present. But this surely does not mean that we are free from self-righteousness.

For example, it is easy to see that those in higher [more liberal, progressive] churches are wrong to have the attitude of "God, I thank thee that I am not like those Old Order people!" But is it possible that the same self-righteous spirit could make us say the prayer in reverse: "God, I thank thee that I am not like those people in the higher churches!"

To be self-righteously proud is wrong, always wrong, even though the things we are proud of may be right in themselves. It is right that we wear plain clothes, drive horses, live separate from the world, have our own schools, and things like that. But just as soon as we become proud about any of these things, we will be condemned right along with the self-righteous Pharisee (Luke 18:11-12).

Self-righteousness is such a sly sin. We need to be alert, watch for it daily, and humble ourselves whenever we have become exalted. Even then we cannot relax, for what is easier to be proud of than of the fact that we are so humble?

("Views and Values," E. Stoll, 12-72)

How to Justify Your Sins

We should feel grateful and thankful toward a person who has reminded us of our sins. But unfortunately, such is not always the case. Too many of us allow our human nature to cause us to react in the wrong way.

1. A mother asked her young, married daughter whether she heard what Eli Miller preached in church that day about reading paperback storybooks, such as romance and Westerns. "Huh," her daughter retorted. "He should preach about that! I happen to know that his daughter Mary has a whole shelf of romance books openly exposed in her room! He should clean his own house first, before he preaches about it in church."

2. A man was kindly admonished in regard to his using tobacco. He justified his habit by human reasoning and twisting Scriptures rather than repenting and turning away from sin.

3. A young man who felt guilty for having unnecessary reflectors

and decorations on his buggy justified himself that it wasn't any worse than one of the preacher's sons.

4. A young mother justified the fancy clothing her baby was wearing by explaining that some "English" folks had given it to her as a gift.

5. A couple who let their daughter work in town instead of helping their own people, justified to themselves that they "needed the extra money."

In all the above examples, people tried to justify their sins in a wrong way. No mention is made in Scripture that we can justify our sins—

- by someone who has committed the same sin.
- because of the deeds of hypocrites.
- because we didn't know better at the time.
- because of material necessities.
- because of someone else's inconsistency.
- because our parents or church don't forbid it.

If we let ourselves believe that we can justify our sins by excuses like these, we will have a horrible surprise on the great judgment day.

(Orva Hochstetler, 3-78)

It Could Happen to You

We know that we can profit from good examples left us by godly men. But we are likely to forget that we might also profit from the *bad* examples left us, those lives that were spiritually wrecked on the highway of life.

Should not fathers point out to their sons the danger of taking their own way, of disobedience and sin? A good way to do this is to tell about the boy who died in a crash early Sunday morning, while coming home from a drinking party. Mention

might also be made of the father with three children who went to an early grave with lung cancer for being a heavy smoker. Or the neighbor who made money his god, until earthly possessions meant more to him than heavenly gain, leading him to leave the church and his faith. Perhaps the suicide should not be forgotten, one who gave up in despair because he could no longer live with a guilty conscience.

The circumstances and details vary, but every community has its share of bad examples we should learn lessons from. At the same time, we should beware lest we consider bad examples with a self-righteous attitude, or with a feeling of contempt that these men and women could fall so far. Bad examples can teach us something only if we view them with fear and trembling and deep humility, realizing that "this could happen to us," as well as it could befall another if we do not watch and pray. ("Views and Values," E. Stoll, 1-76)

Are We Consistent in Our Way of Life?

When we look at the worldly churches, we do not have to search long to find inconsistent Christians. Among those who sit in church pews on Sunday morning are many who profess they know God, but their works deny him.

However, what about among the plain people? Are we always consistent in our way of life? Following are a few examples that should be questioned:

1. Some who consider it a sin to smoke a white cigarette will smoke a pipe or cigar instead.

2. While we will not travel in an airplane, some churches have no restrictions against hiring a motor home, the most modern and luxurious form of land travel there is.

3. Some who refuse to play ball on Sundays will not hesitate to sit down to a game of cards instead.

4. Some who would not think of having a phone in their homes run to the neighbor's place to use his phone, even for calls that are not necessary and for which a postcard could easily have been sent.

5. We don't own automobiles ourselves, but are sometimes caught in hiring a taxi to go short distances when our horse and buggy could be used.

There is no spiritual gain, and we are inconsistent if we avoid one sin only to replace it with another just as bad or worse.

When the world sees us inconsistent in one point, most of our other good points lose their power and influence, and it soothes the world-lings' guilty conscience. (1-79)

Cars and Tractors

The Danger of Horsepower

"He shall not multiply horses to himself" (Deut. 17:16).

We are not conformed to this world. That includes our dress, but it surely also includes our way of making a living. We can believe that it also includes our way of traveling on the road, and our way of working in our fields. What means of travel today is highly esteemed among men? Which means of travel today corresponds with what horses stood for in Bible times?

Our neighbors may pass us on the road with all that "horsepower" under the hood. He works his fields with machinery that has so much more "horsepower" than we are using. Nevertheless, let us be content to stay with our work in a small, honest, and humble way, and not multiply horses to ourselves.

—*An Amish Minister* ("The Scriptures Have the Answers," 12-80)

Machinery, Family, and Community

Today there are many things to consider in deciding whether a piece of machinery is acceptable to our way of living. Most of the plain churches feel they want to stay with horsepower as much as they can. They have ample reason to shy away from modern machinery that seems to lead down the one-way street, on a road we don't want to travel.

It's the responsibility of the church to decide if something is detrimental to the church. If we feel it is, we must take our stand against it the same as we do against such things as TV. The problem is that it's not always such a clear-cut matter. Circumstances can vary in different communities. Also, our understanding is not perfect: some people and some churches consider a certain thing harmful while others do not see it as a threat.

We ought to take a critical look before accepting every new invention that comes along. In the long run, how will it affect the family farm? Will it help to make more use of horsepower and family labor on the farm? Will it encourage working together as a family unit and as a community, to help each other? Or will we have so much money invested in expensive equipment that it may become necessary to take a job off the farm to pay for it?

These things ought to be taken into careful consideration as to whether they are practical in our way of living. This should be of more importance to us than just the dollar signs. After all, riches are fleeting and elusive, and running after them can take us into territory where we have no business being.

[On farming, also see chapter 5, below.]   (D. Wagler, 6-90)

Traveling Time

Shallow reasoning has been used by people who decided it didn't make sense to spend an hour going to town by buggy when they could go the same distance by car in ten minutes. "Why," such people have reasoned, "if we had a car, we wouldn't spend nearly as much time on the road and could be at home with the family more."

By taking one single trip to town and figuring how much longer it would take by buggy, the above conclusion sounds reasonable. But the matter isn't that simple. Instead of spending less time on the road, people who switch to motorized transportation soon discover they are on the road more than before. Since it's easier to go to town, they tend to go oftener and for smaller needs. They soon begin to shop and visit places farther from home. It's just as easy to drive fifty miles as it used to be to drive five, and that's exactly what they do. So they end up spending more time on the road than before.

("Views and Values," E. Stoll, 1-72)

Safer Travel

When buggies and automobiles tangle, the buggy usually comes out the loser. We believe this is as it should be for a people who are nonresistant, since we would rather be the victim than the aggressor. After incidents such as this, we read about the dangers of buggy travel on today's busy roads. We suspect there are some among us who would join the cry and gladly switch to the car, given the chance and a proper excuse.

A buggy doesn't offer much protection against a couple tons of steel and rubber hurtling down the roadway. Yet statistics have not proved buggy travel to be as dangerous as some think. I suppose there are fewer accidents and far fewer fatalities among the plain people (on a per capita basis) than in the society around us. There are a number of reasons for this:

1. We tend to travel far fewer miles than those who drive automobiles. This reduces the opportunity to be involved in an accident. Not only are most of our trips closer to home, but we are just not inclined to go to places where we really don't need to go, because it takes so long to get there. (The more we use taxis, for short trips as well as "vacation," the less this becomes true.)

2. We travel at a far slower speed. When an accident does occur, there is less chance of it being a serious one.

3. There is not usually (I wish I could say "never") alcohol or drugs involved on our part.

4. We strive to practice Christian virtues, such as patience, courtesy, and concern for others when we are on the road.

While our communities vary on how much or what type of lighting, reflectors, and reflectorized tape we use, there can be some general statements that apply to all. When there is something that can be put to a good use, there are usually people who will abuse it. I am not surprised that some communities resist the addition of reflectors and brighter lights to the buggies. We have all seen cases where these were being used as decoration instead of protection. This is where the church can make some guidelines.

Another area where we could all use some improvement is in courtesy on the road. This means giving the right-of-way to cars, even if it does mean pulling off to the side. Let's all consider the fact that we are responsible to conduct ourselves so we aren't a hazard to those around us.

[On cars, see also chapter 6, below.]   ("Staff Notes," 5-92)

Telephones: The Choice of Two Evils

"I wonder which is the worst, anyway?" Fred Hostetler muttered to himself as he sat down at the supper table.

"Worst of what?" his wife, Saloma, asked as she stirred a pinch of salt into the soup.

"I mean, which way would be the worst, to have a phone of our own, or to be continually pestering our neighbors to use theirs?"

"Surely you don't think we should get telephones?" Saloma asked as a frown crossed her face. "Our people have never had them. You wouldn't want to change the *Ordnung* now, would you?"

"No, I wouldn't," Fred answered firmly. "But just the same, I still can't help wondering sometimes which would be the worst. Did you know that they allowed telephones over in the Concordia settlement?"

"You mean there where Atlee Kauffmans moved? I knew they were a little more liberal in some things, but I never thought they would allow telephones."

"They figured it would be a better light to the world to have telephones than to be bothering their neighbors all the time to use theirs."

"But couldn't they explain why we don't have telephones?"

"I guess so, but I've found it's harder to explain that to someone than it is to explain why we don't have cars or radios or something like that," Fred said. "Atlee wrote that the phones are to be allowed strictly for business and emergency only, no gossiping or unnecessary calling."

About five years later, Fred Hostetlers were planning a trip to visit close relatives in Missouri. "Why don't we stop at Concordia on the way back and visit Atlee Kauffmans?" Fred asked.

The Kauffmans were glad to see their old neighbors and welcomed them warmly. "You just come in and sit down. You can visit until dinner is ready," Ruby said.

Fred went out to see Atlee, who was remodeling the cow stable. As the men walked from the barn toward the pasture, a shrill voice came from the house, "*Dad-dy! Telephone!*"

When Atlee returned, he grumbled, "Those seed-corn agents can sure be a nuisance. I told him the other day I'd let him know if I wanted to order anything from him. But he insists on calling me every few days."

After showing Fred around the farm a bit, Atlee said, "We may just as well go in. Dinner should be ready in an hour."

They washed up and went to sit down in the living room. Fred thought he heard a conversation going on, and then saw that Ruby was talking on the telephone. As the men came into the room, she was saying, "Well, I'll have to go now. We've got company for dinner. Thanks for calling. I'll call you back later."

They sat down to visit, and Atlee started telling how his team of horses ran away the summer before. "We let them stand in the hayfield, and they got scared of the baler. Up the lane they went toward home as fast as they could go, until they got to that tree in the lane. Then one horse went around on one side of the tree, and the other one on the other side, and the wagon—"

"*Rrrrrrr!*" The ring of the phone abruptly interrupted the story. Atlee came back and took up the conversation where he had left off. After some time, the phone rang again. Atlee answered it: "Yes, yes. Who? Minerva? Yes, she's here."

About this time the oldest daughter came flying into the room and grabbed the receiver. From the kitchen came the voice of Ruby as she lamented, "Minerva wouldn't have to get so excited every time the phone rings. Now she went and spilled the cornstarch all over the work table. Those Worner girls have a bad habit of calling her any time of the day."

Fred and Atlee got back into their conversation. At 11:30, Ruby came into the room, picked up the receiver, and started dialing. "Hello, Patty. This is me. I hate to bother you, but right now I discovered we're plum out of sugar. We forgot to get some the other day when we were in town. We need some to make the frosting on the cake."

By the time dinner was ready, it was just past twelve o'clock. Ruby had fixed a big meal, and everyone was hungry. As the family sat down to the table, everyone bowed their heads solemnly to give thanks to the almighty God in heaven for his goodness in providing such a bounteous meal. Just as everyone had folded their hands and silently bowed their heads, there was a loud noise. "*Rrrrrrr!*" The telephone was urgently ringing. . . .

As the big Greyhound bus pulled into the station, the Hostetlers hastily bade good-bye to their friends. Soon they were on the last stretch of their journey, heading home.

"Are you still wondering what it would be like to have a telephone in the house?" Saloma asked.

Fred almost had to smile as he answered, "Well, now I know what it could be like, but that's not saying it would have to be like that. I don't think everyone with a telephone has as much going on as the Kauffmans did."

"That could all be," Saloma agreed. "But actually, you only saw half of it. In the afternoon when you and Atlee went over to visit old Sam Miller, the phone was as busy as ever. One time Ruby called Allen Kauffman's wife to ask how much soda she puts in her coconut cookies. Then later in the afternoon, she called her sister to ask what number of thread she uses to sew that blue double-knit material for a dress. That time she talked about half an hour. And Minerva, I think she called up her friends and talked with them several times during the afternoon. She seems to have a lot of friends of all kinds. Are you still unable to answer your question?"

"It looks to me like that would be making a choice between two evils, and I don't think it is necessary to do either one. What I had in mind was the way they do it out in Missouri, but I don't believe that's the perfect answer either."

"How do they do it there?"

"They asked the telephone company to put a phone at the school-house. It's not a large community there, and they can go to the schoolhouse to do their calling. Then they don't have to bother their neighbors so much. They seem to think it's working out all right, and as far as bothering the neighbors is concerned, it apparently is. But I'm afraid there's another danger they may not realize."

"What's that?"

"I'm afraid they're using the phone more than they really have to," Fred said. "By planning their business out ahead, they could often get along without using the phone as they do now. From what I saw in Missouri, I think they could have done a lot of their business by mail, such as ordering feed, and so on."

"But wouldn't it be handier to do it by phone?" Saloma asked.

"Yes, it would be, and sometimes it is about the only way it can be done," Fred agreed. "But a lot of other things would be handy, too. What I was wondering is, Will their children be able to see the dangers in having these things which are so handy, if the parents make use of them so much as they do?"

"I guess there's a danger any way you do it," Saloma said. "But do you mean to say that out there in Missouri, they never have to bother their neighbors?"

"I never said that," Fred answered. "There will still be emergencies, such as someone getting hurt, when they want to get help as soon as possible. I don't think the neighbors object to using their phones at times like that. It's the idea of bothering them continually and for things that don't look necessary to them. That's what gets on their nerves."

"I don't think I'd appreciate that myself," Saloma responded.

"I guess not," Fred laughed, "especially if they tracked their dirty boots over your nice clean floor right after you had done the Saturday cleaning!"   (2-76)

Following are short articles of discussion and debate on a wide variety of issues. A question is often poised in the "What Do You Think?" column, and readers send in their thoughts.

Vaccinations

Does vaccination show a lack of faith in God?

[Four of the five answers felt vaccinations were acceptable. The one negative response considered it a form of insurance. One writer said it is common to vaccinate horses, cattle, and hogs, so why not children? Another reader responded:]

Yes, I strongly feel it's our duty to protect our children from disease when it's in our power. People who say we shouldn't vaccinate remind me of the man who was sitting in his buggy, with his horse hitched up. When someone told him there was a child standing between the buggy wheels, he answered, "Oh, just trust in God. He'll take care of the child." I don't think such attitudes are right. We should do our part, and do what we can.

("What Do You Think?" 5-81)

Social Security

We have asked to be exempt from social security so we won't become dependent on the government. Many of our people signed statements: "I am conscientiously opposed on religious grounds, as taught in Matthew 6:34, to old age and survivors' insurance. I want to put my trust in our heavenly Father for my future needs, as stated in Matthew 6:31-33 and Psalm 37:7-25. Should I, through sickness or otherwise, become in need, rather than accept government benefits, I trust that I will be taken care of through my respected church with alms, as has been our practice since before our people came to America and to this day."

Every year through alms, thousands of dollars are used to help our old and needy. Yet I fear that in the future, more of our Amish people will show up at government institutions unless we can make provisions for our love, dollars, and hands to help share their burdens.

(S., Ohio, 5-68)

Owning Guns: Hunting for Food

The Amish have traditionally used guns to hunt for food and have not had a conscience against it. I am sixty years old and cannot remember that the practice was ever questioned until a few years ago.

Last fall one of my brothers, older than I, shot a deer on his farm and provided himself with a nice supply of meat for the winter. I think the deer is a lovely creature, and I doubt if anyone gets more pleasure out of watching them trot through the bottoms on a summer day. On the other hand, their meat is so similar to beef that I cannot believe they were created just to look at.

For myself, I can see no connection between owning a gun and nonresistance, or between shooting a rabbit and killing a person. Sometimes it's the misuse of a thing that's wrong and not the thing itself. I think there is a big difference between the man who hunts rabbit or squirrel or deer for food, and the one who goes to Wyoming to hunt elk for sport.

("Letter," 8/9-82)

Why I See a Danger in Games and Sports

To what degree is it proper for us to take part in sports and games played within our own communities? Here there does not appear to be easy agreement.

In some communities, married men go to town and play baseball, an Amish team against a non-Amish team. Other communities would frown on that, but would think nothing of married men playing, as long as both teams were made up of members of the Amish community.

Then in still other communities, the married men would not play, but boys with the young folks would play ball Sunday afternoons after church services. Other communities would not permit their young people to play on Sunday, but their young people, both boys and girls, would gather to play ball during the week.

Last of all, some communities teach that playing should be confined to children, and sports to the world. Such communities feel that neither game playing nor sports are fitting for church members, whether married or unmarried.

In the midst of such a variation, where is the correct place to make a line? To complicate matters, ball playing is only one example. The same questions apply to hunting and fishing, racing horses, volleyball, hockey, card playing, and all other games adults play. I will attempt to state my own personal convictions:

1. Playing is for children. It is not wrong for parents to guide and instruct their children in wholesome play; nor is it wrong for parents to join children in play at suitable times. But it does seem out of place when adults spend time playing games with each other.

2. Sports belong to the world.

3. Games promote a generation gap. Some parents have tried to overcome this by advocating that married people should join in freely with games and sports of the young people. I, for one, would be unspeakably ashamed if the judgment day should dawn suddenly and find me, along with the rest of the church (bishop, fellow ministers, parents, young people) playing a game of volleyball.

4. Sports break down our separation [from the world].

5. Sports detract from worthwhile things.

6. Sports destroy a sense of modesty.

7. Sports fail to satisfy.

8. Games are disrespectful on Sunday. If we have any purpose in life at all, any spiritual goals we seek to obtain, we should surely be able one day out of the entire week to find something worthwhile to occupy our time and attention. (E. Stoll, 3-82)

Law and Order

Someone asks, "Should a Christian call or notify the police after he finds his home broken into or robbed while away from home? Does calling the police go against the teaching of nonresistance?"

You wonder how far defenseless Christians should go when thieves enter their house. Inform the police about what took place and answer their questions. That's it. No charges. No prosecution if the thieves are caught. Paul urges Christians to give civil authorities their due, be it in taxes, respect, or in honor (Rom. 13:1-7; Titus 3:1). We should always make sure there is *no* money left at home whenever we go away. Let us not be found guilty of leading weaker souls into temptation. ("What Do You Think?" 7-78)

For Complete Separation

After reading the answers on notifying police in case of theft, I did some thinking. A nonresistant person cannot have someone else using force for him or through his cooperation. If a thief is caught, the person who reported him is helping to bring punishment upon him.

Wouldn't we be like Pilate? He saw "no fault" in Jesus but gave in to Jewish leaders, washing his own hands to signify innocence. Yet in our eyes, Pilate still shares the guilt [since he sentenced Jesus to be crucified; Matt. 27; Luke 23].

Separation of church and state should be complete. We should not use the state for our own purposes, but deny officials when they demand our assistance, such as in armed service or alternative duties. To submit to the government, as we are admonished in 1 Peter 2:13, doesn't mean pulling in the harness with them, but just to obey them as far as our conscience allows. ("Letter," 11-78)

Church and State

This question of what our responsibility is to the government can indeed be a difficult one, and in many areas besides whether or not to report crimes. Recently I happened to be talking with a neighbor who is not of a plain background, but still a professing Christian. He asked me what I thought of capital punishment. That is not an easy question. I never did get it explained so that he was satisfied. He said I was trying to both agree and disagree with it, and that was impossible. The root of the problem was that he could not understand our concept of separation of church and state.

I tried to explain to him that as a Christian, I could not punish anyone or take revenge, much less take a person's life. Jesus taught his followers to forgive and turn the other cheek. That was my position and the position of our church.

However, that is not what God ordained for the government. The Lord ordained government to protect the good and punish the evil [Rom. 13]. The government's role is based on the old Mosaic Law of justice—eye for eye, tooth for tooth [Exod. 21:23-25]. Therefore, I did not condemn capital punishment for the government, as long as every attempt is made to fulfill [the law] in justice.

My neighbor shakes his head and tells me I should make up my mind: either something is good or it is bad; either say yes or no. But this is not a matter of indecision. Instead, I have a firm conviction that the role of the government is different from that of the church. And the two must be forever separate. It is yes for one, but no for the other.   ("Staff Notes," 7-78)

Voting

Someone asks, "Is it right for Christians to vote for those who run for worldly political offices?"

I feel it is wrong to vote. In our country it is required that one must register in order to vote. This would not only go against the teachings of Jesus, but also Menno Simons and Jacob Ammann, who taught separation of church and state. We would be joining our names to the masses of worldly and non-Christian people. Let us not forget—we are but pilgrims in this world.   (F. G., Ill.)

I don't feel Christians should take part in voting for those who seek government office. If we do vote for such persons and help them get into office, we would also be indirectly responsible for their deeds, such as acts of war, and so forth. We ought to obey God rather than man [Acts 5:29].

The Bible does teach us to pray for those who rule over us [1 Tim. 2:1-2]. We should not take part in worldly affairs. This, I believe, is or can lead to the downfall of our plain churches.   (A. H., Md.)

One may perhaps argue that Christians who live in America or Canada live in a democracy, a free country, and hence are duty-bound to take part in the voting process and otherwise support such a government system. Our government does indeed protect and defend our right to worship God freely and in whatever manner we wish. However, as good as any country may be to live in, both Canadian and American systems of government are still much a part of this world. And in James 1:27, we read that pure and undefiled religion means to keep oneself unstained from the world.

Just because a great many Christians do participate in the voting process doesn't necessarily make it right. The Scriptures nowhere encourage one to take part in any governmental system that is part of the world. And in voting, one would in a small way be doing just this.

("What Do You Think?" N.Y., 11-77)

Labor Unions: All We Need Is Your Signature

I am replying to your request for me to join the union [where I work]. I have talked it over with several of my brethren in Christ and also with one of our ministers. None of them felt that it would be a benefit for me or to the church if I joined the union. I will try to state our reasons for not joining.

First, we as Christians must stand out from the world by the way we dress and act. In 1 Peter 2:9, we read, "But you are a chosen generation, a royal priesthood, an holy nation, a peculiar people; that you should show forth the praises of him who has called you out of darkness into his marvelous light."

In James 1:27, we read that pure religion is [to keep ourselves] unspotted from the world. (We don't have cars, radios, TV, electricity, musical instruments, telephones, stereos, and things like that.)

Then in 2 Corinthians 6:14, Paul says we should not be unequally yoked with unbelievers. I'm not saying that everyone in the union is an unbeliever, but some are. By signing up I would surely be yoking myself with unbelievers. Nowhere in the Bible have I been able to find that we as Christians should join any club or organization except the church of God.

We don't think that everything the union does is bad. But they have made the news a number of times lately with their acts of violence and lawlessness. In Ohio, I understand that just recently members of the truckers' union killed several persons. It is true that I can join the union and still not help to do things like that. But I feel that if I join the union, then I will be held partly responsible for what they do since I know beforehand that they do things like this. This is the way I look at it: I can't hold the gun and be innocent of the shooting just because I let someone else pull the trigger.

Generally speaking, we feel that the union's way of dealing with the company is directly contrary to the true Christian way. The union says to the company, "You pay us so-and-so or else," but the Bible teaches us to recompense no man evil for evil [Rom. 12:17]. We are to love our enemies, bless them that curse us, do good to them that hate us, and pray for those who despitefully use us (Matt. 5:44).

In other words, the union uses force, but the Bible teaches us to use love and good works. In our church, we don't try to force anyone to join, but we do try to use our influence so that people will want to join. I believe the union should work the same way.

Last, though I am in perfect agreement with the church in their stand against labor unions, I would still not go against my religious convictions. If I have a job a union member wants, I will exchange jobs with him, and I will not vote against the union. But I think you should have an exemption in your contract for people whose faith keeps them from joining your union.

I do not have any ill feelings against you or anyone else in the union. If there are any more questions, I will be glad to try to answer them for you.   (8/9-77)

Christmas Cards and Valentines

Six-year-old Mary popped into the kitchen all aglow with excitement. Setting her lunch bucket on the cupboard, she raced to mother at the sewing machine. "Guess what Sarah gave me today?" she exclaimed.

"Oh, maybe a cookie," Mother answered.

"Oh, no, it's nothing to eat," Mary said. "It's something very pretty." She jumped around excitedly.

"Then I can hardly imagine what it is," Mother responded.

With that, Mary brought forward the hand she was hiding behind her back. In it was a brown envelope. "Can you guess now?"

"Is it a picture?"

"You're almost right," Mary said as she took a homemade Christmas card from the envelope. "See, Mother, isn't that a pretty donkey? And the baby—Sarah said that is Baby Jesus. Inside the card, she made candles and Christmas packages. She gave Betty and Susannah each one, too. The other girls said they'd make some, too. Oh, Mother, isn't it pretty? I want to make a Christmas card for Mary, too."

That evening Father and Mother did a lot of thinking. Mary was their first child in school. What would come out of this if they let the children make Christmas cards to give away? So they explained to Mary, "It's not necessary to send Christmas cards, for all our friends know we wish them well at Christmas and at other times of the year, too. There is a chance the honor will not be put in the right place. They could easily go too far with it."

The next evening Mary came home a lot happier than she left in the morning. "Betty and Susannah may not make Christmas cards, either," she said.

Mother knew Christmas was to be a time of honor to God. The verse came to her mind, "In all that you do and say, do all unto the glory of God" [1 Cor. 10:31].

Back to her came the thought of her own childhood days. She [and her church friends] went to the big school, but she had been surprised that they were allowed to give valentines. Perhaps then it was because all the other children did it and they went along, but now they had their own schools.

Mother also began to wonder: What's a valentine for?

(Wallenstein, Ont., 2-76)

Photographs

A question was raised about having knickknacks, dolls, and photographs since Exodus 20:4 seems to forbid them.

Also Against Images

It is inconsistent for us as plain people to have small figures, knick-knacks, or photographs standing around. I think we have plenty of other Scriptures against these so that we don't need to make Exodus 20:4 say something it was never meant to say. Exodus 20:4 is talking about making images for idol worship and then praying to them. I'm afraid if we try to apply this verse, we are bound to contradict ourselves.

If this verse is forbidding all images and likenesses and photographs, then we shouldn't use coins with images engraved on them, or postage stamps with pictures on them. We also shouldn't allow an X-ray to be taken, for this is nothing else but taking a photograph of our bodily structure. Worse yet, we shouldn't allow our children to make any pictures at all. Even a simple drawing of a cat would be wrong, for certainly it is making a likeness of something.

Please don't misunderstand me. I also think it is wrong to have images, knickknacks, and photographs. I believe we should all work harder to keep our houses plain and simple and consistent with our dress. I have written this because I feel that only harm and frustration can result from giving a wrong reason for holding a right belief.

("What Do You Think?" 2-71)

No Graven Image

Perhaps it is time for us plain people to examine our position concerning pictures and photographs. Why do we feel as we do?

When we plain people are asked why we are opposed to the use of photographs, someone often comes up with the verse from Exodus 20, the second of the Ten Commandments: "Thou shalt not make unto thee any graven image, or any likeness of any thing that is in heaven above, or that is in the earth beneath, or that is in the water under the earth."

However, does this verse really fit when applied to having our picture taken? The answer is neither a simple yes or no, or perhaps it is both.

If we mean in a literal way, the answer is no. The verse does not apply because the verse says we should not make a graven image or a likeness of anything, period. It doesn't say, "Thou shalt not make a photograph of a man's face, but to trace the outline of a child's foot is all right." Of course, we make likenesses in many other ways. Taken literally, the verse would not allow us to draw a blueprint of a house, our children should not make a picture to color, and *Family Life* shouldn't print a picture on its cover.

Or does the verse just mean photographs taken with a camera? We still have problems. Does that mean we wouldn't object to having our portrait painted, which often looks nearly as true-to-life as a photo? Does it mean we shouldn't permit X-rays to be taken, which are photographs of internal parts of our bodies? If pictures of people's faces are wrong, why do we use things with such pictures every day, on our money and coins, and on our postage stamps?

So if we answer in a literal and direct way, we would have to say no, the second commandment is not talking about taking snapshots. (If it were, what were the poor people supposed to make out of it for the thousands of years before the comparatively recent invention of the camera?)

Maybe someone will say Exodus 20:4 means a graven image, a likeness carved or molded, with a three-dimensional effect. But that wouldn't even include photographs. Besides, we don't observe the graven-image part, either. Check how many toy cows and horses are in your child's toy box.

However, if it is understood in an indirect way, yes, the plain people's traditional opposition to photographs and their tendency to be camera-shy can be connected with the commandment against idolatry. Taken in this indirect way, some of the things that appear inconsistent in our stand begin to make sense. That will then explain why we are not alarmed by the toy cow in the play box, the picture on the postage stamp, but try to look the other way when someone holds a camera in front of us.

We believe that posing for photographs is part of the world's misguided emphasis on glorifying the outward person. The Bible tells us that it is the inner man that is important [1 Pet. 3:3-4]. Fixing up our hair, wearing jewelry, bright colors, fancy clothing—these are the world's ways of drawing attention to the beauty of the created. God wants us to honor the Creator, not the created. The world puts a lot of emphasis on a pretty girl or a handsome boy. As Christians, we should work against this kind of thinking. A person's facial features should not affect our opinion of a person's worth or value.

Thus we believe that letting ourselves get involved in the world of photography leads us away from humility, not toward true humility. We already have problems with too much emphasis on dress and finery at weddings and such occasions. Going to a photo studio to have such occasions recorded in a permanent visual record only increases this temptation toward false values and unchristian adornment. We have enough pride in our hearts without feeding and encouraging it by doing things that tend to increase the temptations.

There is also the stewardship question. Photography is expensive. Once a church becomes involved in it, there seems to be no end to the sums that can be spent for equipment and film. All this to attempt and make permanent what God has decreed shall pass away.

In conclusion then, if we take the second commandment directly and literally, it doesn't make sense to apply it to our opposition to cameras. But taken in a more indirect way, things begin to add up. We don't want to emphasize the outer self, lest we do it at the expense of the inner being. We don't want to exalt self, lest we rob the Creator of his glory.

It follows then that we are not opposed to a graven image in the toy box; few people are tempted to hang their hearts on a child's toy. That explains why we make a difference between a photograph of our backbone, and one of our faces. No proud grandfather has been tempted to impress people he meets by pulling from his wallet X-ray photos of his grandchild's spinal column! (This is also why some church groups allow snapshots to be taken when requested by the government for their files, photos not kept personally.)

No, let us not slip gradually, bit by bit, into the ways that lead to an emphasis on pride and personal vanity. gone, let us be remembered not by how broad were o   , the height of our brows, or the angle of our cheekbones, but by what truly matters—the lives we have lived and the examples we have left.

Dust we are, to dust we shall return [Gen. 3:19]. Why frame and embellish and hang on the wall the pictures of this house of clay in which we live? Let us beware lest we permit self to be exalted, becoming unto us a graven image.   (E. Stoll, 3-87)

A Spoiled Generation

Several years ago I noticed a small cartoon in a newspaper that caught my attention. It showed a picture of a living room in a typical modern home. A brightly lighted and gaily decorated Christmas tree was in one corner. A ten-year-old boy stood in the middle of a wide assortment of toys he had just unwrapped. There was an electric train piled to one side of him, a brand-new bike leaning against the wall, a catcher's mitt at his feet, and in his hands he held a model airplane. The room all around him was strewn with expensive toys and gifts and wrapping paper.

It was a simple cartoon, but it told a complete story. He held the last gift in his hand and was looking around for more, with a frown on his face. Under the cartoon was the caption: "*You mean this is all I get?*"

What a spoiled child! His parents had spent a couple hundred dollars on several dozen toys, gadgets, and playthings. Instead of being awed and grateful, he complained because there weren't more. Instead of complaining, his eyes should have been shining and his lips saying, "You mean I get all this!"

However hard it is to believe that a child could be so spoiled, the truth is that all of us have more in common with this child than we like to think. In a way, all of us have become spoiled children, unbelievably blessed in material things, and yet standing in the midst of plenty and waste and asking, "You mean this is all I get?"

We have life rather easy compared with our forebears. They were hunted, persecuted, tortured, and killed. The government passed special laws against them. We have religious freedom, and the government passes special laws in our favor. [We don't expect to suffer] torture or pain [as punishment for faith].

Our immigrant forefathers toiled with their axes and hoes to wrest a living from thick forests and tree-stump covered clearings. We have rich dark soil, loose and fertile and productive, and teams of horses to work it with. They had to make almost everything, from their ax handles to their homespun clothing. We go to town and buy what we want. No weary hours working into the night carving, weaving, spinning.

Our forebears had a diet with little variety—corn mush, potatoes, meat. Our tables are loaded with delicacies they never heard of—bananas, oranges, and pineapples. They wore clothing that was rough, stiff, and uncomfortable. We have superfabrics with nylon added to last longer, or Dacron to keep out the wrinkles.

We have it easy. We have grown fat, soft, lazy, and spoiled. We have forgotten how to suffer, and we refuse even to be inconvenienced. Everything has to be handy. Our ancestors would walk several hundred miles to visit relatives. They would ride horseback over rough and dangerous trails, taking several weeks or months to make the trip.

Today, Greyhound buses speeding over superhighways aren't fast enough for us. We want a taxi to pick us up at our doorstep and chauffeur us wherever we want to go. It's too much bother to change buses, carry suitcases, and wait in depots. Will our children in turn find it too much bother to hire a taxi, and decide to buy a car themselves so they can go when and where they like?

It does seem to work that way. The luxuries of one generation become the necessities of the next. Let's look at just one area of life, our water supply. When our forebears came to this country, they likely carried their water from a spring. There were many trips for water, morning, evenings, and even through the day. It was tiresome, time-consuming labor, but it was accepted without question because it had to be done.

Gradually, as homes became more permanent, wells became common. What a luxury this must have seemed! A well within a hundred feet of the house. No more long trips down the dusty, winding path for water. Now it was close, convenient, and handy. All they had to do was lower the bucket into the well, and hand over hand pull up sparkling, clean fresh water.

After a generation or two, pumps came on the scene. Ah, once again, how handy it seemed. No more straining backs and tired, aching arms, pulling that rope to bring up a bucket of water. Just grab the pump handle, and up comes the water. It was much quicker and easier.

Nevertheless, what one generation thought was so easy, the next found tiring. They felt pumping water by hand was a hardship and took so long. So up went a windmill. Ah, the whole family was amazed at the utter convenience of it all. No more standing, puffing, and pumping. All they had to do was walk to the well and dip the water from a large wooden tank. It seemed so much easier that this generation never imagined the next might balk at the trip to the well. But that is exactly what happened.

What? Walk to the well and carry all that water! I guess not. So in goes a system of water pipes. Ah, what grand luxury. Water pumped right into the house, water waiting and ready twenty-four hours of the day at the turn of a spigot. Turn it open, and there's water to wash the face, water to cook a meal, water to fill the teakettle.

Fill the teakettle, did you say? What for? To heat water to wash the dishes? Ha, guess again. That's not for us. We're the next generation. Who has time to heat water when we want it? Why, with the water heater installed, all we need to do is turn the tap, and there is all the hot water we like.

That brings us up to the present. What will the next generation want? We immediately think, "But hot water on the tap, that's so handy to wash dishes with, we can't imagine that our children won't be satisfied with that."

No, of course not. Our parents couldn't imagine that we wouldn't be satisfied with *their* luxuries, either. What we appreciate, our children take for granted.

Satan likes to make us believe that if we only had this or that, we could be so much happier. If only the church would allow this, we'd be satisfied. We wouldn't ask for more. We'd be content.

Would it really work that way? Let's look around with our eyes open. If having an abundance of material things would bring contentment, then those who have the most should be the most contented. Who has more material things than the people of the world? Anything they like, they can go and buy. New cars. Fancy clothes. Vacations to faraway places. Anything. You name it, and the world has it. And if they don't, they invent it.

Then are they contented? Are they satisfied with what they have? The answer is obvious. One look at the headlines of a newspaper should convince anyone. Riots. Strikes. Demands. Boycotts. Protests. Marches. Welfare. Unrest. Crime. Divorces. Suicides. Rebellions. Violence. Tension.

There never was a generation that had so much and appreciated it so little. Young people grow up and never raise a finger to work. Still they are dissatisfied and run away by the thousands. No, the people of the world aren't content with all the luxuries they have. Jesus said long ago, "A man's life does not consist in the abundance of the things he possesses" (Luke 12:15).

The time has come for each of us to stop and ask some questions. Where are we as plain people? Where have we come from? Where are we going? What factors have brought us to where we are today? In what ways have we suffered from too much materialism? To what degree do we have the same spirit the world has, the spirit of always wanting more?

What are the solutions? Perhaps the first step is to become aware of how good we really have it, and to realize what spoiled children we have become.

Another thing that would help would be to renew our convictions on the teachings of the Bible showing the importance of simple living. We need to rediscover that a simple way of life, separated and apart from the world, is indeed God's pattern for his people.

However scriptural simple living is, it is not an automatic passport to heaven. Thousands of people live simple lives, with just a roof above their heads and a dirt floor beneath their feet, and so few earthly possessions that they can load them all onto an oxcart. They may still live ungodly lives, wallowing in sin and poverty. Hand in hand with our simple living must be a devout faith in God, honesty of conviction, and an earnest desire for the brotherhood. Olden times were more simple, but that doesn't mean that everything that is old is good. Our goal is not to pattern after the early Americans, but after the early Christians.

Will the same trends and influences that have wrecked families and communities in the world around us, also destroy us in time? If we follow the same route, travel in the same train, we cannot expect to arrive at a different destination. Trailing fifty years behind the world isn't going to get us where we want to be. Those who ride in the caboose are going to the same place as the engineer.

There is constant pressure in the surrounding society to conform in such areas as travel and work. Yet there is plenty of evidence, if we care to see it, that such things as tractor farming and automobile travel are deadly in the long run, eroding the values of brotherhood, simple living, family sharing, and meaningful community relationship.

If we allow ourselves to become like spoiled children, always wanting more and more, we cannot expect long to resist the temptation these and other modern inventions present to us and our children. If our love of ease becomes greater than our willingness to deny ourselves and to sacrifice, we are well down the road of no return, the one-way street of modernism and materialism.

We don't need more conveniences as much as we need more convictions. In this world of emphasis on luxury and earthly possessions, it may be difficult to be content with little. But it is impossible to be content with much.   ("Views and Values," E. Stoll, 7-73)

4
Marriage
and
Family

Perhaps nothing is more vital to the Amish way of life than the family and community. The very title *Family Life* points to its importance. Yet this is also an arena with many challenges, especially since the Amish do not accept divorce. We often hear the promise "till death do us part." For the Amish, it is indeed a promise. But married life is not always wedded bliss, whether we are Amish or not.

In the relationship of husband and wife, the Amish find parallels to those between God and the church. In the family, matters of faith and their application must be played out in practical, everyday terms. Here religion and reality come together in the Amish community, for better or for worse.

Marriage, a Most Sacred Institution

There are three reasons why a wedding is one of the most unique of the services held by our churches today. For one thing, it is the most joyous. The second reason is that a wedding is such a serious event, where a lifetime commitment is being made. The third reason is that it is such a sacred event because it is an *Abbildung*, a representation of the spiritual union between Christ and his bride, the church.

In Lancaster County (Pa.), it is customary for the Amish wedding season to begin after the fall communion and continue until Christmas. The young married couples then spend the rest of the winter in visiting. Uncles and aunts receive an overnight visit. It is the couple's way of starting out on the journey of life together.

I am thankful that in our churches, marriage vows are taken very seriously and are considered a lifetime commitment. If we listen carefully to the words of the marriage ceremony and to the vows exchanged, we find it inconceivable that any provision can be made for divorce and remarriage. I do not believe our churches could have survived and maintained their separation from the world over the centuries if we had not taken the marriage vows so seriously and literally.

We believe reconciliation is the key word to solving marital problems. As long as remarriage remains an option, reconciliation does not get a fair trial. Reconciliation works satisfactorily only when the scriptural requirement is enforced as the only option the church has to offer: possible separation but no remarriage.

("Now That I Think of It," D. Wagler, 1-91)

Questions Asked at the Marriage Ceremony

1. Do you acknowledge and confess it as a Christian order that there should be one husband and one wife, and are you able to have the confidence that you have begun this undertaking in accordance with the way you have been taught? *Answer: Yes.*

2. Do you also have the confidence, Brother, that the Lord has ordained this, our fellow sister, as a marriage partner for you? *Yes.*

3. Do you also have the confidence, Sister, that the Lord has ordained this, our fellow brother, as a marriage partner for you? *Yes.*

4. Do you solemnly promise your wife that if she should be afflicted with bodily weakness, sickness, or some similar circumstance, that you will care for her as is fitting for a Christian husband? *Yes.*

5. Do you promise the same to your husband, that if he should be afflicted with bodily weakness, sickness, or some similar circumstance, that you will care for him as is fitting for a Christian wife? *Yes.*

6. Do you solemnly promise each other that you will love and bear and be patient with each other, and not separate from each other until the God of love shall separate you from each other through death? *Yes.*

[Prayer and wedding passage from the German text of Tobit 7, in the Apocrypha (related to the Hebrew Bible or Old Testament, but written later, preserved in Greek, and included in Luther's *Bibel* as useful reading but not equal to the Scriptures).]

Now we find that Raguel took the hand of the maiden [Sarah] and put it into the hand of Tobias, and he blessed them [as we do here today]: The God of Abraham, the God of Isaac, and the God of Jacob be with you and help you unite, and shed his blessing richly upon you, and this through Jesus Christ. Amen.

(From *Handbuch für Prediger* [Handbook for preachers], 2-88)

Making Marriage a Success

We must think of marriage as being more than a civil contract. It constitutes a bond that only God can bind. Two souls are united into one, to live together as one. The apostle Paul says, "So ought men to love their wives as their own bodies. He that loveth his wife loveth himself" [Eph. 5:28].

The happiness of the husband and wife determines the kind of home the children will be born into.

No one is born a good marriage partner. [Each spouse] must pay the price of being one. The happiest marriages are those in which people do what they can to make each other happy, instead of using each other to make themselves happy. Marriage partners must remember that everyone has faults and needs forgiveness. Therefore, it takes the force of true love to blend two different personalities into one happy union. Love, if it is to grow, must be nurtured. It must not be taken for granted, even after marriage.

Many homes are unhappy because the husbands do not function as partners with their wives. They are quick to quote the Bible verse that says, "Wives, submit yourselves to your own husbands," or "The husband is the head of the wife" [Eph. 5:22-23]. Wives do not become servants, slaves, or puppets.

Woman was not taken from man's head for him to lord over her. She was not taken from his feet so that he could trample on her or kick her around. But she was taken from his side, close to his heart, thus being a loving partner to help him with life's responsibilities [Gen. 2:18-23]. Among [her duties] are allowing the husband to be the head of the house, converting a house into a home, and assuming the responsibilities of motherhood. Certainly the submission of the wife does not mean slavish subjection, but a joyful working together for a common cause. (12-78)

Heirs Together

[Title from 1 Pet. 3:7.] Some husbands get the idea that their position of authority in the home gives them the right to be harsh, demanding, and unreasonable. The answer to this problem is *love*. The apostle Paul writes in Ephesians 5:25, "Husbands, love your wives, even as Christ also loved the church, and gave himself for it." That is a big commandment, for Christ loved the church so much that he was willing to die for it.

It is true that the Bible puts a lot of emphasis on how wives should obey, should submit, should be humble and faithful. Too often men forget that the Bible also says some things about the duty of husbands. More is required of husbands than of wives. It is hard to submit to authority in the right spirit, but it is even harder to use that authority in the right way. To be trusted with a position of authority is not something to be taken lightly. It is not an easy place to fill. Let us remember that those who misuse the authority entrusted to them will someday have to give an account for their actions, just as well as those who are placed under authority and refuse to submit to it.

("Views and Values," E. Stoll, 4-77)

The Head of the Home

Some people think the man some sort of beastly ruler of the home. Probably the main reason why woman has not kept her place of subjection and submission in the world today, in the church, and in the home—is because man has failed to take his place. The apostle Paul says that Christ is the head of man, and man is the head of woman [1 Cor. 11:3]. One of the greatest needs of our time is men who will assume the responsibility that God has placed on their shoulders.

Brethren, no matter what we do or say, the responsibility of headship rests upon us. If we are going to assume the responsibility of establishing a Christian home, God expects us to assume the headship of the home. The Bible teaches that men are primarily responsible for the way things go. Not to accept that responsibility is to lie down on the job, to fail God's will. The woman should help the man wholeheartedly, but she should not be the head. Where we turn the teaching over to the women, we cannot expect God's richest blessings on the home or the church.

(6-71)

The Place of Women

Women in the Church

The modern housewife who thinks everything in marriage is a fifty-fifty proposition ought to read Ephesians 5:21-23. And the husband who thinks himself the household dictator ought also to reread it. Christian marriage, unlike Greek, Roman, and Jewish marriage, is not built on a foundation of feminine inferiority. Women are spiritually equal to men in God's plan of salvation. There is equality of partners. In these two respects then, it can be said that Jesus' teaching on marriage is revolutionary. He did raise the position of women immensely. Jesus erased the inferiority of women, but not their position of being subject to men.

Were not the apostles, the seventy disciples, the New Testament writers, and the early Christian missionaries men? Where in the Bible is there any teaching conferring official positions in the church on women? There isn't any such teaching. If a woman were ordained, she would then be the head of men, and her husband and other husbands would be subject to her. This is not the order God has given to his church. Women ministers in the Mennonite Church in the Netherlands? Yes, seventeen women who do not understand God's will for his church. (D. Luthy, 8-68)

Distinct Roles

It's not a question at all of whether or not women are as good as men. The Bible teaches us clearly that men and women are equal. But being equal in worth does not mean being the same in calling. This is where modern women make their greatest mistake. Men are still men, women still women, no matter how equal. Each has been assigned separate and distinct roles by the great Creator.

If marriage were to be fifty-fifty, that would result in two people being the head of the home. Not only is that not scriptural, it isn't even workable. As one writer summed it up, "In any kind of relationship involving more than one person, there must be the head of the relationship. Further, no organization, large or small, commercial or philanthropic, secular or religious, has more than one president, ruler, or head."   ("Views and Values," E. Stoll, 3-77)

Subordinate but Not Inferior

Subordinate does not mean inferior. God has set up authority everywhere, such as in government, the church, the school, and the home. The citizens shall be subordinate to the government, but this does not make them inferior. Lay members shall be subordinate to the leaders of the church, but this does not make inferior people out of them [Heb. 13:17]. Even the most brilliant pupil should be subordinate to his teacher, but this does not make him inferior. The same thing applies in the home between children and their parents, and between man and wife.   ("Editor's Note," 1-76)

Starved (for Affection)

I noticed in the weight-watchers article that several of the women said their husbands didn't want them to be overweight. Perhaps the underlying reason a lot of women are overweight is because of a lack of affection and understanding. If they would get all the love they need from their husbands, they wouldn't keep trying to fill that void within themselves with food. If supplying the affection is too much trouble for the husbands, they can just forget about voicing their opinions about that extra fat.   ("Letter," 8/9-79)

A husband wrote to ask what others do when the wife gets a crying spell. "Do you comfort her lovingly, or just ignore it all and hope she will get over it again?" Here are two answers:

Mutual Encouragement in Marriage

Meeting Each Other's Needs

Since the husband cared enough to write for advice about his wife's tears, I want to say, "God bless him. Talk to your wife! Work toward an honest, open relationship." My husband loved me but couldn't handle his emotions. If I cried, he would yell at the children or start a tirade of how inconsiderate they are to me. Most of the time all I needed was a strong shoulder to lean on, or a sympathetic ear.

Don't condemn. Wives pretty well know their shortcomings. Working at home alone gives one time to think. We need to know that we are not alone, that we can't be expected to be a tower of strength every moment of our lives. Be her protector, her comforter, her friend. You can be sure that if you understand each other's needs, she can be these things to you also!

("What Do You Think?" MI, 5-78)

In Favor of Sharing Problems

In the most common situations, the husbands of the weeping women have about as many fears and as much lack of confidence as their wives. I guess to really prove my sympathy to my wife, I should share my feelings and weep with her. But I try to keep my balance and avoid extreme feelings. I know from experience how completely weak and drained a body can become with the habit of being afraid of the future or others, and of myself.

The most important thing is for the wife to talk to her husband about her fears when the load gets too heavy. Being afraid to talk about our fears is more than anybody can live with for too long.

My guess is that if all the men who have gone into the silo and cried alone would write to *Family Life*, we would also have many letters.

("Letter," 10-78)

To My Beloved Wife

I think of times some twenty years ago when we were going through our courtship and first years of our marriage. We were in love then. We worked together, played together, laughed together, and mourned together.

It seems in recent years, you are giving most of your love to the children. Is there not enough love in your heart that a little might be left over for the two of us?

I know I have failed you many times, but with God's help I am trying to do better. If I touch your arm, you tend to turn away. You seem to treat me as an object rather than as a human being. I am indeed human and need your love and understanding.

My heart is not made of stone. Really, it feels like it is getting more tender as the years go by. Surely the coolness that has come between us is not the way you like it. In many ways, you do your duty well. You work hard to provide a home for me and the children, and you are very unselfish in many ways. You have many flowers and they all seem to be very well cared for, except one. It is called a bleeding heart of . . .

—*Your Loving Husband, John*   (3-79)

For the Hurt Husband

I feel sorry for you and your wife. You are the one who started the courtship, and no doubt she was pleased with you then, so you got married. When did your courtship end? Perhaps it is five or ten years since you have touched her arm, and it pleased her very much, but it embarrassed her because she didn't want to be touched or because she wanted to hurt you. Maybe she even turned away to hide a few tears of joy.

I don't think there is a woman in the world who will not respond and become quite lovable once she is very sure she is still being loved by the man she married years ago. Take her into your arms and fondly tell her what your heart is longing to say. The next time she goes for a rest on Sunday afternoon, go join her. Perhaps she's lonely and shedding a few tears because of the same gap that is troubling you.

—*Just Another Wife*   (8/9-79)

The Long Divorce

For the past several months, Lester and the rest of Valentine Zook's carpenter crew had been working on a new house for Dick Waffles and his wife, Pam. When they arrived at the house they were building, Lester saw at once that something strange was going on. Valentine called Lester and the others over to him. His face was solemn.

"You probably noticed that Dick was here," he began bluntly. "He was pretty upset, and I guess he had reason to be. Pam left him last night, and she plans to file for divorce. Dick doesn't want to spend any more money on this house, so he wants us to finish up a few things we started, and then he'll put the house up for sale as it is."

Married one day, divorced the next. Lester kept shaking his head. "I wonder how it would feel to wake up one morning and be told your wife is leaving you, is going to file for a divorce," Lester asked himself. He turned to John. "I just can't get over this."

John shook his head. "It does seem sudden to us, I guess," he said. "But don't let that deceive you."

Lester felt sick at heart. "I took my frustrations out on Lavina and was too proud to apologize and admit how unreasonable I had been." He had hurt his wife for hardly any reason at all, just because the baby cried, and farm prices kept going out of sight.

[As they worked, John shared his thinking.] "There's no way a man and wife who have a good relationship today are going to get a divorce tomorrow. People just can't do that when love and affection is there. I'm afraid Dick and Pam were divorced for a long time—not on the outside, not legally, not according to the law. Of course not. But on the inside they've been divorced for a long time. They must have been. The inside divorce always comes first.

"Our people don't believe in divorce and that is good, as far as it goes. But I'm afraid we have some divorces among us and don't know it. Husbands and wives still live in the same house, but that is about all. Their love for each other is missing. They don't feel close or loyal to each other. On the outside they are married. On the inside they are divorced. They argue. They disagree. They work against each other. [For this separation to happen,] there must have been a long time of misunderstanding, of quarreling with each other, of not apologizing, of refusing to bend to each other."

Three o'clock in the afternoon found the work completed on the Waffles' house. "Would you mind stopping in town a bit on the way home?" Lester asked John. "My wife needs a stand for the bedroom. She said she'd do without, and we'd save the money and put it toward buying a farm. I just decided today that I'd surprise her and make a neat little bed stand for her."

They poked the boards into the back of the buggy box. Then Lester said, "We're all set, I guess, except for a few items I need at the grocery store." He went straight to the freezer. For himself, he'd rather have butterscotch ripple or just plain vanilla, but he knew that his wife's favorite ice cream was maple walnut.

John's horse stood patiently while Lester unloaded the boards and bag of groceries beside their small house. As soon as John drove away, Lester opened the door and ran into the house. Lavina was at the sink, stirring something in a large mixing bowl.

"Are you baking something?" he asked. But then he knew the answer. He saw it in her face and all over the kitchen sink. She was planning to bake a carrot cake, a cake she didn't really care for, but which was his favorite. She was doing it as a special favor for him.

All of a sudden, his throat felt tight and funny, but he struggled to control himself. He took her by the arm, led her silently to the window, and pointed out at the things he had brought home from town.

"You remembered!" she said, her face lighting up.

"There's everything I need to finish it tonight, I hope, even if I have to work late. But most of all, I wanted to say, I'm sorry."

She didn't let him say more. Sure enough, she was crying again. Only this time he was crying right along with her, and he wasn't even ashamed of the tears, only sorry that he had waited so long.   (1-77)

Maturity in Marriage

Before we were married, we discovered we both loved pizza, so we decided we had a lot in common. (Of course, we didn't base our marriage on that.) Now, after fourteen years and six children, there have been times I have wondered, "Do we have *anything* in common besides that?" But in my more sane moments, I know we do. First, we love each other.

How I tried to reform my husband, the poor soul! He likes to get up late in the morning, start the day slowly, then commence to be really on the ball around 11:00 a.m., sometimes not until after dinner [lunch]. By then, he may have decided which of his numerous jobs he will work on that day. Some of the jobs have been started for days, some for weeks, some for years. He is never excited or upset. He takes everything as it comes. He has no concept of time. He is very forgetful, and sometimes is sure it's Tuesday when it's really Friday. He loves to go anywhere, day or night. And oh, he loves popcorn.

Now the extreme opposite—*me*. I get out of bed with a hop and a skip, the earlier the better, ready to tackle the job I have already planned the night before. I work at it diligently until it is finished. I work full speed all morning and into the afternoon. Then toward supper time, I start slowing down and by 8:00 p.m., I'm ready for bed. I'm prone to outbursts of alarm, distress, or even anger. I continually watch the clock; everything must be on time. I despise being late, especially to church, which I enjoy going to. Otherwise, I am happy to stay at home. And I dread popcorn.

By now you're wondering how we can stand each other. It took a while, but one thing we have always been able to do is talk things over. That's one of the keys—communication. I remember well the time he told me, "How would you like to be like I am?"

"Impossible," I answered.

Then he explained to me that this is what I am trying to do to him, trying to make him like I am, and he said that's impossible, too. I began to realize we can complement each other. In many areas, we compromise. It is essential to give in to each other, but it is not necessary to lose one's individual identity.

Even if we are extremely opposite, we seem to have exactly what the other needs to make a well-rounded union of two personalities combined in one.

However, the very thing that gives us this understanding of each other, the very vital part of our marriage, is praying together. Come what may, we have an anchor for our souls. Even if there are stormy times, we know we have a sure foundation. I don't even begrudge him his popcorn once a week. But please, not *every* day.   (2-75)

Question from a Young Mother

We are a young couple with our first, perfectly normal baby boy. Since his arrival, I feel very much deprived of the freedom I used to have since I now am tied down to all that goes into caring for a baby. Because of this, I feel I don't love our baby the way God meant for us to love children.

I feel guilty while caring for him because of the resentment I at times feel. I would not want to give him up, but my own selfishness still bothers me.

Can I help my husband raise our baby in a God-fearing way without God's contentment in my heart? Have other mothers had such feelings? If so, did you overcome them and how?

—*Tied-down Young Mother*   ("What Do You Think?" 11-82)

Mothering

Mothering is an art and a growing experience. Some young mothers seem to sail into motherhood without any problems, while others need time to grow into it. But remember, you can never be a perfect mother, nor can you have a perfect baby, so don't expect too much.

It is natural to sometimes resent the tiny baby, especially one who is fussy. Unless you feel a constant resentment, I think you should accept your feelings and realize they will pass.

Truly, loving your baby will take time, just as loving your husband came gradually. I feel sure you can help your husband raise your little one in God's way. Some day soon your little one will give you a hug and a kiss and say, "I love you." Then you will feel amply repaid for motherhood.

("What Do You Think?" E. R., Denver, Pa., 11-82)

Childless

Longing for Children

You say you are deprived of your freedom you had. Freedom for what? Freedom to help others in your spare time, do errands, or visit the sick and elderly? Or freedom to go to Tupperware and Stanley parties, or garage sales, to read books, or to go to the neighbor's place on evenings to play games?

Yes, perhaps one would have a little battle with tied-down feelings. But perhaps if you had empty arms for several years, aching to hold your own child, or had doctor bills to pay just because of trying to discover why your longed-for children are not on the way—you would be glad for tied-down feelings.

Perhaps, of course, I do not know how you feel, for we are . . .

—*Childless*   ("What Do You Think?" 11-82)

Acceptance Is the Answer

I don't feel God chose us couples to be childless because we're unworthy. Why don't we meet this childless state as a challenge from God to see what we make of it? Are we going to waste our time being bitter and filled with self-pity? Sometimes I wonder if we childless couples' biggest problem might be hurt pride. Do we feel odd or like outcasts because we can't have what most couples have? If we can't be happy without children, what makes us think we'd be happy with them? If we can't meet the challenge of *not* having children, what makes us think we'd be capable of meeting the challenge of having children?   ("Letter," Ont., 5-87)

Discipline of Children

Old Enough to Spank

I never like to cause or see disturbances in the room where church services are being conducted, such as slapping a child. If pinching the earlobe doesn't get the results needed, I respect the mother who takes the child outside a little distance from the house until she can come in with a more sweet-tempered boy, having done the job well.

This reminds me of the time I decided our one-year-old should learn to be more quiet during family prayer. When prayer was finished, I gave him a slap on his seat, which started him crying in rebellion. I spanked and talked to him until I felt my strength and heart faltering and failing me in accomplishing the needed discipline. The next Sunday, I had such a different child in church. Then I wondered why I had put it off so long, thinking it was just a minor thing.

How old does a child need to be to be old enough to be spanked? It varies, of course, but my mother always said, "If he's old enough to show rebellion, he is old enough to be spanked." That is often when they are just babies yet.

For some, it takes more than others to reach the point when they are fully yielded and the self-will completely surrendered. May our lives also be more fully surrendered to the Lord's will so that we may daily be a better example and light to our children.

("Letter," Mrs. Lester D. Miller, Shipshewana, Ind., 8/9-82)

On Spanking

Our August issue seems to have done a good job in stirring up some differences of opinion about spanking children. Here are some conclusions we might draw:

1. Spanking a child is sometimes necessary.

2. A child should never be punished in anger.

3. Spanking should reinforce patient, loving, consistent Christian teaching, but *never replace* it.

4. Spanking should be done to teach a child that certain behavior is bad, but should never leave the impression that *the child's self* is bad.

5. Spanking should be humane and merciful.

6. Finally, before bringing things to a showdown, be sure, doubly sure, that your child is old enough to know why you are applying punishment.

Sooner or later a child comes to a point of knowing what the parents want, but chooses not to obey. When you are sure the child's refusal to obey you is because of not thinking it is necessary to obey, the time has come. Discipline administered with love is not cruel. It is kindness in disguise, a way concerned parents have of sparing their children from discovering that disobedience ends in far greater pain and tragedy later in life.   ("Staff Notes," 12-82)

Are the Children His or Hers?

Our family is four-fifths male. The boys are "mine" when there are diapers to change, heads to wash, clothes to mend, Band-Aids to put on, clothes to wash, cookies to make, apples to peel, and small quarrels to stop.

The boys are "his" when there are baths to take, hair to cut, trips to make to the feed or parts store, toys to fix, a new calf being born, enough snow for toboggan rides down the steepest hills, or extra-firm discipline is needed.

They are "ours" when we have family devotion, go for walks or wade in the stream, attend church, or visit grandpa's; when they get sick at night or enter school life; when we do farm chores or we sit around the table for a meal.   ("Maturity in Marriage," 11-75)

An Indiana Grandma Remembers

I am now a grandmother, with not so many chores and no little children to take care of. We raised nine children, and nearly all of them are married. When they were small, we would get up at 4:30 or 5:00. This gave us time to chore together, have breakfast, and have a little work done before the little ones were up. If they were awake when we came in, Daddy would lend a helping hand while I got breakfast. After breakfast, all who could toddle would go out with him until he was ready to go to the field. Then they would come in or play in the yard. As the noon hour neared, I would fill the horses' mangers with hay and dole out oats for them.

When Daddy came in for dinner, the children all came in with him. He would see to it that each one was washed and at the right place around the table. Sometimes one would not want to eat this or that or was naughty. They would go to the porch. All the other children would not say a word, but sympathize with the one on the porch. When Daddy and the child came in, the eats tasted good. But this did not have to happen often.

After dinner, Daddy would take the little ones under school age for a nap. Toward evening, at 4:00 or 4:30, I would quit my work and start choring. We worked together. Often after supper, they all went out to play in the yard. A lot of times I would think that Daddy would have many other things to do instead of playing with them. I always worked. Now I can see where he was a better Daddy than I was a mother. They remember and treasure this more than anything else he could have done for them.

("Maturity in Marriage: The Children His or Hers?" 11-75)

The Family That Plays Together

Children are born with imagination, and all they need is a chance to develop it. A rag doll is just as good as an expensive wind-up beau-

ty. The imagination of children can soon give dolls the ability to cry, drink, sleep, and wet. Yet most parents find it easier to buy a box of "performing" toys than to take time to help their children with something that requires their presence and interest, plus imagination.

So in choosing a game for children, look for something they can do things with, rather than something that will do things for them. A half-dozen chairs lined up behind each other will create an instant train that children can ride to all sorts of places. Such a train can "chug-chug-chug," whistle at the crossings, load and unload passengers. The battery never runs down, though after half an hour the parents may wish it did!

Beware lest you spoil the child's natural knack for imaginative play. Two of my brother's boys were playing in our yard. We had an old discarded lawnmower without the cutting blade. They had this lawnmower, and one was hitched to the front, pulling it with a twine string, while the other grasped the handle. No grass was cut. I felt a bit of pity for them that they had to keep imagining they were cutting the lawn.

"You got the lawn mowed?" I asked them after a while.

They stopped and looked at me in surprise, amazed at my adult ignorance. "Why no," said the younger of the two, "we're not mowing anything. We're plowing this field!"

Properly put into my place, I retreated, realizing that I still had a few things to learn before I would be worthy of helping children play.

("Views and Values," E. Stoll, 3-78)

Not Mine, but Ours

Somehow the family should be such a close-knit unit that sharing is the most natural thing in the world. Sharing cannot be difficult where there is a strong feeling of love and appreciation for each other. Learning to share our toys and childhood belongings should be the foundation for easy sharing on a wider scale in the adult world.

However, families are not only for sharing material possessions. More important yet is the sharing of feelings, of problems, and of joys. In the shelter of the home, we should be able to discuss with frankness our hopes and disappointments, knowing that we are speaking to those we can trust.

Another thing that should be shared within the family is work. No home is without work, and it is fortunate that this is so. Any child who doesn't grow up helping with dishes, or doing chores, or running errands—has been cheated out of a good start in life. The family should be the place to learn to work cheerfully and well, even eagerly. Work should be shared by everyone willingly chipping in, and not by a legalistic insistence that each does an earmarked portion.

A happy family life requires giving of ourselves. We must learn to sacrifice, learn to give up our will for the other.

Some families are just so many individuals with the same last name, living in the same house. They seem to lead separate lives, go their own ways, each independent of the other. If you ask where another member of the family is, they rarely know. Apparently, they don't know where the rest of the family is, or what they are doing. Each is busy living their own life. They lack the essential elements of a joyful family life—love, togetherness, loyalty, sharing.

These sad little groups of lonely individuals are not families at all. They are failures. They are missing out on one of the greatest challenges on this earth—building a meaningful family relationship where work, possessions, and even feelings can be shared in love and trust.

("Views and Values," E. Stoll, 11-77)

Mother's Musings

Cleaning and scrubbing can wait till tomorrow,
For babies grow up, we've learned to our sorrow;
So quiet down, cobwebs; dust, go to sleep;
I'm rocking my baby, and babies don't keep!

(5-79)

5
Work

Farm Versus Factory

For readers who have never lived on a farm, the following selections will give you a feel for the Amish love of the land. They are concerned about a future in which fewer and fewer young men become farmers. As land became scarce and expensive, many of the Amish had to turn to other occupations to earn a living. Attempts to go elsewhere to buy farmland and start new settlements were often unsuccessful. In some of the larger Amish settlements, only about half of the men earn a living as farmers.

The Amish manage to keep much of the modern world at a distance. But when it comes to work and the technology used to earn a living, run a business, or operate a farm, the Amish have had to adapt, change, and compromise. The use of bottled gas, hydraulics, pneumatics, compressed air, diesel and gasoline engines, and car batteries is now common in many Amish communities. These forms of power may be used in occupations as diverse as dairy farming and furniture making. They have also made their way into the home.

The Amish are asking the logical questions that arise from this work revolution in their communities. As fewer Amish become farmers, will they lose that connection to the land that is so much a part of their culture? Will the rise of Amish businesses, some grossing in the millions of dollars, threaten their very ability to be Amish? While most Americans seek prosperity, many Amish see it as the single biggest threat to their way of life. (On tractors and machinery, also see chapter 3, above.)

Why Do We Farm?

Take paper, pencil, and calculator in hand,
And first punch in the high cost of land.
Add painting, repair bills, and taxes, too,
And sky-high interest that always seems due.
Figure in the long hours that we have to work,
At wages that would make a city guy smirk.

But, oh no! Farming is much more than that!
With our patched-up shoes and our battered-up hat,
And the smell of the stable clinging to our clothes,
To make the nonfarmer wrinkle up his nose.
Farming is the smell of the soil being plowed in the spring,
While the north-flying geese let their music ring.
It's the wobbly legged calf on a dewy summer morn;
It's a good stand of alfalfa, a nice field of corn.
It's the super-sweet smell of freshly stacked hay
That fills the entire barn for many a day.
It's a nest of new kittens with fur smooth as silk;
It's a sputnick* filled to the brim with warm milk.
It's being your own boss from day to day,
Making your mistakes in your own special way.
It's a soft, gentle rain when you really need one;
It's being up in time to see the rising sun.
It's resting after lunch with the hat pulled low,
Beneath the shade trees where the soft breezes blow.
It's seeing the first corn sprouts pushing through,
Realizing God's promise is still holding true.
As long as the earth remains, it never shall cease,
Sowing and harvest, frost and heat,
Summer and winter, day and night, . . .
The march of the seasons so perfectly right.
[* Sputnick: container for carrying milk to the cooling tank.]

    ("Homespun Verse," David Z. Esh Jr., Gordonville, Pa., 12-81)

Windmills

Windmills and the Weather

Windmills are for pumping water. The cold, hard facts will bear out the statement that dollar for dollar, it will pump water cheaper than any other method under the sun. When we bought the farm, we found that a fifty-foot windmill had been here, but the previous owner had cut it down, sold it for scrap iron, and installed an electric system. After pumping water with a gasoline motor for a few years, we erected a windmill. It was a used mill and cost $50 plus $10 to erect it. During this time, it has pumped an estimated two million gallons of water. This would figure out at a rate of 10,000 gallons of water for a penny. (D. Wagler, 1-68)

Windmills on the Way Back?

Perhaps it is not proper to say windmills are coming back, since among the Amish people they have been there all the time. It is estimated that throughout the Amish communities, half the water is pumped by wind. The other half comes from natural springs or is pumped by water wheels or motors powered by gasoline or diesel fuel. Lancaster County (Pa.) is estimated to have at least five hundred windmills, in spite of the fact that there are dozens of water wheels going the year round.

When windmills went out of style, the Amish were able to buy them at their own prices, ranging from $25 to $50. In recent years, they have become scarce and more costly. Now a good used mill in some communities may bring up to $400. What is the cost of new windmills? A mill and tower can be erected for a little more than what a diesel engine would cost. The Baker Company lists a 40-foot tower at around $600, and an eight-foot mill at about $400.

An eight-foot mill pumps about 500 gallons of water an hour with a 40-foot lift in a 15-mile wind. Aermotor makes mills up to 16 feet in diameter. This size will pump up to 3,000 gallons per hour, which is nearly a gallon a second.

In Lancaster County the Aermotor mills are sold and serviced by Samuel U. Zook, a farmer who has a windmill repair shop near New Holland. Most of the servicing consists of changing oil, done only once every year or two, requiring two quarts of oil. About 80 percent of the mills in Lancaster County are Aermotors.

The Aermotors begin to operate in a five-mile-per-hour wind. The recommended capacity is reached at 15 miles per hour. When velocity reaches 25 miles per hour, there is a safety device that throws the mill out of the wind to prevent damage to the mill.

Most farmers have a fairly large storage tank, since there will always be times when the wind does not blow for a day or two. Railroad tank cars are set on end. Oftentimes, one tank car is cut to make two storage tanks. Others use discarded stainless steel milk truck tanks, especially where the water is used for household purposes.

Once a system is properly working, there is no cost for fuel and little upkeep. Many mills have been operating for 10 or 20 years with only a change of oil about once a year. Figuring 800 gallons of water per day, this would be a total of nearly a third of a million gallons per year. With a little more figuring, this adds up to an operating cost of one penny for every 2,000 gallons of water pumped. Is there any other method that will put running water on the farm at that price, and with no worry about fuel costs or pollution?   (8/9-74)

Farm and Field

Is managing on the farm these days so much different than it was forty years ago? There's not as much difference as some people try to make themselves believe. The management is much the same, but the people have changed. Forty years ago, the floors didn't have to be painted or varnished, the buggy didn't have to be shined, the pretty things didn't have to be on the walls, gifts weren't so freely given to those who were not in need, "fancy" gifts or expensive clothes weren't bought so much, the children didn't have to have two pairs of shoes, people didn't travel so much, and many other things weren't necessary that today "must be had." It is well when young farmers ask advice from successful elderly farmers.   (11-75)

Problem Farmers and the Community

A family started farming on one of the poorer farms. After about ten years, they were in such financial difficulties that it seemed they would have to give up. This would have meant selling the farm and seeking employment in town.

At this point, happily, a brother in the church offered assistance. He practically took over management of the farm, dictating to the farmer what to do and what not to do. It must be said to this farmer's credit that he was willing to listen and obey. Otherwise, the plan would never have worked.

In a few years' time, the farmer was once more farming on his own. His family was saved from destruction through the foresight and charity of a fellow church member. Because the farmer was humble enough to accept help, he profited greatly by it.

There is a definite relationship between the farm-oriented family and their support of the Old Order Church. No other atmosphere seems quite equal to the farm. Where it is necessary to take off-the-farm employment, the closer the work is associated with farm life, the better.

(12-74)

Choring Together

I just finished reading about women helping their husbands do the chores in the barn, and how some wives feel a bit like slaves. Although it has been quite a struggle, I try hard to be thankful that I am able to help with the work. I am also thankful we plain people still have the privilege of having our own farms. Just the same, too many times I feel like this poem I wrote:

The Milking Time Blues
The alarm is set every morning at four,
And then it's out to the barn to chore.
The milking's got to be done,
On time—the cows, every one.

Before we're done, the baby's awake,
To cry as though her heart would break.
(When the children wake, how I'd like to be
In the kitchen warm to greet all three!)

Again at four at night, to the barn we go
For another hour and a half or so;
The dishes get left sometimes till late,
And the fussy baby, too, must wait.

I love to sew, to cook, to clean,
To bake, to mend, to fix, to glean;
What fun it is to trim the yard,
And plant the flowers, working hard.

But more important than all the rest,
Are the precious children, all in the nest;
To leave them alone makes my heart ache so,
Especially in winter when cold winds blow.

I shouldn't complain, but my heart's not in it;
I can't force myself to enjoy every minute.
I know we need cows to pay our dues,
But *how* can I shake the Milking-Time Blues?

—*A Mother*   ("Letter," Lancaster Co., 5-79)

Farming as an Occupation

We feel our occupation should be home and community centered.
Our occupation should do at least four things:

1. Provide some useful service or product.
2. Provide an opportunity for children to work with parents.
3. Permit the father to be at home most of the time.
4. Provide an income.

In the fall of 1977, a detailed study focusing on Lancaster Amish
was published: "Occupational Differentiation Among the Old Order
Amish." The study was done by William H. Martineau and Rhonda
Sayres MacQueen of the Department of Sociology, College of William and Mary, Williamsburg, Virginia. It appeared in *Rural Sociology*, volume 42, number 3, pages 383-397.

Of 1,633 males in the labor force, 1,052 or 66 percent of the total
were "identified simply as farmers." It was also reported that the percentage of farmers varied from church district to church district, from
a high of 96 percent to a low of 36 percent. A farming level of 60 percent or more was found in 70 percent of the districts.

A number of daughter settlements have been started by families
leaving Lancaster, due to young people wishing to farm but unable to
buy land near home. If these daughter settlements had been included
in the study, undoubtedly the percentage of farmers would be still
higher.   ("Letter," 3-80)

Finding a Farm

Probably most of us, if we really consider the matter, would agree that working in factories is not good for building up the church. The following points, as a general rule, do not work for the good:

1. Working with worldly people who practice smoking, swearing, telling dirty stories, and so on.

2. Men and women working together, especially under such conditions.

3. Fathers away from home, many times leaving too early to have devotions with the family.

4. Too much money available. Many people would say they want to work away so they can get started farming, but it seems the number of farmers are getting fewer and fewer.

The list of disadvantages in factory work would be long if everything were included. The good points (for lasting good) are hard to find. There is no easy solution to the problem [of finding a farm], but we would like to make a few suggestions:

1. Spread out. In most of our settlements, farms are available on the edge of the communities at a much cheaper price. But still the miniature farms are popping up in the center of the settlements.

2. If you want to buy a farm some day, then begin now to live simple and save money. Don't try to keep up with the Joneses (or the Beilers, the Burkholders, or the Millers).

3. In many communities, there is a good market for truck farmers or specialty crops. This could provide profitable employment for the children and can be done on a small acreage.

4. There are always older people who are well established financially. Why not help the young people get started instead of putting money in the bank? Who is it helping if you put it in the bank?

The high cost of living, or perhaps it would be more correct to say the cost of living high, makes it difficult to start farming today and to keep on farming. As far back as we can go in the history of our people, we find they were an agricultural people. In Old Testament days, the Israelites, too, were an agricultural people, as seen by the many laws and commandments given them, nearly all based on a rural people. To change this now would be taking a serious step.

If we consider what effects [leaving the farm would] have on the home and church, the question is before us: "Do we really want to change it?"   (Sam, 7-72)"

The Changing Farming Economy

That the farm economy in general is in a hard place these days is plain to nearly every observer. We see our high-tech neighbor with the latest equipment, farming more acres quicker, and getting higher yields and production than ever. He is also going deeper and deeper into a spiral of debts that eventually bankrupt him. How is it then that the plain people have been able not only to continue farming, but actually to expand their total acreage (often on smaller and smaller farms)?

The answer is in farming practically. We have mostly resisted "buying into" the system that has driven most American farmers off their farms in the last half century. If we wish to remain a rural people, we will have to continue to resist the salesmen of modern agriculture. It hasn't done our neighbors any good, either financially or spiritually, and it won't treat us any better. We need to stick with practical farming.

In this column last month, we discussed how small changes in society go almost unnoticed from year to year, but add up to big changes in a couple of decades. These changes often have a bigger effect on our communities and our way of life than we care to admit. These changes are as plain to see in agriculture as anywhere else.

As markets and commodity prices change over time, we are forced to make some adjustments to stay in business. We may react by expanding a certain part of our enterprise, by dropping some others, or by adopting a new practice.

A recent letter in *Die Botschaft* is a good example of this. It gave statistics for changes in agriculture in Lancaster County since 1960. As expected, in these three decades the total number of farms in the county dropped from 8,000 to 4,775, a loss of 41 percent. (Lancaster fared better than the nation as a whole, which dropped from four million to two million farms during the same time, a loss of 50 percent.)

While the number of farms dropped 41 percent, the total acreage only dropped by 20 percent. This 20 percent represents land taken out of production for development. The remaining change corresponds to an increase of average farm size in the county, rising from 62 to 85 acres per farm. This is a little hard to believe since many, if not most, farms in the area occupied by the plain people have been divided at least once during these thirty years. But apparently farmers in the tractor-farming area in the western part of the county have expanded their operations enough to make up the difference.

In crops, the big gains in Lancaster County are in corn production, where the grain corn acreage has increased by 75 percent and silage acreage has quadrupled. (Corn now fills well over half the farmland.) The only other major crop to increase was alfalfa, which is up by 40 percent. This crop represents about one-sixth of the total cropland, hardly what we call a sod-based rotation. The big losing crops were tobacco (not a big loss, in our view) and wheat, both of which have just a third of the acreage now as in 1960. Potato production has also been cut in half. Although no figure was given for pasture, I suspect a lot of that new corn land has replaced what used to be pasture.

All that extra corn and alfalfa is being fed to livestock. Dairy cows have increased by 50 percent to 99,000. No figure is given for beef cattle. Hogs have gone up a whopping 8.2 times. A big increase is in laying hens, which [almost tripled in number, to about nine million; and broilers surely increased, too].

Changes like these make it obvious that life on the farm isn't what it used to be just three short decades ago. The real question that plagues us is this: "How have these changes affected our communities and our way of life? Can we still neighbor like we used to? Are we letting our values slip away as we try to keep up with the times?"

While there is no pat answer to these questions, I suppose most of us would have to admit that they are showing up not only in our social life, but in our religious life as well.   ("Staff Notes," 10-92)

Amish Shops

We remember how a few years ago, predictions were being made in some circles that we Amish people wouldn't be able to hold out much longer in our stand against modern farm machinery. The argument was that soon all the horse-drawn equipment would be junked or worn out, and then, "What will you do?"

The last while, one rarely hears those kinds of gloomy forecasts. One reason: we are demonstrating that if something isn't available commercially, there are Amish shops that can make it. If the tool that is needed never did exist, someone will invent and design a tool to do the job. There seems to be a small industrial revolution occurring among the plain people. We are building everything from buggies to kitchen ranges.

Our foundries melt down chunks of cast iron and transform them into large kettles or tiny harness rings. Leather shops produce harnesses and even manufacture collars. Blacksmith shops turn out plows, manure spreaders, and buggy fifth wheels [metal undercarriage part letting the front axle pivot for turning].

A second reason some old-fashioned items are again becoming available has nothing to do with what we manufacture ourselves. It is due instead to the swinging pendulum trends in the world. A lot of people are turning away from the latest technology and are going "back to the land" in an effort to become more self-sufficient.

Perhaps one reason more Amish shops today are manufacturing the items we need has nothing to do with the difficulty of buying the items elsewhere. That reason may be the high price of farmland. Traditionally, the plain people have encouraged farming since that was the most logical and suitable place to bring up a family. On a farm, there is always work to be done. Children aren't in the way; instead, they are wanted and needed. Also, children growing up on a mixed farm learn to do many things well, which helps them grow into capable adults possessing varied skills. They learn to do what needs to be done, whether it is delivering an oversized calf or repairing the barn door.

However, with the frightening and almost numbing leap in land prices during the last ten years, a certain number of people have turned to shops and home businesses simply because the cost of farming is too high. They may agree that farming is still the best place for a family if possible, but if not, a business at home is certainly better than a factory job.   ("Staff Notes," 4-76)

The Doom and Gloom of Future Farming

The old saying that all a farmer needs is a strong back and a weak mind is no longer true. It is more accurate to say that the farmer needs a broad back and a keen mind—a broad back to carry all the debts, and a keen mind to manage and make wise decisions.

The old people had a saying, "Don't put all your eggs in one basket." This meant that a farmer should have a few chickens, a few pigs, and a few cows. If the price of one goes flat, then hopefully the others make up for it. This is another saying that no longer holds true. It might be better to say, "If you have your eggs all in one basket, you'd better take good care of that basket." It is useless to jump from one thing to another and try to hit the market at the right time. By staying in one thing through thick and thin, a farmer usually has a fairly good average.

There are few young people and even fewer older ones who do not see a danger of working in town for a lifetime. That is why we see more and more home shops and businesses. As the businesses grow, they also provide work for others in the community, giving them a chance to make a living without being in a poor environment.

Then there are the many new settlements starting in areas where the land is cheaper. The young people must realize that if changes have taken place in the life of their parents, they will continue to take place in their own lifetime. The day may easily come when they too will be baffled and troubled because of the future outlook. One old farmer once said, "If a person can't cope with one dry year, he had better not be a farmer, because there will surely be some more."

The important thing for all farmers is to not set their sights on the wrong goals. The words of a song express it well:

This world is not my home;
I'm just a-passing through.
My treasures are laid up
Somewhere beyond the blue.

(Pa., 11-80)

Costly Farms

A salesman was talking with the writer one day and stated, "Today only rich people can be farmers."

I shrugged off his remark with a laugh and said, "Either rich people or deeply in debt, like myself."

Ten or twenty years ago, farm people were considered unfortunate and poor, maybe even ignorant, certainly not people to be envied. How are these changes going to affect the plain people in the future? For some time now we have been asking, "How will our young people be able to continue buying farms?" Is it possible that we should also be asking what it will do to us if we *are* able to buy farms? Can we expect to continue leading simple lives and pay off farms costing several hundred thousand dollars?

At the same time, we feel deeply that the farm is the best environment for our children in which to grow up. It is important that children have work to do, that they feel needed and wanted and not in the way. Few things in life are simple. Certainly this problem is not one of them.   ("Staff Notes," E. Stoll, 7-79)

New Settlements

The Amish population in Lancaster County had been doubling about every twenty years. If the Amish population of Lancaster today is 15,000, and we double the figure every twenty years, we will have 480,000 one hundred years from now, and nearly a million just twenty years after that. Before the end of a third century from today, there could be more Amish in Lancaster County than there are people in the United States now.

At this rate, four hundred years from now the Lancaster Amish will be three times the present population of the entire world. Lancaster, are you ready for fifteen billion? [By 1997, the Lancaster Amish population approached 20,000, easily on its way to doubling in twenty years once again.]

I suppose it is fairly obvious that, if the Lord tarries, we are going to be in for some mighty big adjustments in the future, one way or another.   ("Staff Notes," R. A., 7-91)

Farmers Not Needed

Recently I received a letter from an Amish brother in another community:

"Two young Amishmen in this community recently got married. The one bought a farm, since he came from a rich family and was able to pay for it. The other man was unable to get money to buy a farm, so he is working for an English farm operator, driving big combines, tractors, and so on. Some people are talking of working in factories. Most of the unmarried girls work in cities and towns around here. All this is beginning to show effects.

"I understand that within twenty years, four thousand young married Amish couples will be looking for farms. The greater part of this cannot take place in their home communities. So those who do not want to become urbanized will have to settle elsewhere, either where there is cheaper land in the USA and Canada, or in other countries."

This flocking to cities hasn't caught the plain people yet, but another move in some communities is catching us more and more—the move of the cities out into the country. Many of our settlements are not the quiet, rural areas they were ten or twenty years ago. Examples are Geauga and Stark Counties, Ohio; Lancaster County, Pennsylvania; and parts of Elkhart and LaGrange Counties, Indiana. Factories have sprung up, new houses are lined along the roads, and farmland has become expensive and hard to buy. Traffic on roads is heavier every day, and the land is becoming crowded and noisy.

What effect does all this have on the plain churches? Are we riding the same train, going the same way, but just in the caboose? Our concern should not be so much "Can we make a living on the farm?" as "Will our faith survive off the farm?" But of course, the two go together.

There may be several solutions. One has been to move out of the larger, crowded settlements to areas where farmland is lower priced. The last fifteen years have seen many new settlements in Missouri, Wisconsin, and other states, and in Ontario.

Another answer is intensive farming, specializing in fruits and vegetables that require much labor but fewer acres.

Surely there are lands that need hardworking farmers worse than the United States does, or than Canada does. Shouldn't we give consideration to having some of our families that want to farm, and want to live their faith and raise their children away from the modern mad rush, go as immigrants to countries with underdeveloped farms and hungry people? Meanwhile, the USA is paying its farmers to quit farming and let the land lay idle, and the people are eating better than any people ever ate before. Where, do you suppose, does the farmer count the most?   ("Fireside Chats," J. Stoll, 9-69)

New Settlements

We live in a time of many new settlements among the plain people. We also live in a time of soaring land prices. We asked our readers to comment on this subject.

We have many serious problems in our bigger Amish settlements, especially among the young folks. But I would advise anyone considering a move to a new settlement to ask themselves honestly whether they are really seeking a spiritual improvement in their lives. Perhaps secretly, deep within their heart, they are moving for good, cheap land and perhaps a few more modern conveniences than the new settlement will allow.

Many of the answers pointed out perhaps the most important consideration of all: most people who move to new settlements are not looking for financial gain. They are seeking cheaper land not to make their bank account grow, but to make possible a plain way of living in a Christian atmosphere centered around the family farm.

Many times it's not just a matter of price. Farms are simply not available in the home community at any price. So new settlements often represent not only cheaper land, but available land. Without that land, more and more families would have to turn to some other way of earning a livelihood. This may take the father away from his family all day, leave children in the home with nothing to do, and bring ready cash with temptations to buy unnecessary items.

From Ontario

From the financial point of view, I must think that it is much easier for a young man to get started in farming in a smaller community where the land is cheaper, if he is willing to work hard, make sacrifices, and not spend money unnecessarily. He should also be meek enough to ask for advice.

For instance, I know a young man who is buying a 60-acre farm (55 tillable) with good buildings on it for approximately $30,000 in a smaller [newer] community. Let's say he has $10,000 to pay on it, and borrows $20,000 at 10 percent, which would be $2,000 a year in interest.

The same farm in a large [old] Amish settlement might be worth $70,000. If the same young man wanted to buy it and had to borrow $60,000 at 10 percent interest, it would come to $6,000 a year interest. Would he have a chance to make it? My guess would be no.

From Lancaster County

The soil type is something not to be underestimated. Buildings can be changed with time, and low fertility can be corrected, but some types of soils will not respond. Last but not least, the trip to the home community for business, weddings, funerals, and visiting may have more of a financial impact than we realize. In conclusion, I would be the last to discourage anyone from moving. But before you move, weigh the different angles and don't expect a cure-all.

[In 1993, a Lancaster County Amishman paid $435,000 for a 66-acre farm, about $6,400 per acre. By the late 1990s, some farms were selling for $10,000 or more per acre.]

From Pennsylvania

Can't we look beyond today and think of the future generation and the future church? Can't there be those who are willing to give up the idea that the bright, fertile spot they grew up in is just a bit closer to heaven than the rest of the world? Can't you see that if you have only one home farm and have seven children, and they each have a family, that you must have enough love for them not to keep them close to you as you would wish, but to let them go? After all, a journey of a thousand miles takes no longer than a hundred miles did a hundred years ago.

Most of those who moved to new settlements did so against the will of at least one set of parents, and sometimes both. Often there were bitter words from relatives that took a long time to be forgotten. I have often wondered why these things couldn't be discussed sanely and sensibly.

Sure, the young people who move will face problems, just as the older ones are ever ready to point out. But sometimes it seems as if the older ones do not realize that there are always problems in this life, no matter where we are. (12-76)

Horse and Machine

Farm and Field

Among the Old Order Amish and Mennonites, the question is often asked, "What can be done about horse-drawn farm machinery, and what does the future hold in this respect?" Very little has been manufactured since 1940.

The draft horse was chiefly used as a beast of burden in the field of agriculture for over a century [relieving the ox]. Therefore, horse-drawn farm machinery was manufactured on a large scale in the United States. After the turn of the century, steam engines were used for belt power. By 1930, they were being used for experimental purposes in the Midwest wheat-growing country to pull gang plows, discs, and combines. They replaced as many as twenty or more horses in one team, but never became very popular because of the large amount of coal and water needed to feed the boilers. Also, the weight of these rugged machines was a problem. Steam-powered engines never replaced the horse.

The gasoline-powered tractor was first designed for belt power only, but was later used in agriculture for plowing or whenever heavy equipment was used. As late as 1930, it was still often called "the farmer's folly."

At that time nobody thought horses could be replaced by machinery to do general farm work. Not until tractors were built in light weight and on rubber tires was much interest seen in using a tractor instead of a horse. It also was not practical to have a tractor pull machinery designed to be horse-drawn. Often it was necessary for two people to operate the rig [one on the tractor and one on the implement], whereas with horses one man could do it. The tractor didn't make headlines in agriculture until equipment was manufactured to fit the power used.

From 1945 to 1955, farmers across the United States became tractor conscious. The change in this ten-year period was almost unbelievable. One farmer with a few men to help him can now operate a thousand or more acres if he has the right equipment.

By 1950, farmers who continued to keep horses to do their farming could buy equipment at their own price. Never before could an Amish farmer buy equipment and operate as cheaply as he could in the fifteen years following World War II.

About 1960, the trend was changing; far less horse-drawn machinery was offered for sale. By 1970, to keep supplying the farm with these implements, it was necessary for the dealer to travel to other states in an area of six to eight hundred miles, searching for [used] horse-drawn implements. It is only natural that the prices jumped considerably.

Here is a list of farm machinery with the cost in 1937 compared to the estimated price if still manufactured today:

	Retail, 1937	Est. Retail, 1975
Frick Thresher	$2,200	$16,000
Walking Plow	24	195
Manure Spreader	175	1,500

In those days, one man in the community owned a steam engine or tractor with a threshing machine, silo filler, and probably a fodder shredder. He went from farm to farm, serving as many as twenty to thirty farmers with one outfit. No one knew anything of Amish farm boys working in commercial jobs such as factories, road building, railroads, etc. (Gideon L. Fisher, 8/9-75)

Modern Machinery
Machines now mow the hay and crimp,
In order the curing time to skimp.
Next day comes baler with thrower attached,
Which tosses the bales up into the racks.

A power-driven elevator stows it away.
Oh, this is the modern way to make hay.
All this big machinery makes the man
Want to buy and farm all the acres he can.
Machines equipped with glaring lights
Enable him to work far into the nights.
Oh, he's so busy with things of the sod,
There's little time left to think about God;
If there is no time for the Lord, my friend,
This kind of life meets a horrible end!
Praise the Lord, there are still men tilling the soil
Who have time for God in their daily toil.

(Ella A. Hostetler, 7-68)

Rules for Farming

For twenty years, we have tried to emphasize the dangers of modernism, and the spiritual blessings of leading a simpler and plainer lifestyle. At the same time, we have tried to promote consistency, honesty, and openness, basing our life and practices on the principles of the Scriptures.

We say we encourage farming, yet often the church rules are more restrictive for farmwork than for shopwork. That has the effect of encouraging people into shopwork instead of farming. It also has a secondary effect of making many farmers feel dissatisfied with the restrictions that apply to them.   ("Staff Notes," 4-87)

Agreeing on Standards as the Needs Arise

There is no ruling against some things we use today that are just as worldly as other things the *Ordnung* (church rules) has us do without. Certainly a diesel engine powering a sawmill is not less worldly than one that is pulling a plow.

However, as the industrial revolution brought changes to all phases of American life, the church responded according to the things that affected the church the most. Since most plain people are primarily farm people, church rulings had the hardest affect on changes toward progressiveness in the farm community.

In our church standards, there is nothing mentioned about owning railroad locomotives. Of course, plain people have used railroads a long time for transportation, but no Amishman has ever tried to buy or own one that I know of. Therefore, the question has never been raised.

To an outside observer, as well as to some inside, our set standards are obviously impractical. Yet as we know, the *Ordnung* wasn't made in a day, but as the need arose.

As for machinery in shops and small businesses, I believe things like sawmills have always been an important part of a plain community. On the other hand, tractors and barn cleaners were new inventions in their time. The modern sawmill we see today has been improved through the years. It was not brought into question at any point in its development.

In our church, tractors have been in common use since their introduction. Then when we decided against automobiles, we also decided against the rubber tire. Back in those days, it was not hard to understand because most tractors came on steel wheels from the factory. Now, however, our young people find it hard to understand that a tractor on steel wheels is tolerable, but that it is "worldly" with tires.

I conclude that it is not our *Ordnung* or our adherence to it that is our faith. Instead, *our Ordnung is an agreement* among the church members and not just imposed on us by the ministry, an agreement that certain things may be a detriment to our faith. When we joined the church, we were well aware of this agreement and endorsed it. For our salvation and the redemption of our sins, we depend not on our own works, like keeping a law or rules, but on the shed blood of Christ.   (I. Shirk, Pa., 6-87)

Old Order Shops

A large number of small shops are springing up in Amish communities as a result of farmland being so high-priced. In connection with this subject, we call attention to a directory of these shops. It is a 72-page booklet compiled and published by Joseph F. Beiler of Gordonville, Pennsylvania: *Old Order Shop and Service Directory*.

In his introduction to the directory, the compiler points out that an estimated 60 percent of the shops among the Amish have opened since 1970! He says the oldest tend to be the blacksmith shops, with one dating back to 1870. Next oldest are perhaps the buggy and harness shops, and after that the furniture shops, becoming popular in the 1950s. Machine shops began to open up on a wide scale in the early 1960s or slightly before.   ("Staff Notes," 5-78)

The Lunch-Pail Problem

We asked our readers to join us in a discussion of the lunch-pail problem—fathers working away from their families. As we expected, there are no simple answers.

I have just sent my husband out the door with his lunch pail. That is the way it has been for the last four years. It is not the way we would both like it best. We have three boys, the oldest is ten, and they should have their father at home. But we have five acres here, not enough to think of farming. The idea of buying a farm with no savings is not practical. So I guess we will go on as we are for now and hope interest rates and farm prices will come down some day.   (Mo.)

I think the man's personal attitude toward his work and his family makes a big difference and determines whether there is a lunch-pail problem. Those who work away from home need to gear their life so they will have several special hours a day together with the family. It can be done. I feel I have seen cases where the busy young farmer did not succeed as well as the happy factory worker or carpenter.   (Ind.)

Here in our new community, most of the families are farming or have shops. There are many blessings to living on a farm. But some of our farms are too big. So Mother is out helping to milk and chore for several hours. In cold weather, the children are alone in the house, with the oldest coping with demands and frustrations. In those families where the father carries the lunch pail, at least the children have one parent who stays in the house with them.   (N.Y., 4-82)

Maybe not all Amish settlements have so many mobile home factories in the area as we do. Here conditions have come to such a head that many are now compelled to work in factories as the only way to make a living. Some of our factories have such a high percentage of Amish workers that it is no longer exactly rubbing shoulders with the world. It is actually because of the available Amish workforce that many factories have flourished here. The easy money made home buying easier and small plots of land more expensive. The small farmer down the line was hurt because the increased value of small homes and farmland forced him to work in the factory part-time to supplement his farm income. Have we become victims of industry, fast easy living, and our own growth? (Ind.)

Some blame inflation for the hard times and high prices of today. Yet I believe we can make inflation worse by bidding up land prices. Several years ago our local paper said that the value of farmland in our state went up 10 percent that year. In our county made up of half Amish, the prices rose 25 percent that year. It seems to me this is the result of overcrowding. Maybe this is partly why we have a lunch-pail problem—our reluctance to spread out. I am sure there are still many places out there with farming opportunities. (5-82)

One problem is often the easy-come, easy-go spending policy, often resulting in much finery in homes, clothing, and more and more modernism and luxurious living. Another problem is the degrading language and worldly attitudes that can creep in, depending on where we work. "Evil communications corrupt good manners" (1 Cor. 15:33). In addition, factory-type jobs tend to sever community sharing. Also, it is becoming more difficult to hire or get help for tasks that one man can hardly manage alone. (Mo.)

Solving the Lunch-Pail Problem
Here are some ways I have seen families successfully solve the lunch-pail problem. Their work is at home. These home businesses are exactly like farming; they must be conformed to church standards. They should not become too large. The livelihood should serve our needs; we should not serve the livelihood. We can become a slave to our farm; the same can happen to a home business. We must not

replace the lunch-pail problem with a no-time-for-family problem.

Many of the businesses have to hire help, a plus for the young folks who can then work with church members instead of away among outside influences.

A widow and her nearly grown family operate a flourishing poultry-slaughtering service. A husband-and-wife team operate a successful sewing machine sales and service. Another, a bicycle sales and service shop. A young family of eight operate a busy little shop making horse and pony bridle blinds for harness makers. Quality and good workmanship are important if we are to be successful in a home business. We must be competitive.

Other examples are tailoring (making plain suits, etc.), fix-it shops, small-engine services, accounting and preparing tax returns, estate

planners, dry-goods stores, homemade bakeries, salvage grocery stores, butchers, sawmill operators, woolen mills, appliance sales and service, alternator and generator repairing, upholstery repairs, manufacturing baskets and bushels, blacksmithing, boat building, bookbinding and printing, selling homemade cheeses and other home foods.

People sell and service heavy canvas and timepieces, offer health-food services [with bulk foods and home remedies], greenhouses, small nurseries, small foundries (for making buckles, bits, snaps, farm machinery parts, etc.), gunsmithing, binding buggy wheels, manufacturing stovepipes, gutters, and downspouts, and selling air-operated items (such as deep well pumps) and floor covering.

They are also making cabinets, farm equipment (such as flat wagons, harnesses, gates, horse-drawn manure spreaders), mobile homes, sheds, woodstoves and kitchen ranges, pallets and skids (plus repairs), ceramics and glassware, rubber stamps and signs, toy novelties. They run small-animal shops, restaurants, construction projects (trusses, sawhorses, and other wooden specialties); and so on. (Pa.)

Why I Am a Carpenter

Some of the lunch-pail carrying jobs do create a problem with the U.S. Social Security [or Canadian Social Insurance] system and the tax that has to be paid. I am thankful that the U.S. government has permitted self-employed people to be exempt from this tax. This exemption has also made it possible for several people to work together as a partnership and, as each one is then self-employed, they don't have to pay the Social Security tax.

Even if we would have to pay the tax, we still don't have to collect the benefits when we retire, although I expect that not all our people feel that way. When the time comes to retire, the temptation to apply for and collect the monthly Social Security [or Canada Pension] checks is rather great if we need the money.

Most of our people do not believe in accepting government payments and subsidies available if we go along with certain soil conservation practices that help in saving our precious resources—the top soil. Most of these practices should be used anyway, since we are the stewards of the soil for future generations. Getting paid by the government to follow such practices is another matter.

However, there is another government subsidy that most of our people would not have accepted ten or fifteen years ago. Due to high land prices, many of our people are now accepting it. That is the Federal Housing Administration (FHA) loan available to farmers who cannot get enough credit locally through a bank or a production credit office. These loans are low-interest money subsidized by the government. Many of our people have not intended to use that money. But so often a farm is bought, then the new owners find it is almost impossible to get a local loan, so they end up getting an FHA loan.

We should not have a business where we think we need to hire young Amish boys with cars so we can get our crew to work, or where we need to hire non-Amish workers so we can own the tools and equipment the *Ordnung* does not permit.

Doesn't it all boil down to staying small, whether in farming or whatever? (Just so we don't define *bigness* as meaning only those who are at it bigger than we ourselves are. I have to watch myself on that!)

Not long ago, I was talking to a minister about how so many of our people work away from home. He said he was concerned that many of them do not dress at work as though they attended a plain church. I fully agree on that. A faith that is genuine is not only for Sundays. Our work through the week should also be a part of our faith. (6-82)

A Priceless Heritage of Faithfulness

Our mission in life is not to go to some far-off foreign land, but to work at home and in our churches and home communities. Our goal should not be to leave behind riches and possessions, farms and homes for our children, but a priceless heritage they will cherish enough to work fervently to pass along to their children. It has been done for generations, and with God's help it can still be done.

—*A Minister*   (3-79)

Contentment

Let us try to keep our hearts in heaven while we have our hands at work, and we can be content wherever we are.

("Letter," Mrs. S. Hoover, Clifford, Ont., 7-82)

6
The Young
Blessings and Problems

Every society recognizes its young as its future. The family and school are integral in producing a "successful citizen." In the Amish community, where private one-room schooling is the norm, parents are involved in the lives and education of their children through the eight grades. They also know that not all of the skills and lessons for life are learned sitting behind a desk.

The Amish, like parents everywhere, have their successes and failures when it comes to rearing children. They, too, worry about being too strict, or too liberal. Like most parents, their emotions can sometimes get in the way of making the best decisions for their children, and they suffer great pain when a child goes "astray." These writings are some of the most touching and compelling to be found in the pages of *Family Life*.

Children Are Treasures

Menno Simons made a statement on the way parents should feel about their children that is so strong most of us today would hesitate to express it so forcefully: "This is the chief and principal care of the saints, that their children may fear God, do right, and be saved."

Perhaps herein lies the greatest single difference between the teaching of the plain churches and that of the more liberal churches—the degree of emphasis on child training. This concern for [bringing up and educating] our children is best summed up by the German word *Kinderzucht*, not matched exactly by any English word.

With the loss of *Kinderzucht*, many other things get lost rapidly from our families and churches. Our very lives center around our families and our children. They are our future church, our most treasured possession. This is in direct contrast to the world around us, where children are in the way, especially in large families—meaning any family with more than two children, in today's society. Worldly parents often find children getting on their nerves and under their feet. They want longer and longer school terms so the children will be out of the way. When the children are at home, the TV set is often used as a babysitter.

In our way of life, however, children are useful, needed, and wanted. They help with the work around the farm and do household chores, learning to be useful at a young age. Instead of sighing with relief when the school term begins in the fall and groaning when it lets out in the spring, Amish parents react in reverse.

Probably no theme comes up in our sermons more frequently than the great responsibility that parents have to bring up their children in "the fear of the Lord." We have all heard again and again the saying that "Children are the only treasures on earth we can take with us to heaven."   ("Across the Editor's Desk," E. Stoll, 11-76)

Unfair Grading

Recently an eighth-grade teacher gave his pupils strict orders to watch a certain TV program that evening: "Now don't forget to watch it."

The next morning he gave them a test on the program. When the Amish children handed in blank papers with the notation "No TV," the teacher was exasperated: "Well, at least you have radios, don't you?" Again the answer was no. "Then you deserve a big fat *F*."

—*A Concerned Parent*   (6-68)

Concerned About Schools

The greatest threat against our schools does not come from the outside but from the inside. If we are careless and unconcerned about who is teaching our children and what they are teaching them, then our schools will soon reach the point of no return. If we do not realize the need for our *own* schools and the dangers of sending our children to public schools, then unfavorable rulings from the courts cannot do us any real harm. They can make us suffer for our convictions. But the faith that's not worth suffering for is not worth living for.

(5-68)

Parental Responsibility

Government officials would like us to believe it is their right to give our children secular education. This is false. The Bible teaches that it is the parents' duty to provide or oversee all of their children's training, religious or secular.

Can you control what is taught to your children in the public schools? Can you see to it that their teachers will not be atheists, evolutionists, immoral, or unqualified in some other way? Very unlikely. In a private school, we can control what is taught and by whom.

The government not only tolerates us in exercising this privilege, but also grudgingly admits it is our right. I know it costs us more, but to what better use could we put our money? I also know there is risk of a private school getting out of control, but the public school is already far out of control. It teaches our children gross untruths about our origin and the creation. It also exposes them to all kinds of vice and sin. With proper direction and control, we can safely operate private schools. (4-79)

A Waste?

"Mr. Troyer," said a public school teacher a few years ago to an Amish father, "do you realize that your son, Bennie, has an exceptional mind? He always gets straight *A*'s without even working. You should certainly see that he goes to high school and college. It would be a shame, a terrible waste, if he didn't."

The Amish father shook his head. The schoolteacher shook his, too, though for a different reason. He went home muttering to himself, "A terrible waste. All that talent, and all he'll ever amount to is an old-fashioned farmer, sweating in the field, tilling the soil with his hands like a common peasant, when he might be a doctor or a dentist. Who knows, maybe even an artist or a poet."

A waste? Yes, Bennie might get on in the world. He might well reach fame, wealth, and pleasure. But what if he lost his soul? Would that not be the greatest waste of all? (3-75)

Amish Schools

It is estimated that about two-thirds of the Amish now attend parochial schools. Another 20 percent attend one-room public schools where nearly all pupils are Amish. According to these estimates, there would only be about 15 percent still going to town schools. How are

the parochial schools working out?

Wayne E. Miller, from the University of Michigan, along with several other recognized authorities in the field, tested a number of Amish and public school children to compare the different groups. The purpose of the survey was to determine whether Amish school children are getting the education they need later in life. They tested in the following subjects: vocabulary, reading comprehension, spelling, word usage, knowledge and use of reference material, and arithmetic.

Five different groups of children were examined:

• Children in Amish parochial schools.

• Children in public schools that are 100 percent Amish.

• Amish children in public schools with less than 50 percent Amish children.

• Non-Amish children in public schools with less than 50 percent Amish children.

• Non-Amish children in schools with no Amish enrolled.

When the final results were in, they showed that the pupils from the parochial schools had the best rating. Second highest were the pupils from the public schools with 100 percent Amish students. Third place went to the schools with no Amish students, while the mixed schools came in last. One noticeable part of the survey was the poor showing made by the parochial school children in using reference material. [Only Midwest rural schools were tested.]

Amish schools in North America: four in 1940, six in 1945, twenty in 1950, fifty in 1955, ninety-seven in 1960, then 152 in 1965, and 309 in 1970. [By the 1990s, there were over a hundred Amish one-room schools in Lancaster County alone, and the total number of Amish schools had passed a thousand.]

("Across the Editor's Desk," 8-70)

Special Education

Several years ago here in Lancaster County we started a "Special Education School" for nervous, hyperactive, slow learners, or any other children who couldn't cope in regular school. Classes are held in the basement of a regular [one-room] school. Thus these children have recess at the same time and can play with the other children.

The two teachers have about sixteen pupils. They need to have much patience with their pupils, but the results are surprising. Children who would have little chance in a regular school learn arithmetic, and learn to read and understand what they read. Evidently outsiders felt we would not be qualified to operate such a class. It did look like a big mountain to the board that was elected to get it started.

Though I am not closely associated with the class, I can still say that the results appear to be very good. For some of these children, I believe it is like filling a bottle that has a small neck. It is possible to fill such a bottle, but it takes much time and patience. For children who otherwise would not learn, it opens a new world to be able to count and read, even if it's only some of the simplest books.

("Letter," D. F., Pa., 6-80)

What Troubled Linda

Linda was discouraged with teaching. It almost seemed to her that it was pointless to have parochial schools. What was the use of going to all that effort and expense to shield the children from harmful companions if later they associated freely with young people who seemed to undo all the good accomplished in school?

Surely it is good and right that we have our own schools. We seek to teach and train children in what is upbuilding, and to shield them from the harmful company and environment of public schools. But it is too bad if we are not concerned in providing an equally upbuilding environment later, among the young people. Are we concerned only about our little children and not about our big children?

It seems that the greatest reason why not more is being done about this problem is simply that we don't care enough. If we really cared, would we or could we casually visit together about our crops and neighbors all Sunday afternoon? Meanwhile, in the room upstairs, our young people are keeping the air blue with smoke and playing cards and entertaining each other with off-color jokes. Would we as parents, if we really cared as we should, go ahead week after week, washing and ironing clothes for our young people, which they wear in disobedience to the church?

If we really cared, would we let our young people go away in the evening without knowing where they are going, or what they will be doing, or with whom they will be spending their time? Would we go to bed on Saturday evening, with our daughters upstairs and the house unlocked so boys can enter and leave at will? This is a setup so evil that it is shameful to mention. One can hardly imagine parents so unconcerned as to tolerate it.

It is time we looked around and asked what kind of teachers our children have when they reach their teenage years. A teacher is anyone we learn from. Who will our children learn from more readily than the friends and companions they are with?

("Views and Values," E. Stoll, 8/9-72)

Generation Gap

One of the basic rules of life is that it takes time to build strong emotional ties. For strong ties of friendship to develop, people need to spend a certain amount of time together.

No doubt our children spend more time in the company of their peers than any other generation before them. Our people have certainly been right to resist consistently any government demands to send our children to high school. It is already bad enough that they are away from their parents for eight school terms. Perhaps we have already gone along too far with today's educational system.

Three hundred years ago children were at home with the family during all of their growing years. We would not want to go back to that. In those days, few could read. At the same time, we should be aware of the danger in children being away from their parents too much, and in the company of their peers. We have our own schools, and that is good. This is our way of guarding against bad company for our children. But perhaps it is time for us to see that even good company, if it detracts from the ties between parent and child, can also be a harmful thing.

This same thing is true beyond the level of school years. Yet even many of the most well-meaning parents see no danger in young people being together too much. In fact, some parents call for *more youth activity* as a solution to the problems of our young people.

There is a motto that "the family that prays together, stays together." That says a lot in a few words, but it doesn't say enough. It is surely an oversimplification. A family needs to do more than pray together. It needs to work together, visit friends together, read together, plan things together, eat together, share their joy and sorrows, hopes and disappointments. In short, the family needs to *live together*.

It is true that young people need something to do. But parents should look harder for things they can do with the family that will serve to strengthen the ties between children and parents, rather than between children and their peers.   ("Views and Values," 1-78)

Scriptural Reasons for the Rules

Maybe one reason parents ease their rules is due to a lack of having a sure foundation or solid scriptural reasons for the rules. There may be nothing wrong with the rules themselves, but there may be something wrong with the reasons or motives behind them. This is like having a good house built on a poor foundation. There are several wrong foundations:

• Not being too concerned about the actual things parents are forbidding, but more concerned that the children will not disgrace their parents. This is pride (James 4:10).

• Feeling that dressing plain, good behavior, or church membership will earn our salvation. It won't (Eph. 2:8).

• A lack of asking God for help (Prov. 1:7).

Children quickly detect these underlying motives and reject them because they don't want to be like their parents.

These will form a sure foundation:

- Separation from the world (Rom. 12: 1-2).
- Decency in dress (Rom. 13:14).
- [Fleeing desire for] earthly treasures (1 Tim. 6:6-11).
- Purity (1 Cor. 9:27).
- Obedience to parents (Col. 3:20).
- Obedience to God (Heb. 12:25).

("What Do You Think," Sugarcreek, Ohio, 2-77)

Responses to a question on how parents handle money their children have earned: ("What Do You Think," 12-82)

Earning Money

When the opportunity came to earn money outside the home, my parents let us have half and invested [it] in savings accounts. With our own children, because we have a large family with physical handicaps and large family responsibilities, our children had to take adult responsibilities at a young age. Therefore, we started giving them an allowance for being on time or doing their chores well. We then allowed them to spend half of their earnings under our supervision, also teaching them to remember the poor.

—*A Father*

It's the child's duty to work for his parents until of age, though a small weekly allowance might be all right. I think it's fine for the child to establish a savings account, but no checking account. The father should keep the bank book till the child is of age. I know of parents who allow their children a certain percent of their paychecks (money earned away from home—10, 15, 20 percent, or whatever the parents decide), to invest in savings. When the children are twenty-one, with the accumulated interest, what a surprise they will have.

(A. W., Millbank, Ont.)

In some homes, when children reach sixteen years of age, they are allowed to keep half their earnings till twenty-one. I feel it fair for children to keep all their wages at eighteen and be encouraged to save it for starting housekeeping or farming.   (A. H., Md.)

I am satisfied with the way my parents taught me to handle money. I went through four stages:
• Penny bank: I had a yellow piggy bank, where all my money went, whether from gifts or rewards for doing special jobs.
• Savings account: When I had accumulated enough money, my piggy bank was emptied. Dad sawed it open, helped me count it, and took it to the bank. Before I was of age, I couldn't withdraw any money without his signature.
• Ten percent: When I was old enough to hold a paying job, I was allowed to keep 10 percent of what I earned.
• Checking account: Dad knew I'd need a checking account once I handled my own expenses and went on my own. He introduced me to checking, and my savings account remained untouched. What I earned went into the checking account.
Thus I was taught to save before I was taught how to spend.
(Laura Z. Martin, Pa.)

Our children handled little money till they were twenty-one. We wrote in an account book what they earned in their younger years. When they worked out, 10 percent was supposed to be for them, but it was all written down, and they didn't get it until they were twenty-one. When they did something extra, like weeding or hoeing, we told them to write down something like five cents a row. It is sad to see how many young folks go wrong when often there is too much money. If they wouldn't have the money, I believe many of these things could be avoided.   ("Letter," Lancaster Co., Pa., 3-73)

Hired Girls

Scarred

Today was our communion service. It was a peaceful day outside, as peaceful as the hearts of those inside who partook of the Lord's

Supper. The minister's words were inspiring and a blessing to all listening ears. I kept looking at the stern expressions of these folks in our small community. A few silent tears escaped my eyes, and I felt a heavy heart.

My heartache was made worse two weeks ago when I was punished at council meeting, but it didn't start there. It didn't even start two years ago. In fact, it goes back much farther.

In our family, I was second in line. My parents never had a lot, but we never went to bed hungry, or wore patched clothes to church. They tried to teach me right from wrong, and I'm thankful to God for my Amish heritage.

I started working out at an early age. My first job for non-Amish people was at the tender, vulnerable age of thirteen. My parents didn't realize the years of heartache I would live through by letting me have a better-paying job. I have an outgoing personality, which makes it easier for me to accept different people. I had little or no problems adjusting.

For two solid years, I was gone from Monday morning until Friday night. I had every convenience imaginable. In no time, I could control every switch and knew how to push every button. Of course, I had free evenings, and I soon had my favorite TV shows. I could recognize a radio station by hearing the DJ's voice. I learned most of the songs and often sang along. I read newspapers and books of all kinds. I adapted to their views and ideas. Without realizing it, I was living two different lives.

Now I'm twenty-eight, and I realize my many years working out have been somewhat of an exception. I've been employed by the families of an air force pilot, a policeman, doctors, and even a professional football player, plus other more-common people. I've been acquainted with just as many different religions and attended church at least once with most of them. I've had opportunities and encouragement to go into nursing, dental assistance, secretarial, and other types of work from all the well-meaning people who always told me I had too much intelligence to waste on housecleaning or babysitting.

I began joining church at sixteen and was baptized at seventeen. I really have tried to live up to the rules and regulations of the communities I've lived in. In spite of this, there [seemed to be many] times when I was making confessions in church for misdeeds. Now I'm beginning to see or understand that no one is doing anything to be cruel. But for the church to be pure, it must remove any leaven of evil [1 Cor. 5].

I am the one who must change, but after all this time, it seems impossible. How can I change the inside of me to be the Amish person I should be? How can I undo the influence of all those years?

I pray to be like the girl down the road who gets up at five o'clock in the morning and milks seven or eight cows, and who doesn't have to be away from home day after day after day. I only hope more parents realize the dangers in letting their young girls go out, away from home and under the influence of the world. Believe me, it's not worth the money.

All I can say is that it's a miracle I'm still Amish. I'm not sure I can stay in my beloved community. The Lord knows I want to stay, but my best may not be good enough. I'm at the crossroads of my life, and I don't know which way to turn. The scars will always be with me. I'll suffer the effects for the rest of my life.

If my letter can help just one parent realize the danger in working out, if I can save just one girl from all the heartache I've been through, this letter will have been well worth my time.

(M. B., Ohio)

Sacrificing

I often feel that the single Amish girl is discriminated against. Why does she always have to do all the sacrificing? Granted, young couples are struggling to make ends meet, making payments, and so on. But the single girl's struggles are much harder if she ever wants to see any of her dreams come true, especially if she's making three or four dollars a day. She might as well forget it.

I'm single and on the shady side of twenty-nine. I skimped and saved for over twelve years before I was able to obtain a home of my own. Sad to say, I did not earn my money working for the Amish. This is sad, since I realize that spiritually I would be much better off working among my own people. Most older girls had to sacrifice their biggest dream of all, that of having a family of their own. So why should they be asked to sacrifice a home as well?

—*Puzzled*

Not Worth the Money

We have seen two different times since we were married that we didn't have as much as a dollar. One time I had to borrow money so we could buy groceries for another few weeks, not having any idea when we would be able to pay it back. At the same time, we had nearly more feed bills than income, because milk and hog prices were low. Then one of the cows got sick, and when the sows farrowed, the pigs got scours and nearly all died.

At times like this I've said, "I'd be glad if I was making only three or four dollars a day." Many a hired girl now helping a mother with a family of small children, may herself in a few short years be the one needing a hired girl, and having a financial struggle.   (1-77)

Courtship and Wild Oats

The Right Time for Courtship

It is hard to look around the plain churches today and not get the feeling that we have far too much courtship *before* marriage, and not nearly enough *after* marriage. Young people who make every effort to win each other's love before marriage, often do not put forth much effort after marriage.

Young men will travel miles before the wedding day to show how devoted they are to their special one. Ten years later, they find it too much of a task to get up from the table to help her with the dishes. Boys who stayed up all night with their date refuse to take their turn to wrestle with a sick baby at midnight.

Ah, if only we could get a little more courtship into marriage, how much happier would be many of our homes.

Marriage, to be worthwhile, requires intelligent thought and continued effort. Good marriages do not just happen. They do not result from having married the "right" one as much as from the blessings of God, persistent work, and loving labor to make ourselves the "right" one.   ("Views and Values," 11-80)

Striving for a Hundredfold

Here in Lancaster County, we have many young people, so many that they can't all gather at one singing. At least ten different groups have been formed, from the plainest to the wildest. This leaves every boy and girl who turns sixteen with a wide variety of groups to choose from. None of these groups is perfect.

—*A Young Mother* (5-79)

Seeing It Different

On a typical Sunday evening, from two to three hundred young folks come together for a so-called singing. While only a small number are inside the house to help sing, the rest are usually outside, scattered in other buildings, entertaining themselves with drinking, smoking, and other acts of disorderly conduct. How can such a gathering be to the honor and glory of God?

The young folks in our community were divided whenever church districts were divided, as far back as I can remember. They attend the singing in the same district where they have attended church that day. If they don't go to church that day, they also stay home from the singing. We feel it works well to have it this way. In a small group, each one feels needed to help sing, and not nearly as much visiting during the singing is apt to be done.

Young Myself

I think it's more than the size of the group that makes young people act disorderly. What they need is an inward conviction against wrong. They need self-respect and parents who truly care and are a little more strict.   ("What Do You Think?" 5-79)

How to Be Accepted and Have Friends

A boy turns sixteen and starts going with the young people. He soon sees how some of the boys seem to be leaders in the "gang," and gets an ambition to be one of these. So he decides that if he takes a drink (just a little, he thinks), he too could be funny and "the life of the party." That is how he starts being a slave to the demon alcohol.

He may think that if he gets a car and takes the other fellows and girls for a ride, he will be popular. If so, he has a shallow idea of popularity. He is playing with a temptation that has taken young people, and later their descendants after them, down the road forever, away from a church that stands for nonconformity in the world.

In other words, he is seeking the answer to a problem all people have, not just young people: he wants to be accepted and have friends. But the answer to that problem is so simple that few people will believe it really works. It is in these few words from the Bible, "A man that hath friends must shew himself friendly" (Prov. 18:24). In other words, to have friends, you must be one. You must let it be shown that you are friendly.

That is the answer to our quest for friends—to think more of others than of ourselves. It is shallow and cheap reasoning to think that lasting, deep, durable friendships can be built by trying to do things to impress others.

If we are sincere, we will find that those who are sincere will be our best friends. If we stop trying to impress people and forget about "keeping up with the Joneses," if we listen more to what *other* people say and think less about what *we* want to say—then we will find deep, satisfying, and lasting friendships with sincere people.

("The Scriptures Have the Answers," 8/9-81)

Hard to Forget

Not all our youth are involved in these [rowdy] happenings. No, not half. But too many are. Sometimes such parties bring in young people from different states and communities. When I actually saw what took place, I was shocked.

There is still a vivid picture in my mind of a boy and girl walking hand in hand down the lane, the girl carrying a beer bottle and talking boisterously. It made me think, "And this is a Christian community known far and wide for its plain people." Yes, it happened at one of their farms.

As another car approached, the couple slipped over the grassy bank. I stood watching them. Paris hairdo, miniskirt, sheer hose, college haircut, checkered shirt—surely it had to be a dream. It was hard to believe that only hours before the couple had attended a plain church.

Knowing nothing of the planned party, some friends and I had spent that evening in a nearby home. Since we had tied our horse where later they parked their cars, we suddenly found ourselves in the center of the activity. As the shadows lengthened over the scene, cars were lining up, one after the other, five, ten, fifteen, up to a total of twenty-five cars. Dirty talk filled the evening air. The roar of stationary racing motors became louder as dusk shed its blanket over this shame. At the very moment, Mom and Dad were probably lighting a lamp.

Some people will be saying, "Such things are not for the public to know about." I wish, too, the public didn't know, but in this case, they knew all too well. A local paper had a write-up on these doings. With cigarettes in one hand and beer in the other, these young people could hardly be imagined as the future church. Now and then, religion was heard mentioned, in mockery.

Within the last two years, at least a half dozen boys in our community didn't get time to quit sowing "wild oats." Death suddenly snatched them from this life. While drunken and rebelling, all died in violent car accidents.

Still the parties go on. It seems to me that for too long youth problems have been allowed to take second place, while petty church misunderstandings get the most attention. If we are unconcerned while sin is dragging down our youth, a harvest of misery and regret is sure to follow. Facts are facts. Facing them is the only scriptural way. And face them we shall. If not now, some day.   (Anon., 7-69)

Our Inexcusable Silence

Sometimes ignoring something is the best solution. But many times it is not. One problem too many of our plain churches have been ignoring for generations is unclean talk and low courtship and moral standards of their young people. I can think of no other problem in our churches about which so many people are silent. Parents ignore it. Whole communities of ministers and bishops ignore it. But there is no longer any hope that if we just pretend the problem isn't there, maybe it will go away.

It has been getting worse for generations. Yet there is a terrible disease, a spiritual plague spreading in too many of our communities. There are even some communities where there is hardly any shame or disgrace any more for couples to come to marriage with purity gone. That is a terrible foundation upon which to build a Christian home. (Thankfully, there are also many communities where such conditions are unheard of.)

If we ignore low courtship standards and pretend they aren't there, the day will surely come when we will have to answer for not only the shameful problem itself, but also for our inexcusable silence about it.   ("Views and Values," E. Stoll, 10-77)

We Don't Have to Sow Wild Oats

I read "Our Inexcusable Silence" several times. It must be our community that you are writing about. There are parents who feel that sin committed by youth is not so serious. God will overlook and excuse young people. They even defend their children by saying, "They'll get over it."

I know some children do not listen if they *do* come from good homes. But so many don't know things they should. It is not true that we have to sow wild oats. Such attitudes often lead young people into lifetime regrets and eternal judgment.   (12-77)

So-Called Amish

I was both shocked and surprised one day last week when our neighbor boy came over and said, "My friends and I really saw something last evening."

When I asked him what it was, he said they had stopped at a gas station up along Route 23. A car pulled in with three Amish boys and three Amish girls in it. He said the boys were dressed in "loud" clothes, and the girls jumped out and ran for the rest rooms. They were soon back with their hair hanging down to their shoulders and dressed in skirts which he said were "real short."

They drove off down the road. These boys were curious to know where these so-called Amish young folks were going. They followed them up the road and saw them pull in at the fire hall, where a dance was being held. There they were laughing and talking among the worldly people.

I just had to wonder, where were these young folks' parents? It seems to me, these young people should have been at home that evening. Things like this hurt me very much when I hear them. I believe that surely the Lord must also be grieved.   (Anon., 5-77)

Allowing It
We tell others we don't sanction what our youth do. But there is one thing sure—we allow it.

("Letter," Levi J. Schrock, Sullivan, Ill., 5-81)

For Purity
Not everyone took kindly to us mentioning an Amish community with a high rate of pregnancies before marriage. We did not state the location of the community. What really disturbed us was that more than one community thought we had them in mind. Apparently, things are worse than we thought, in more places than we knew.

("Staff Notes," 12-83)

Not Guilty on Monday
I wish someone had told me when I was a young girl of sixteen that it is possible to have a date *without* feeling guilty on Monday morning.

When I turned sixteen, it was the accepted thing that I would join the young folks, start going to the singings, date, and do all the things the young folks did in our community. I almost shudder to write this now, but even necking or petting was expected as the accepted and normal way to have dates. My parents said nothing against it, but rather expected us to have our dates this way. They did have strong rules against bed courtship. But they expected us to sit in a living room without lights, and also that I would wear no head covering.

Thus, my dating years began.

By the time I was eighteen, I had gone steady twice, but each time I had quit the fellow. I felt guilty on Monday morning, even though I was abiding my parents' rules. Nothing was satisfying.

Then about this time, a very nice girl came in from another community to stay a short while, visiting relatives. We found out that she felt strongly that our way of dating was wrong, and that where she came from, petting was not allowed. The couple would sit on separate chairs in a well-lighted room, and visit or read something worthwhile together.

I felt very much alone with my thoughts. It was not until some time later that we found two other girls who shared these convictions with me. People started talking, and soon there were reports out that we were "missionary minded." Even my parents were suspicious of my motives. They were afraid such convictions would lead to changing churches.

Today I'm married, and we have a family. We are members in the church of our parents, and our convictions are stronger than ever to teach our children pure courtship standards.

I feel sorry for the young people in our Christian churches who never were told of a better way, and who are still going with the trend.   ("Things I Wish Someone Had Told Me," 7-83)

Taking Responsibility

Young people sow their wild oats, living undisciplined and lustful lives until they want to get married. Then all of a sudden, they decide to join the church. Many people suspect deep down inside that they are joining the church to get married, and not because they have repented of their sins. Yet parents and ministers go along with this mockery, remarking to one another how thankful they are that the young people still have a desire to join the church. Sure enough, they are barely baptized until they get published and married.

What is important is that for too long, too many of us have been taking the wrong attitude. We have been excusing ourselves with the lie, "One man can do nothing." Why don't we all make up our minds to do what we can, however little that may be? We might be surprised over the years what the total may add up to.

("Views and Values," E. Stoll, 12-74)

Cars

Minding Your Own Business

Many people have asked me, "Why don't you have cars?" I found no one who was unable to understand when I said, "We do not feel cars are wrong in themselves. It is the misuse of them that is wrong. How many sixteen-year-olds do you know who own a car? Is it not usually that the car *owns them?*" (Pa., 7-89)

The Faded Flag

A visitor once related how he was visiting relatives in another community. He noticed that many of the Amish homes had a car parked in the driveway. In the course of his visit, he had the chance to ask one of the ministers in that district about this.

"Yes," the minister explained, "we feel parents should allow their son to live at home with his car if he has one. That way the parents can still talk to the son, and explain to him how wrong it is for him to have his worldly life. The parents don't ride with the son, of course."

The visitor was somewhat satisfied. That evening, he happened to be a supper guest in a home where a son was at home with his car. All evening the son was laughing and talking with his young brothers and sisters about radio songs and sports events. Worse yet, when the visitor was ready to go to another place for the night, instead of the parents hitching up and taking him over, they said, "Our son will drive you over with his car. You don't mind, do you? The church doesn't want us to ride with him, but it won't hurt if you do."

The visitor was stunned. Was this how the parents admonished their son for his wrongdoing, by asking him to transport visitors with his car? What message were the parents giving their son? They would have claimed that they were waving a red flag to their son. But who could blame the son for thinking the flag looked more like a white one that told him to proceed, the way was clear?

[On cars, see also chapter 3, above.]

("Views and Values," E. Stoll, 3-74)

Untaught Years

I, in my untaught younger years, had a car because almost everyone else had one, and my parents went with me freely. By God's grace, I put it away and changed my ways. But my younger brother was not so fortunate. He lost his life in a car accident and went to his grave without Christian baptism. ("Letter," 8/9-74)

To the Boy Who'd Like a Car

How will a car help you? To get a date with a girl who said she won't go with you in a buggy? Do you realize what kind of wife she would make? She would never be content until she had the very best (or is it the worst?). You might never be able to afford a home the way she would want it, so she'd always be complaining and dissatisfied.

You say you want it so you can be away from home. You can go across the world and back again and never find a home like you left. Where would you find people who care what you do, provide all your meals for nothing, keep your room cleaned and your closet filled with clothes?

Tired of your chores! Would you rather get up in a messy apartment, hunt for something clean to wear, and wish for a breakfast like Mom's, but instead end up eating some cold cereal?

You want to prove Dad and Mom can't keep you from getting a car if you want to? No, maybe they can't. But neither can they keep you from going to a fire that burns forever.

You may think that as long as your parents keep praying for you, you'll be all right. Don't forget, you'll have to make your own wrongs right. You can't expect your parents to make it right for you if you get killed in an auto crash.

Are you just planning on having your car a couple of years? Remember, a car will take you farther and farther from home. What if you get so involved you can't come back to your home? If you do come back, marry, and have a pleasant home, what will you tell your children when they want a car, too?

—*A Girl with an Aching Heart*

(Ind.; from Pathway's *Young Companion,* June 1972)

Leaving the Community

Are You Really Going?

Tomorrow is the day, the parting of the ways, and you must make your decision. No one else can make it for you. God ordained it so.

When you were young, we carried you. We helped you over life's rough places. We thought we led you onward on the path, the narrow path, the path that leads where all of us will want to go. But now the time has come. You have said that you will go away. Tomorrow is the day.

My thoughts go back some twenty years, and sweep and search and grope. If only I could find the seeds [and know] from whence they came, the seeds that separated in your soul and grew and grew and brought such harvest that today we weep.

Your closest friends have tried to tell you not to go. The ministers of your church, ordained of God to answer someday for your soul—they're urging you to stay. Do not go away. We need you, and you need us, too.

Perhaps you think when you have left us that we can just tear out your sheet, and all will be as though you never had been here. But you are young, my child. You cannot realize the bonds that bind, and bind, and bind.

Now you say you've found a better way. You want to do great things. You're confident of what you're doing, and you're anxious to go on. Beware lest you become entangled in the snares of this vain world. It promises so much, but in the end it cannot give you what you want.

Now that you are grown up, think of those little feet that follow yours, your little brothers and sisters. See those trusting eyes that look toward you. How can we tell them why you've gone away? How can we explain so they will understand, that you have gone of your own free will? You turned your back on all you once held dear. Your chair is empty at the far end of the table, and no one can take your place.

Sometime there well may come a day when the enthusiasm of your newfound life will wear away. Perhaps the day will come when all this glitter will vanish from your life. Then you may see your highest hopes were nothing, and all the things you sought were vain.

We hope your thoughts will then turn back home, the home where once you too were happy doing what you could. Don't be afraid to turn your steps and come on home.   (7-69)

Answers to a mother wanting to know the feelings of others whose children have left home and church:

Lonely and Sad

How do parents feel when children leave home? It is so heart-breaking. At first I cried and cried, and when I got over that, it just made me sick. Still, I had to do my daily work.

Sometimes I feel I didn't treat them right when they were growing up. I didn't show enough love, didn't talk nice and kind, didn't teach them enough about God and to pray, and so on. Whenever I think about it, such as now when writing about it, it brings tears to my eyes. We can't change what already happened. I will keep praying for them as long as I live.

—*A Lonely Mother*   (1-75)

From Shock to Rejoicing

We, too, had a taste of this. We had a child leave home. We did not know where he had gone, why he had left, or what he had gotten into. When I found him missing, I was shocked. I asked myself, "Where have we failed? What have we done to cause him to leave home?" At a filling station, they told us he had been there, filled up his car, and headed north, away from home.

We prayed and prayed, for he was constantly on our minds. Time and again, I asked God to send his angels to protect my son and bring him safely home.

Then a week or so later, I saw him come into the lane. I was never so glad to see him. When he came in, I smiled and asked, "So you decided to come home? Did you run out of money?"

He admitted he did and couldn't get a job. When he saw he couldn't

get work, he turned around and started for home. He didn't have
enough gas to come home. Several times he picked up hitchhikers
who gave him a little money to buy gas to keep going.

He wasn't home long until he asked, "Do you have anything to
eat?" We gladly prepared food for him, although we didn't have a
fatted calf. Yes, there is much rejoicing when the lost return home
(Luke 15:11-32). Today he is a member of the church, is married, and
has a family.

—*Reason to Rejoice* (1-75)

Sorrowing

We lived on a small farm as renters. Needing more income, it was
decided that Dan would work out. When a non-Amish man asked for
help, Dad let Dan go. The man he worked for had modern machinery, and Dan soon learned how to run the tractor and then the truck.
Soon he was driving a car. By this time, Dan didn't care to stay at
home anymore, nor do I believe Dad would have allowed it because
of his influence on the other children.

Dad was seriously ill, and his sufferings were severe, but Dan seldom came home to see him. More than once, Dad called from his death-
bed, "Dan! Dan!" But Dan did not hear. He was miles away, enjoying the pleasures of this world. Then Dad died.

Dan drifted from one thing to another. He married an "English" girl.
Dan never complained, but we think he had many regrets. After some
years, we heard that they were going to dances, playing cards, and
drinking. I sent them a book telling them how wrong it is to live the
life they were living. Later I found out that it only made them angry.

Dan loved Mother, although he seldom came to see her. Mother is
still watching and waiting, with a prayerful and sad heart. She recalls
the sorrow she went through when a little son was laid to rest. Many
tears were shed for the innocent little child, but many more tears have
been shed for Dan.

I know that today my mother is still sorrowing, not for the one who
died, whose body is asleep in the grave, but for the one whose body
is still living but whose soul is dead.

—*An Observer* (1-73)

Mothers, Do Not Weep for Your Babies

We, too, were blest with a beautiful child like yours, a son. We taught him from the Bible, we attended church together, we had family devotions, and we worked together.

When our son grew up to the years of accountability, we looked for fruit. At the age when most young people begin turning to Christ, we saw no indication of his turning that way. We waited and worked with mounting anxiety as the years sped by and the heart became harder, the will more stubborn, the face more sullen.

Tonight we weep in sorrow for his soul. No, he is not asleep as your little one in the grave. He is in a spiritual sleep, in death, nigh unto eternal death.

If you could look with us into that hovel which our son calls "home," you would see a long-haired creature wallowing in rock music, weird lights, pornography, TV, cigarettes, and beer. What more, we do not know. Has he forgotten his childhood teachings? Does he ever think of God, or eternity, or his sorrowing parents?

Our home is quiet, a place is empty at our table, and a space is void in our hearts. The room that should be his contains an empty bed. The clock ticks steadily through the silence of the night, a grim reminder that time keeps moving on.

What if the summons that called your son home should come to ours in his present state? Are you surprised that we weep?

Tonight, as many times before, we wonder how we have failed. We bow ourselves before our heavenly Father and ask for forgiveness. We pray for wisdom that from now on we might be better able to do his will.

Fathers and mothers, do not weep for your babies who have gone before. They can never be lost. Compared to other scenes in this world, a baby's grave is a peaceful picture.

—*Another Mother*   (10-73)

The following three stories are true, but with names changed:

Andy Zook

Andy was a young, rebellious boy who lived in a community where disobedient children were not allowed to stay at home. After a while away from home, the longing to see the family, especially his young brothers and sisters, grew so intense that he finally mustered enough courage to go home. As he parked the car beside the barn, he heard the door slam. Looking around, he saw his father running with an up-raised hammer, straight for the car. He immediately put the car in gear and drove back out the lane. The next we heard of him, he had enlisted in the army and, sad to say, a few of his younger brothers followed him.

Adam Yoder

Adam was much the same as Andy Zook. One difference was that he could stay at home. One thing led to another, and the time came when he was in trouble with the law. Running through a red light, he struck another car. He was searched, and drugs were found in his possession. When his father found out that his son was in jail, he immediately paid the $500 bail and took him home. What will become of his boy in time, I do not know, but as of yet he has not changed his course.

Eli Miller

Eli was another boy much the same as the two already mentioned. Although he was not forbidden to stay at home, the sad faces of his father and mother haunted him so much that he didn't spend much time there. After a few years of rebellious living, he ended up in jail for drunken driving. There he had lots of time to think.

His jail sentence expired on a Saturday, and he was free once again. But where would he go? Practically penniless, he knew he would find no friends at the tavern where he had spent so much of his time. There seemed to be only one place to try—home. The sad face of his mother invited him to stay for supper, much like you would invite some special company. After supper, he was admonished that he should go to church the next day, and the relieved feeling at being accepted at home made him think he might go.

However, when he awoke the next morning, that feeling had left him. He got out of bed and looked out the window. To his surprise his horse, which he had not driven for so long, was patiently standing at the hitching rack, all hitched up. Suddenly the kindness of his parents overwhelmed him. Yes, he would go to church, even if he had to face the people as a jailbird. This was the beginning of a new life for Eli.

Today Eli is a married man with a family. He has often mentioned the sorrow he feels for his wasted years.

("Letter: The Wisdom of Jethro," Daniel L. Hershberger, Millersville, Ohio, 10-85)

The Wrong Kind of Love

It was a cold rainy day in March that Roman Troyer happened to glance out the window and notice his neighbor, Delbert Yoder, coming up the front walk toward the house.

"Come on in," Roman called out.

Delbert entered. "Good afternoon. I'm going around to a few of the neighbors, taking orders for clover and alfalfa seed. The mill lets us have it a lot cheaper in a large order, so I figured we might as well pool our orders and get the price break."

"Sure," said Roman. "That's a good idea."

The men did their business and then talked farmers' talk for a while. It was time for Delbert to move on, but there was one more thing he wanted to ask. He shifted on his chair and cleared his throat as if he didn't know how to begin.

"Ah, er, ah, I . . . I was wondering if it's true your Andy has a car now?"

Roman's face saddened. He sighed. "I'm afraid it's true," he said heavily. "Seems he was always such an obedient boy until about a year or so ago when he turned eighteen. Just wants to have his own way now and be his own boss."

"Where's he planning to stay?" Delbert asked sympathetically.

Roman looked up, as if surprised at the question. "Stay? As far as I know, he'll be here at home."

"Aren't you afraid that Andy won't be a good influence on the other boys if he is right here at home with his car?"

"I know," Roman said soberly. "It's not the best, but what can we do? It wouldn't be right to chase Andy away from home either."

"No, not to chase him away," Delbert said. "But surely you have the right to say under what conditions he can stay at home. I don't think you would be chasing him away if you took the stand that the only way he can be at home is if he doesn't have a car."

"But what if he didn't put it away?"

"That would be his choice. Then he would know that he chose to have his car rather than his home."

Roman's wife couldn't keep silent any longer. "But do you know where Andy would be staying if he couldn't stay at home? He would be with that gang in town, and you know what those boys are like. At least as long as he's at home, we can talk to him and keep trying to get him to see his mistake. I think we should pray for him and show him love, and try to nourish that little bit of love back to life instead of stamping it out and driving him farther away."

As their conversation with Delbert showed, the Troyers based their decision on the following reasons:

1. *Andy was too old to be forced.* But if Andy was too old to be forced against his will, why were his parents not too old to be forced against their will? Our actions must stand behind our words. Why are we all so afraid of forcing young people to do right, that we let them force us to do wrong?

2. *Andy still had some good in him.* If we must wait to discipline a person until there is no good left in him, we will never work on anyone. What we so often fail to realize is that firm discipline at home and in church, when done consistently and in love, does not drive people away, but draws them.

3. *It is better for Andy to be at home than in town.* There is no end to the things one can justify with this reasoning. With that kind of standard, things in our homes and churches can only get worse and worse. Let the boys decorate their buggies if they wish; it's better than getting a car. Let the young folks play ball on Sunday; it's better than being at a beer party. Or let them go to the beer party for that mat-

ter; it's better than if they go completely out in the world. Let the girls wear their coverings way back on their heads; it's better than wearing no covering at all. As long as we measure ourselves with wrong things, we can only move in one direction: losing ground. Why not do the reasoning in reverse? Why should we permit decorated buggies? Wouldn't it be better if they were plain?

4. *Andy needed time to see his mistake.* The longer a person lives in sin, the harder it is for him to break with it. The disobedient do not need more time nearly as much as they need more encouragement not to put off their repentance another day.

5. *They loved Andy too much to chase him away.* We do not have the right kind of love for our children when they are in spiritual danger and we do not do all we can to bring them to safety. The wise man Solomon said, "He who spares the rod hates his son; but he who loves him chastens him promptly" (Prov. 13:24).

("Views and Values," E. Stoll, 4-85)

Welcome to the Club

Every community is full of fences, high ones and low ones, tight ones and loose ones. It seems like parents and ministers are repairing or building new ones all the time. All one has to do to belong to the club is just find out what fences your local church and parents have put up, then crowd those fences and encourage others to do the same.

Jonas became interested in the crowd-the-fence club before he was very old. Of course, at home he didn't have many fences to crowd; his parents just let him do as he wanted and didn't build many fences.

The ministers felt the influence of the radio harmful, so they put a fence around it. Finally, he broke through the fence entirely and bought a radio of his own. It gave him ideas and taught dirty words and suggestive tunes with which to express them.

Now that he had the radio fence crossed, Jonas started crowding the fence of bad companionship. He sought out the kind of friends that could talk the language he learned on the radio.

The horse-and-buggy fence didn't stop him long. When Jonas was eighteen, he rattled home one evening with a secondhand car. Now Jonas could roar through fences [break rules] at eighty miles an hour.

He could go where he wanted to, and he did.

He remained faithful as an active fence-crowder all his life. Right to the last, he worked at gathering fresh members and introducing them to the club. It was too bad he had a wreck one Sunday morning at three o'clock, when he drove out into the path of a truck on a busy highway. The police found two empty bottles smashed beside his crushed body.

So now you have your invitation to join the club. But don't think you have to crowd the fence as far as Jonas to be a member. It wouldn't be good for the club if all the members cursed and drank and tore around with a car. The club needs you just as much as it needs the Jonas kind. If we all stick together, we'll all go to the same place. And Jonas will be there to greet us.

"Enjoy yourself, youth. Do what your heart desires, but know that God will judge you" (Eccles. 11:9, abridged).   (2-69)

A Hard Decision

I was raised in an "English" home. I decided to join the Amish church. I believed in my heart that this was the thing that God wanted me to do in life.

When my parents found out, they were very hurt and disappointed in me. They kept telling me that one of the commandments is to "honor thy parents." At times I felt that maybe I'm wrong and maybe I should give it up. But still I didn't dismiss the idea and longing to join the faith that I felt was walking closer in the footsteps of Christ than what my parents and I were.

While reading and studying the New Testament, I found two verses that fit me and my life: "He that loves father or mother more than me is not worthy of me; and he that loves son or daughter more than me is not worthy of me" (Matt. 10:37). "If any man come to me, and hate not his father, and mother, and wife, and children, and brothers, and sisters, yea, and his own life also, he cannot be my disciple" (Luke 14:26).

Through these verses and others, my decision was made. It was *hard*, and only those who have gone through such [a struggle] know what I mean. But through prayer, in time my parents are no longer bitter. They are still hurt that I'm not with them. But they feel that if this is what I think the Lord wants me to do, then it's the best. I am thankful to the Lord that they feel this way.   (12-71)

Our Deprived Children

In a recent report from Ottawa, I came across a statement that caught my eye. According to Statistics Canada, over a million children lived in poverty since 1984. Since that time, the child tax credit has been increased to $565 per child, with a $200 supplement for those under six years old, to ease the burden of poverty.

What base was used to determine the child poverty level? Upon investigation, I found that a rural family with five children and less than $24, 209 annual income was considered to be living in poverty. (If that boggles the mind, in a city the size of Toronto, Canada, the same-sized family would need an income of over $32,960 annually to get away from poverty!)

The plain people, who do not accept family allowance payments or other government subsidies, would be depriving themselves and their children of an additional sum. I would not even venture a guess at the amount. Oh, our poor, deprived children! I have no figures to prove it, but I guess that the greater number of them are being raised in poverty, according to the above calculations!

Besides, we deprive them of "certified" teachers in our schools. We deprive them of education beyond the eighth grade. We even deprive them of that greatest of educators, the television set. They are deprived of the opportunity to attend theaters, exhibitions, circuses, baseball and hockey games. They do not have the privilege of going to the beach, the cottage, or the youth camp during the summer.

Instead of having all of the above advantages, they are expected to feed the chickens, sweep the floor, and fill the wood box after walking home from school. On Saturdays and holidays, they have to help with planting the garden, and later with picking berries and cherries, peas and beans, corn and potatoes. They drive a team of horses for loading hay and grain. Truly, they have little leisure time.

Of course, there is no sign of deprivation. They enjoy the rides on the loads of hay. They pop the occasional berry and cherry into the

mouth. Possibly they do eat more and better food than children in the cities do. Most of their food is homegrown, home-cooked, and as fresh as possible. The work they do builds up a healthy appetite. They go to bed early without watching TV, and they sleep soundly.

Nor do they seem to be hampered in their studies by their lack of TV education. In fact, what they learn by other sources is possibly at least as beneficial to them as watching TV would be. They learn German in infancy, and become truly bilingual by the time they leave school. They are far from being illiterate. Their teachers make up for a lack of academic skills by their dedication to their calling. After the eighth grade, our children are "apprenticed" to their parents to learn their trade by practical application. Their farming experience seems to serve them as well as a college degree would.

On a more positive note, we also "deprive" our children of the evil influence of TV, the exposure to crime, violence, immorality, liquor, and drugs. We deprive them of the addictive pursuit of pleasure, of becoming sports or entertainment fanatics.

Instead of all manner of public entertainment, our children find enjoyment in nature on the farm: the baby chicks, cuddly kittens, and playful puppies. They learn to know and appreciate the wild animals and birds abounding in woodland and meadow. They swim and fish in pond and stream. Above all, they enjoy learning by doing.

Being deprived of many of the pleasures of this world is a spiritual blessing. Our children seem to be just as happy as those who are deprived of nothing.   (Isaac R. Horst, 1-91)

7

The Amish Congregation

A Look Inside

For the Amish, whose ancestors in Europe worshiped while hiding in homes or caves to escape persecution, the church is still a community of believers, not a building. Where they gather to worship, there is their church.

Few outsiders ever get to experience an Amish district church service as held in the home of a member. Some non-Amish friends and neighbors have been to weddings and funerals. Yet much of what takes place at church, baptism, and communion services is something an outsider will never see. Writers have described these services in books, often in clinical detail, but they often miss the emotion and feeling of what it is like to be there.

In this chapter we can truly "get inside the heads" of the Amish, share their thoughts, their human reactions, and thus gain a measure of the strength of their faith and community. For those who say the Amish are more worried about religious form and rules than spirituality, these writings offer another view.

Of all the stories I have read in the thousands of pages of *Family Life*, perhaps my favorite is the one titled "Only God Knows." It captures the personalities, feelings, fears, suspense, and emotional release experienced when a new minister is chosen by lot. Here we see the Amish not only as part of a group, but as distinct and very human individuals with hopes, strengths, fears, and sometimes doubts. In other words, they are not unlike you and me.

Amish Meetinghouses

We believe that the people are the church, not a certain building. When the Amish immigrated to America, they brought with them the practice of holding church services in private homes.

In Europe, the government would not have allowed them to erect meetinghouses, even if they had wished to do so. They were also forbidden ownership of farmland, and certainly not land on which to build a meetinghouse. They were tenant farmers on other people's estates.

It is likely that every family could not host the church service since they did not own their homes and could not construct them to accommodate a large gathering. In one large European Amish congregation, Montbeliard in France, the church record book indicates that only several tenants' homes with large rooms were regularly used for church services.

When the Amish became established in America, where they could own their farms and construct large houses, the worship services rotated between families. While permission could easily have been obtained from the government to construct meetinghouses, these early Amish immigrants were well content to continue meeting in private homes. After all, their Anabaptist forebears had been denied permission to assemble, having to meet secretly in forests and caves. The freedom to worship in America in their own homes was a privilege indeed.

With time, some Amish decided they wanted meetinghouses. As time would tell, it generally was the progressive element that wanted them.

During the last half of the 1800s, a liberal movement developed within the Amish churches in America. During this period, the term *Old Order Amish* originated, referring to congregations keeping the *alte Ordnung* and the older traditions, such as worshiping in private homes. The liberal or progressive congregations became known as *Amish-Mennonites*, which was a fitting title, since they were yet somewhat Amish but also traveling in the Mennonite direction.

One Mennonite historian, John C. Wenger, has estimated that [over] half of the Amish went with the Amish-Mennonite movement. The introduction of worshiping in meetinghouses was only one of the many differences between the Old Order Amish and the Amish-Mennonites. Much could be written about the divisions in various states and the construction of more than eighty meetinghouses.

The present Amish settlement in southern Somerset County, Pennsylvania, extending over the Maryland line, dates to 1769 or perhaps earlier. In 1881, it was decided to build four meetinghouses for the large settlement, two in each state. By 1895, there was a church division. The two Pennsylvania congregations remained with the Old Order Amish.

Today, when Lancaster County Amish visit the Somerset County group, they do not preach in the meetinghouses even though the buildings are one hundred years old. They insist on preaching in private homes in Somerset County, and their wish is granted. The Somerset County Amish are unique.

Nearly a hundred meetinghouses have been erected by congregations whose roots are Amish. Only the Somerset County group has remained Old Order Amish, proving the truth of Harold S. Bender's statement that meetinghouses are evidence of a "break between the progressive and old order elements."   (D. Luthy, 8/9-91)

A Costly Church

If we Amish think it's expensive to build and pay for our own schools, we should just be thankful we don't have the church expenses some people do. According to a recent survey made of a large church in Winnipeg, it costs $30,000 a year to provide a one-hour service each Sunday for the worshipers of that church. That figures out at more than $500 an hour. At that rate, an Amish church service of three hours would cost $1,500!

It's not hard to understand why we get by a good deal cheaper. We don't pay our ministers thousands of dollars per year to prepare and deliver the sermons, as this church does. We don't pay a choir $6,812 a year to sing. Nor do we need a $727,550 church building in which to meet. We also get along without a $77,851 organ or $25,000 worth of stained-glass windows, not to mention skimping on the $3,000 worth of carpets. Our communion vessels don't come anywhere close to costing us $3,727, nor do our pews and pulpit cost us $27,875.

With a budget like we have, we even save the $240 this Winnipeg church spent on twelve brass collection plates!   (8/9-73)

A Typical Sunday Morning
Four-thirty in the morning, it's get up and go;
I comb my hair first, if I'm not too slow.
Out to the barn with hubby to chore;
I help to get started, but not much more.
One by one, the cows come in.
Scrape down the *Misht** where they've been.

Tie them and wash their udders clean.
Cows are contented, but one seems mean.
I head for the house and when I arrive,
I glance at the clock; it's after five!
I quick change clothes and put on my *Kopp*,*
Tie on an old apron to catch the slop,
Get breakfast ready, with eggs to fry,
Cold cereal, too, and a piece of *shoofly*.*
Call the rest of the house, they're soon alert
If I tell them we are going to church.
Omar goes to the barn; the girls get *Gma** dressed.
They'd look all right, but their hair's in a mess,
So I comb them for they are only three;
I had made Becky *bobbies** on Saturday eve.
Quick! Get the eggs fryin'—the men are coming in;
They sit at the table, on down to Mim.
Breakfast is eaten, and all have their fill,
With the usual fuss, and likely a spill.
From the bedroom comes a cry out loud,
So the baby's brought out to join the crowd.
Table is cleared off, dishes washed in a hurry,
With the help of Eli, Ruth, and Mary.
I'd run wash the milkers if I'd have time,
But I don't, so Ben will, for he won't mind.
A round with the washcloth on faces and fists,
In spite of all this, there's *Kutsle** you miss.
The men get dressed; doesn't take them long;
Pop helps the little fellow with his shirt on wrong,
Puts on his jacket, through his hair runs a comb.
Then comes a voice, "Are you ready, Mom?"
But there's *Schatzlin** to button and *Kopplin** to tie.
We straighten the kitchen, and then with a sigh,
I tear off my apron and slip on my shoes.
I'm about ready, not much more to do,
Tie my bonnet and then patiently wait,
I glance out the window—oh, they're at the gate!

I lock the doors; Pop must think I'm slow.
Quick grab the baby, and away we go.
On the way to church, I have time to think
And thank the Giver of all our blessings. . . .
A lovely morning, so quiet and serene,
Beautiful flowers, grasses so green.
I look over my shoulder, happy faces in a row;
I wouldn't trade places with anyone I know!

[*Misht*, manure. *Kopp*, *Kapp*, prayer covering. *Shoofly*, pie made of molasses and brown sugar. *Gma*, *Gmee*, church. *Bobbies*, little girls' hair tied in a special way. *Kutsle*, a food smear. *Schatzlin*, small aprons. *Kopplin*, *Kapplin*, prayer coverings for little girls.]

(Mrs. B. H. King, 5-78)

Children and Church

Children at Church

Church ought to be one place where children are *welcome*. When your little three-month-old baby cries and the one-year-old at the same time, you hear talk after church, "What a racket!" Please, older mothers, why not *help* a young mother with her hands full? She can't nurse the baby and at the same time give the one-year-old his need. Make the mother with a lot of children welcome, even if her babies get fussy.

I've happened to see a young married man not singing, chewing gum, and looking over the church. That bothers me a lot, more than one of the small angels playing, but no fuss is made of that. Every story has two sides to it.

—*Just Another Sister*   ("Letter," Ind., 1-77)

Observed at Church

Little dolly in a basket, plastic bolt-and-nut set, large and small plastic animals in a pocketbook, plastic folding comb, horse-and-chariot set, tractor, pull-apart beads, book and pencil, small picture books, diaper boxes, plastic case full of midget toys, plastic clothespins, rain bonnet case with candy, steel truck, play money.

You may ask, "Is this a public sale bill?"

No, it is not. It is a mother's supply of toys to keep one little girl's time occupied while church is in session.

Oh! Oh! Here comes Mrs. Dan Erb, and she has that paper bag with toys again. I'll watch so I won't sit near her or I can't hear Preacher John Lehman.

There comes five-year-old Danny to sit with his sister, and the bench is already overcrowded. I know it doesn't matter too much, because he doesn't sit long anywhere. I see he is already going over to his father.

Opening the door and coming in quietly and in a meek and humble manner is Mrs. Abe Troyer with her little girl. She usually has one string of beads and buttons on a string for her daughter, and the little girl is still satisfied.

What was it the minister once said? "I can see that mothers who take many things to church to satisfy their children seem to have the most unruly ones."   (M., 2-69)

Hymns and Hymn Singing

The Ausbund

It is a bright, warm Sunday morning. The living room and kitchen of the Yoder's farmhouse are filled with people sitting quietly and expectantly on the wooden benches. The first hymn has just ended, and there is a pause, a moment of rest before the next hymn begins. Then a deep-throated voice from the men's benches calls out, "Seite Siwwahundert und Siwwazig" (page 770). There is a wave of motion among the people as they open their songbooks. But there is little rustling of pages. The well-creased books seem to open automatically to the announced hymn.

"O Gott Vater, wir loben dich" (O God the Father, we praise you). The words rise and lower as the leader intones the song. Such a beautiful song, a perfect song to be sung while the ministers are in an upstairs bedroom preparing for the morning service. First God is praised and thanked. Then the singers pray for the ministers, that they may speak God's teachings. Next they pray for the congregation, that their hearts and minds may be receptive to the service. Finally, they ask God to be present during the service. Yes, it is a meaningful song, this second hymn sung at Amish church services.

After a quarter hour, the second hymn ends and the ministers are heard descending the staircase. The members close their songbooks and tuck them away. A little boy, Bennie, is sitting on his father's lap. He reaches down and touches the black book that was just placed beside his father. Bennie tries to lift the book, but its two-inch thickness is too wide for him to grasp. The young man sitting beside Bennie's father sees the little boy's interest in the book. He picks it up and taps Bennie's hand gently and playfully with it. The cover drops open, exposing the title page. The young man gazes at it: *Ausbund das ist Etliche schöne Christliche Lieder* (An excellent selection of some beautiful Christian songs). His attention leaves the open book, for the minister has begun to speak.

The young man did not look at the title page of the songbook for more than a few seconds, but it was long enough for a few questions to enter his mind. He could remember that this songbook had been used ever since he was little Bennie's age. But had it been used when his father was a boy, or when his grandfather was young? Had it, perhaps, always been used in the Amish church? Who wrote the songs, and how long ago?

("Four Centuries with the *Ausbund*," D. Luthy, 6-71)

Leenaert Clock's Songs in the Ausbund

Leenaert Clock, a Mennonite minister and a native of Germany who settled in Holland, probably before 1590, has greatly contributed to Amish singing. His hymn "O Gott Vater wir loben dich" is always sung as the second song in Amish church services, except funerals. And his hymn "Lebt friedsam" (Live ye peacefully) is often sung as the final song. In 1625, he published a Dutch edition of his prayers. Many are commonly used in Amish family devotions as well as in church services.   ("Yesterdays and Years," D. Luthy, 11-88)

Michael Schneider's Songs in the Ausbund

The *Ausbund* is often called in German *das dicke Liederbuch*, the thick songbook. But that would not have accurately described the first edition printed over four hundred years ago in 1564. It was not thick, nor was it even entitled *Ausbund*.

The first edition of 1564 contained only fifty-three hymns written by a group of Anabaptists known as the Philippites. They were similar to the Hutterites, living in colonies and sharing all things in common. In 1535 their bishop, Michael Schneider, and some sixty followers left their colony in Moravia because of persecution. They entered Germany, hoping to reach the place where they had lived before moving to Moravia. But the entire group was captured by the Catholic authorities and imprisoned in the castle dungeons at Passau, on the Danube River in Bavaria. During their imprisonment, the Philippites wrote hymns. Michael Schneider himself composed twelve.

After their release from the Passau prison, where all had been tortured but none put to death, the Philippites disbanded. Nothing is known of what became of their leader, Michael Schneider, but some of his followers united with the Swiss Brethren and abandoned communal living. Naturally, they brought with them the songs they had written while in prison. The Swiss Brethren then published the fifty-three Passau hymns in 1564. By 1583, quite a few other songs were added to the original set, and also the title *Ausbund*, which apparently means "special" or "select."

Today the Passau songs are found between pages 435 and 770 of the *Ausbund*, making that section of the hymnal the oldest. While the 1564 songbook contained fifty-three Passau hymns, the present-day *Ausbund* contains fifty.

The Old Order Amish are the only group that still uses the *Ausbund* for church services. Even so, not all of the lengthy songs are familiar to the Amish, nor are all the verses of the familiar songs sung.

Several of Schneider's songs are favorites of the Amish and are sung at important times. His song "Wohlauf, Wohlauf, du Gottes G'mein" (Rejoice, rejoice, you church of God, no. 97) is sung at weddings. When an excommunicated member reunites with the church, number 99 beginning with verse 20 or 21 is used the first time the person comes to church. Then, when one is received back into full membership, verse 30 is sung: "Es ist auch Freud im Himmel" (There is also joy in heaven).

A few Amish settlements do not use the *Ausbund*. For example, the large settlement in Kalona, Iowa, uses the *Unpart(h)eiische Lieder-sammlung* (Impartial collection of songs), first published in 1860 by Johan Baer of Lancaster, Pennsylvania.

Most people have likely failed to even notice the initials "M. S." at the beginning of Schneider's songs in the *Ausbund*, and some may have mistakenly thought them to stand for Menno Simons. Yet the time Michael Schneider spent composing the songs in Passau prison was not in vain. While his personal fate is unknown, the songs he wrote are still alive today and appreciated by the Old Order Amish.

(5-78)

The History of Our Amish Church Tunes

It is likely that our Anabaptist forefathers developed their own style of singing within the first generation. Although the hymns were their own, the tunes were likely borrowed from various sources. Since they came out of the Catholic Church, they must have been acquainted with the Gregorian chants. Although many of the tunes were borrowed from Lutheran and secular songs, likely even those were influenced by the beauty and depth of the chants.

No doubt as the years went by, their singing evolved into the kind they felt best suited to obtain true humility and a prayerful attitude on the part of the whole congregation.

If we say that our singing must be easily understood by a listener, we imply that the power is in the words alone and that the music is of little or no value. If this were true, then we might as well forget about the singing and have someone read the verses. Since the Amish changed the least over the years, it stands to reason that they are the only ones to preserve both the hymns and the tunes down through the centuries.

Ancient church music was always sung in unison. Over the years, as congregations grew larger and music became faster and more elaborate, this gradually changed for most of Christendom.

Why do our old German church songs not have notes with them to help us sing them? Because the tunes we sing are much older than the system of music and notes used in the modern hymnbooks.

Perhaps there is no better way to end this article than with the words of John Umble, who was a professor at Goshen College:

"No one has yet written these tunes in conventional music score and, even if it were possible to do so, it would be impossible to teach anyone to reproduce their tone and spirit accurately. The Amish sing them with a depth of sincerity, a feeling of true Christian piety difficult to imitate. It is literally true that even if anyone should know the tunes, he could not sing them as the Amish do. Anyone wishing to reproduce the tunes must first of all be sincere in trying to know and understand the Amish people. He must understand and feel the context of the words."

[In *Amische Lieder* (1942), Joseph W. Yoder gave musical notations for selected German hymns, some from the *Ausbund*. Ben Troyer Jr. published *Ausbund and Liedersammlung Songs with Shaped Notes* (Sugarcreek, Ohio: Carlisle, 1997). Pathway Bookstore (LaGrange, Ind.) also offers *Notes for Ausbund Hymns* and *Notes for Funeral Hymns from Ausbund*. The Amish Library of Millersburg, Ohio, prepared *Songs of the Ausbund* (1998), an English translation of 69 of the *Ausbund*'s 140 songs.]   (D. Wagler, 12-85)

In Praise of Singing

A feed salesman stopped in at the Amos Yoder farm. Before leaving, the salesman started asking questions about the plain people's faith and beliefs.

"Do you use an organ or piano in your worship?"

"No, we don't have any musical instruments in the church," Amos answered.

"Oh, I see. You just clap your hands and stomp your feet."

"No. We sing without a beat."

"Do you harmonize, singing in tenor and bass?"

"No."

"How about quartet singing?"

"No, we sing in unison of voice."

"That's interesting. I guess you just sing old gospel hymns like 'Amazing Grace' and 'The Old Rugged Cross.'"

"No, the songs we sing were written two or three centuries ago by people who were persecuted, imprisoned, and martyred for their faith.

We sing them in slow tunes that have been handed down from generation to generation."

Historically, it has been said that the slow singing originated with the Anabaptist Christians. They would sing to their death while being martyred for their faith. In mockery, the people would dance to their singing. Because of this, the Anabaptists started singing slow tunes.

Singing that worships and praises God and spiritually edifies people doesn't have to be sung in four parts, harmonized, or have a musical background. When these things are added to our singing, there is a danger of putting emphasis on the voices and music rather than feeling the message and inspiration the words contain.

Romans 12:2 tells us we are not to be conformed to this world, but to be transformed by the renewing of our minds. This should be applied to our whole life, which would certainly include our mode of singing.   (Orva Hochstetler, 2-79)

Some Thoughts on Singing

What is the reason singing in parts is being accepted in some areas among our plain people? If we are singing just to see how nice we can sing, we aren't singing to God's honor and glory. When we have our minds on the tune to make sure every phrase works out just right, our mind can't very well concentrate on the words we are singing. Another thing about singing like this is that someone with a better voice can be heard above the rest. Soon that person will be getting praise for the fine voice, forgetting Who gave the voice. When voices blend in the same notes, it will not be so much this way.

—*A Young Girl*   (Ky.)

Singing the Old Songs

Singing the slow tunes as they are sung in Amish churches today is indeed a special assignment. The Amish have kept up and handed down these tunes from generation to generation, for hundreds of years. Singing these old hymns can be likened to the final harrowing before planting the crop. It should help in getting our minds into a prayerful, receptive mood.

Indications are that this type of music grew out of the early Anabaptist church music. Without beat or measure, time or rhythm, it depends upon depth and devotion, appealing to the nobler sentiments of the heart. The song leader sings the syllable of each line alone. Since there are normally two to five notes to each syllable, this can be a major undertaking, especially if he is not well acquainted with the song. The secret of singing any slow tune is to be able to tie the last syllable of each line to the first syllable of the next one.

In most Amish church districts throughout the Midwest, someone is appointed to announce the songs and ask someone to sing them. The Swartzentruber churches go a step further and have a *Vorsinger Tisch*, a table at which the song leaders sit. The *Vorsinger* is usually one of the older brethren who is fairly well acquainted with the church tunes. There may be problems in getting it started. If so, he must be prepared to either start it or ask someone else to start the first line. Then the one who was originally asked to lead will take over. It is the *Vorsinger's* responsibility to decide how many verses of a song should be sung.

Practice singings are held in many communities, where young and old get together to practice these old songs. Most tunes are sung for various hymns and at different times during the year. Most of the counsel meeting and communion tunes are not sung at other times.

Each community has its own variations of many of these tunes. At a wedding, the marrying couple and their families usually decide who is to lead the hymns.

All four verses of "Das Loblied" are sung [the hymn traditionally sung second at most services]. I am always interested to note how long it takes to sing it. Twenty minutes is about the normal time for most Amish communities. For some of the plainer churches, it takes 24 minutes, and the Swartzentruber groups may take up to 28 minutes.

Many years ago when I was in a Swartzentruber service and was asked to lead "Das Loblied," I soon detected that their tune was slightly different. But what really threw me was when the first and third lines ended up on a different note than I had ever heard before. I thought I had done pretty well in not getting stuck until my host told me on the way home, "Two weeks ago there was a man from Pennsylvania, and he did even worse than you did!"

Since memory cannot be depended upon [to guide rotation], many of the *Vorsingers* keep a card file with the name of each [song leader] on a card. When he leads a song, the date is recorded on his card, and it is put in the back of the pile.

The singing may even have an influence on the sermons that follow. If the ministers appreciate the singing, how much more do we hope that it will ascend and be heard and accepted by the One in whose Name we have gathered to worship.   (D. Wagler, 7-88)

Musical Instruments

Musical instruments have been used by popular churches for a great number of years. Those who do so claim they have been of value in promoting spiritual experiences. We should take notice that we have no mention in the New Testament of Christians using instrumental music. On the contrary, we do have Scripture on the evil of music, its natural rather than spiritual effect, prophecy of its condemnation, and use as a shadow rather than the real. "Woe to them that . . . invent to themselves instruments of music like David" (Amos 6:1-5).

Those who defend musical instruments because they were used in Old Testament worship would have as much Scripture to justify war. The apostle Paul compares spiritual deadness to the sounds of musical instruments (1 Cor. 13:1; 14:7).

Instrumental music tends to draw attention to itself through its natural beauty, distracts our thoughts from the meaning of the words we sing, and entertains us rather than glorifying God. Also, instruments of music are an expensive luxury. Much money is wasted that could be put to better use.   (2-80)

The Amish practice believers baptism, for those who are old enough to understand, believe for themselves, make lifelong vows, and be accountable. According to custom, applicants for baptism are at least sixteen years old.

Baptism

Is It Merely Joining the Church?

Why would anyone want to join church without being born again? [I hear various comments.]

"My friends are joining church, so I want to, also."

"I'm grown up, and my parents and relatives keep bothering me until I do. Then when I have joined the church, the pressure will be off, and I can do more as I please."

"My parents want me to be baptized so that if anything happens to me, I can go to heaven. I don't want to go to hell, so I better join church, and then everybody will feel better."

When I was taking instructions for baptism, there were several in my group who were not permitted to date until they were baptized. On the evening of the day of their baptism, all of them dated. How sad that they should cast a dark shadow of suspicion upon their motives for being baptized.

Applicants for baptism have been seen coming for instruction dressed in immodest clothes and wearing unbecoming hairdos. Yet they claimed they were saying no to the world.

When such things are seen, is it not a sign that the Christian faith has degraded into a Christian culture? Anyone who is born again will live for Christ, but those who are merely living a Christian culture, are living for themselves.

When we are born again, we have the desire to be in fellowship with others of God's children. The ceremony of baptism has been given us so that we can testify to the church as well as to the world that we are now God's children. We are members of Christ's body, the church. Joining church is a consequence, not a cause. It should be the result of a change of heart, instead of being considered the change itself.

(David E. Miller, 10-68)

Wrong on the Inside

As a young father, it doesn't seem long ago that I was in the preparation class myself. I must say that I didn't attain much of the new life until after baptism, but it wasn't the ministers' fault. How could they know, when everything seemed in order on the outside, that something was wrong on the inside? But what puzzles me is, if the candidates can't even come up to what the rules require on the outside, what hope can we have that things are right on the inside?

In our community, there is a theory that we don't want to be too harsh with our young folks, or we'll chase them out into the world. A lot of our young boys are permitted to have their cars at home because the parents say that is a better environment for the boys than it would be to live in town. But light and darkness will not mix. I have seen where the parents were partaking of darkness more than the boy was being enlightened. Then when the time for baptism comes around, we comfort ourselves with what a big change they have made. Yet they may still be far from what the Scriptures require.

What is the result of baptizing members who have the wrong motives in seeking church membership? Too often there are members who are inside the fence, but wish they were outside. Is there any wonder we hear of married men smoking, drinking, and playing cards in their homes or at the factory? (Ind.)

Proper Preparations for Baptism

Can water make a Christian? Can church membership make a Christian? If it were possible to make Christians by simply baptizing them, then we should do as they did in the 1400s—use the sword and force people to be baptized, or run mobs through a river like a German king did. We realize that this would be ridiculous and not scriptural.

Exactly what did out ancestors believe in the line of baptism and church membership? Menno Simons writes, "We are not born again because we are baptized, but we are baptized because we have received the new birth. He who seeks remission of his sins through baptism rejects the blood of Christ and makes water his idol."

If we wash the bowl only on the outside, but not on the inside, we will never be anything but worldly, sinful, wretched, miserable, poor, blind, and naked (Rev. 3:17). (Ind., 8/9-79)

Faith, Works, and the Anabaptists

The Anabaptists were strict on the conduct question. Unless applicants showed evidence in daily life of being born-again, they simply were not baptized or accepted as members. A tree is known by its fruits. Christianity is a practical thing.

Because the Anabaptists were practical, they soon had a reputation as "good" people. Even their enemies, who persecuted them, admitted that their conduct of life was more holy than for any other group. The Anabaptists became so well-known for their good works that anyone who rebuked sin or left off sinning was at once suspected of being one. In the same way, people were sometimes cleared of Anabaptist charges by their bad behavior.

(**"Fireside Chats," J. Stoll, 2-70**)

Questions Asked at the Baptismal Service

1. Can you confess as the Ethiopian eunuch confessed? *Answer: Yes, I believe that Jesus Christ is the Son of God.*

2. Do you acknowledge it to be a Christian order, church, and fellowship of God, under which you now submit yourselves? *Yes.*

3. Do you renounce the world, the devil with all his doings, as well as your own flesh and blood, and do you desire to live for Jesus Christ alone, who died on the cross for you and rose again? *Yes.*

4. Do you also promise in the presence of the Lord and the church to support these teachings and regulations, help to counsel and work in the congregation, and not to forsake the faith, whether it leads to life or death? *Yes.*

(Then the applicants for baptism kneel [forward] for a prayer, with the congregation standing.) [Next, the bishop lays his hands on the head of each kneeling person in turn and baptizes each, saying:]

Upon your faith, which you have confessed, you are baptized in the name of the Father, the Son, and the Holy Spirit. Amen. [While speaking, the bishop cups his hands over the head, and the deacon pours water through them onto the head. After all applicants are baptized, the bishop greets each one.]

In the name of the Lord and the church, I extend to you the hand of fellowship. Rise up.

[The bishop gives a handshake to each and a holy kiss to each young man; the bishop's wife greets the young women likewise.]

(From *Handbuch für Prediger* [Handbook for Preachers], 2-88)

The Holy Kiss, Sacred Symbol of Love

What exactly is the purpose for the holy kiss, and what does the Bible teach about it?

In 1 Thessalonians 5:26, Paul says, "Greet all the brethren with an holy kiss."

The kiss was a common secular greeting of that day, but the Christians practiced a special version of it, the holy kiss. What made it holy? It was sanctified, first of all, by the devout lives of those who practiced it. Second, it was imparted with a prayerful blessing, "Peace be with you" or "God be with your spirit."

The holy kiss is rooted in history. The Anabaptists practiced it. Menno Simons mentioned it in his writings. Today almost all Amish churches retain traces of it, proving that it was once universally practiced by the plain people. Those traces vary from community to community. In most places, ministers still greet each other. Other communities have retained a bit more, and the ministers greet each other plus the older members. Other communities go still farther, with the ministers greeting each other and all other members.

In some churches, it is practiced as Paul commanded it: all members greet each other, regardless of age or calling, the sisters greeting the sisters, and the brothers greeting the brothers. We believe in practicing the holy kiss because it is a Bible-commanded symbol of our spiritual bond of love.

The holy kiss is a sacred command, one of the most meaningful symbols of love and good will that exist in the world today. God forbid that we should either continue to neglect it, or permit it to become an issue of contention and disunity among the very people it was meant to unite, the children of God.

("Views and Values," E. Stoll, 2-80)

Foot Washing: Our Dusty Feet

The practice of foot washing, as Jesus commanded in John 13, is one of the Bible's most neglected and forgotten doctrines. If so many churches don't practice it, why do we? This is much more than just an outdated practice carried over from Bible times. The doctrine carries a deep and important spiritual meaning for the Christian church throughout all the ages and in every culture. Its spiritual meaning is twofold:

1. The practice of [paired and reciprocal] foot washing among the entire brotherhood dramatically underlies Jesus' revolutionary concept of humility. He chose the most extreme example of servitude. He, their Lord and Master, stooped to wash the dusty, sweaty, smelly feet of common fishermen and tax collectors! No king before ever had such an idea of how a great ruler should reign over his subjects, by serving them! Our world today, as greedy, haughty, and self-serving as ever, still needs that truth demonstrated.

2. The second spiritual lesson taught by foot washing is that we still *do* get dusty feet. We may not always get them physically dusty, but it was the spiritual dust Jesus was most concerned about anyhow. Jesus spoke of two washings, that of the feet being one, and of the hands and head and the rest of the body being the other. There is the washing that occurs when we are first converted [a full cleansing]. The second washing, that of the feet, signifies removal of the dust we pick up from our daily walk of life. Our weak flesh, our dusty feet, need daily washings. We cannot expect to walk through this world and not get some of it on our feet.

To stoop at communion service and wash the physical feet of my brother [or sister with sister] is not nearly as hard as the spiritual washing it symbolizes. When I see my brother [or sister] in an error, it is my duty to go to him and with love and good will and above all humility, tell him about it, and admonish him. Ah, that is the true foot washing.

Our attitude toward our brother [or sister] must be that of a servant, feeling ourselves of less importance than the one whose feet we wash, the one whose error we help to overcome.

There is no room for the holier-than-thou feeling here. Washing is gentle, washing is cleansing. Some of us, when we see a brother in error, forget to wash, but go for the cleanup job with a wire brush. There are certainly plenty of dusty feet, but the servants willing to stoop and wash them are hard to find.

("Views and Values," E. Stoll, 6-79)

Leaders in the Church

A Survey of Amish Ordination Customs

Several years ago an Amishman who had just been ordained bishop was congratulated by his non-Amish neighbor. The Amishman was dumbfounded, not knowing what to answer when congratulated. No one else had ever congratulated him, but many brethren had wept with him. The Amishman, like any newly ordained Amish bishop, wept. The burden of his office felt too heavy.

Amish ordinations, whether for deacon, minister, or bishop, are solemn and serious affairs. Amishmen do not attend a seminary seeking ordination. They do not seek it in a political way. They never ask to be ordained. It is thrust upon them by lot. This practice of ordaining by lot is based on Acts 1:23-26, where lots were cast to see who would replace Judas as the twelfth apostle.

When he joins the church, every Amish boy knows there is a possibility that he may some day be ordained. In fact, in most Amish settlements, the bishop asks the boys who are joining church whether they are willing to accept the ministry if the congregation should some day ordain them. Their answer must be yes, or they cannot be baptized.

The full count ["full bench"] of ordained men in each Amish congregation is considered to be one bishop, two ministers, and one deacon. When the bishop feels the congregation is in a position to hold an ordination, he announces so two weeks before the *Ordnungs-Gma* (church counsel meeting [semiannual service in preparation for communion]). This two-week period is called *Besinn-Zeit* (time to think it over and pray about it). Most congregations require that the members be 100 percent agreed to hold the ordination. The ordination usually takes place two weeks later, on communion Sunday. [Each district holds services on alternate Sundays, as listed in Ben J. Raber's *Almanac*.]

[Following the communion service, in most cases,] the bishop in charge stands and says a few words about the seriousness of the occasion. He then reads 1 Timothy 3. (In some areas, Titus 1 is also read.) The bishop does not specifically mention that the person must be a married man, but such is taken for granted.

When the [scriptural] qualifications have been mentioned, the bishops and other ordained men leave the congregation and go into an adjoining room of the house. One ordained man (often the deacon) remains with the congregation to see that all the members come forward one by one to say who they feel should be in the lot. Another ordained man stands just inside the ministers' room, with the door slightly open so as to hear the name whispered to him by each member.

Each [baptized] member of the congregation goes to the door, men and boys first, then women and girls. Each time the minister at the door receives a name, he closes the door and repeats it to the bishop in charge, who then writes it down. Each time the same man's name is mentioned again, he places a mark beside it.

Each Amish congregation has its own rule on how many *Stimmen* (voices, votes) are needed to place a man in the lot. Some congregations require two, while others require three. This is based on Matthew 18:16, where Jesus said, "In the mouth of two or three witnesses, every word may be established." No members, even husbands and wives, are supposed to discuss for whom they are going to vote.

The average number in the lot in a large congregation is around eight; four is an average number in smaller congregations. The presiding bishop determines which men are in the lot, takes an equal number of [identical] songbooks, and places them before him. Inside one of the books, he places the lot, a slip of paper with German writing on it. (In Lancaster County it reads, "The lot is cast into the lap; but the whole disposing thereof is of the Lord." Proverbs 16:33.)

In Lancaster County, a large table is used, and the men sit around it with the [shuffled] songbooks in the center. When all are seated, they reach for the songbooks, one by one. In some areas, they take the books beginning with the oldest man first. In other places, it is done in the order their names were announced, in the order in which they received the required *Stimmen*. [Next, the bishop examines each book.] Once the bishop comes to the book containing the slip, he reads the words on the slip and says the man's name so all the congregation can hear.

Only ministers may advance to [be ordained as] bishops. Generally [if there is no bishop in a district,] there are three ministers, and usually all three are included in the lot [for bishop]. But in Lancaster County, there is a major difference from anywhere else except the daughter settlements [of people from Lancaster]. Verses 4 and 5 of 1 Timothy 3 are more strictly applied. To qualify for the lot [for bishop], each minister must have children who are church members, or at least one child, and all their children must be in good standing.

Deacons are ordained by lot in the same manner as ministers. Their duties, however, differ. A deacon is in charge of the *Armengeld* (money for the poor), enforces the *Ordnung* (rules) by talking with disobedient members, counsels couples wishing to marry, reads Scriptures at the church service, and gives *Zeugnis* (a testimony) to the sermons. In the majority of Amish congregations, he does not preach. In some areas (such as Lancaster, Lawrence, and Mifflin Counties in Pennsylvania, among others), the deacon's office is looked upon as so strictly separate that he may never leave it for [other leadership] ministry.

If the lot is cast, it is up to God to see where it falls.

(D. Luthy, 3-75)

Physician, Heal Thyself: Ministers as Examples

The Bible refers to those who are ordained to the ministry as messengers (Mal. 2:7; 2 Cor. 8:23). Not only the young people need to be led to a higher standard. We ministers do, too. Too often the root of church problems lies within the ministry. If the ministry is unconcerned or divided, problems in the church cannot be solved. Down through history, God has always held the leaders primarily responsible for the conditions of his people.

We are to be *watchmen* [Jer. 6:17; Ezek. 3:17]. It was the watchman's duty to detect danger when it was still far enough away that people had time to run inside and close the gates securely. Today we also need to be alert and to have foresight, to detect spiritual dangers and trends in time that the people may be spared.

We are to be *shepherds* [1 Pet. 5:1-4]. We are called to be *servants* [2 Cor. 4:5]. We are called to be *intercessors* [Isa. 59:16]. The list of descriptions the Bible gives to ministers is too long for us to give in detail. In addition to those already noted, we are called to be *teachers* (Eph. 4:11), *fishers of men* (Matt. 4:19), *defenders of the faith* (Phil. 1:7), *ambassadors for Christ* (2 Cor. 5:20), *preachers* (Rom. 10:14; 1 Tim. 2:7), *soldiers of Christ* (Phil. 2:25; 2 Tim. 2:3-4), *stewards* (Titus 1:7), and *sowers* (Ps. 126:6; Matt. 13:3-8).

Sometimes we are referred to as *Prediger* (preachers) instead of *Diener* (ministers [servants]). But we should not for a moment permit ourselves to think that preaching is the main part of our calling. There is something that is much more important: living the gospel as we are called to preach. If we do not live consistent Christian lives, what we do and what we are will speak so loudly that the people will not be able to hear what we are saying when we stand up to preach. Nothing has spoiled as many good sermons as a poor example. Ours is a calling fraught with danger and filled with responsibility. Thankfully, we know that God's strength is made perfect in weakness.

("Views and Values," E. Stoll, 12-85)

Qualifications of Those in the Lot for Ordination

The Bible has left us clear and precise directions on what qualifications to look for when ordaining men to the ministry in the church. When considering a person to be included in the lot, we should give attention to the following qualifications mentioned in the Bible:

1. *His reputation.* He should have a good reputation, even among outside people, based on 1 Timothy 3:7: "Moreover, he must have a good report of them which are without."

2. *His way of making a living.* Those who give themselves to the work of the church must be especially careful lest their souls be taken captive by the possessions of this world. If we are to proclaim the riches of another world, we must not be overly concerned about the possessions of this world.

3. *His personal habits.* One of the first to come to mind is the admonition "not given to wine" (1 Tim. 3:3). Whatever justification the impure water of biblical times might have given for the use of a little wine then, there is certainly no reason for the use of alcoholic beverages among any of us, much less among those who are ordained. I cannot help feeling that he should also be a man who is free from the

use of tobacco. A man in the ministry should not be a man with his temper out of control, or stubborn, or quarrelsome (1 Tim. 3:3; Titus 1:7).

4. *His marriage partner.* A happy husband-wife relationship is a priceless treasure and a valuable asset for any man who enters the ministry. Pity the poor soul who must labor without it.

5. *His children.* Just as a wife can spoil a good sermon by her inconsistent example, so can disobedient children (Titus 1:6).

6. *His past morals.* Although this may be a somewhat controversial point, it is my feeling that no one should be taken into the lot who has had a "one-flesh" relationship with any other than his wife, or with the one who became his wife. This conviction is based on the threefold mention in Scripture that an ordained man is to be "the husband of one wife" (1 Tim. 3:2, 12; Titus 1:6). Considering the moral laxity of our plain churches in many communities, it is only reasonable that we look to others to lead the church out of the quicksand we have sunk into.

7. *His talents.* The ability to teach is important for those within the church and also important when dealing with those outside, and those who would oppose sound doctrine.

8. *His hospitality.* Those ordained to the ministry should be willing hosts, able and ready to entertain visitors (Titus 1:8; 1 Tim. 3:2). Hospitality is one virtue our forebears were especially careful to leave for us as plain people. We travel from community to community with the confidence that wherever we go, we will readily find food to eat and a bed to sleep in.   ("Views and Values," E. Stoll, 3-85)

The Minister's Pay

Is it scriptural for a minister to accept or demand wages for his labor in the gospel? Why have the plain churches shunned a financially paid ministry?

First of all, sin comes under two different categories:

1. Things that are absolutely sinful.

2. Things that are not wrong in themselves, but their overall influence leads to evil rather than being spiritually edifying.

The practice of paying ministers is just one of the many evils that have crept into the churches because the thing itself is not wrong.

Paul says, "When I preach the gospel, I may make the gospel of Christ without charge, that I abuse not my power in the gospel" (1 Cor. 9:18).

While many of today's modern preachers are preaching for the money, we as plain people can give our ministers something that is far more valuable. We can give them love, respect, obedience, and submission [Heb. 13:7, 17]. If we donate these Christian virtues to them, we will have the highest-paid ministers in the world.

(Marshfield, Mo., 2-81)

Advice to Young Ministers

True humility is not thinking meanly of ourselves, but in not thinking of ourselves at all. No member in the church dare be so little that we disregard them, or anyone so important that we bend the rules to suit them.   ("Views and Values," E. Stoll, 1-86)

Experiences of a Bishop's Wife

Being a minister's wife for many years, I can well detect the expressions on my loving companion's brow and the sighs that go with it, whether it is only tiredness from work, or if it is a trouble at heart. Then while lying beside him in bed, I can hear his heavy breathing, trying to fall into a relaxing sleep. The next morning, with a heavy heart, I carry his damp pillow to the stove for drying.

—*A Bishop's Wife*   (6-73)

In a long article on suicide, its causes, and its prevention from an Amish perspective, was this letter from a woman whose husband, an ordained man, had taken his life.

The Greatest Gamble

We were just an average family, with an equal number of boys and girls. Dad was very serious minded, and his aim was to live the life of a Christian. But it seemed that the last year before he died, it was a burden for him to live. He was an ordained man, and it seemed there was more than the usual trouble in the church. He just couldn't get over it. Family cares, debts, and church troubles all loomed so big for him.

I, in my ignorance, did not realize how serious this was. He would tell me that he just couldn't take it any more. Over and over he would say, "Mom, you just have to help me."

Sad to say, I didn't know how to help. It was an unhappy situation, and this only added to his cares. We often had to speak twice to get his attention. Finally it came to the point where he couldn't sleep anymore. If only I had known more about sickness of the mind, maybe this story would not have to be written.

With God's help, my children and I are carrying on with the farming. There is no turning back. But friends, when your loved ones become depressed, can't sleep, become shy, feel inferior to others, and work becomes a burden, then they need help. You may think it would be too hard to put your loved one into a hospital, but *don't wait too long*. For me, it would seem a very simple matter to visit at the hospital instead of going to the cemetery.   (via D. Wagler, 11-71)

Only God Knows

Who, oh who would it be? The ministers had just come in, and now the old, white-haired bishop had arisen. He stood before the congregation. "Those chosen in the lot are . . ." His voice faltered and he paused. He needed a moment to steady his voice. His heart went out in sympathy to the brethren whose names were written on the paper in his hand. How solemn this ceremony was, this choosing of God for a man to preach the Word!

Most of the men sat with lowered heads. William Yoder shifted his feet. Before he was married, he had been reckless and defiant. He had done some deeds that he now longed to erase from his mind forever. It was true, he had settled down later and gotten married. He was a concerned husband and father. But it was not easy to live with a burdened conscience. After services, he would watch his chance and talk with one of the ministers or a bishop. It no longer mattered that he might have to make a public confession. He was more than willing.

He sighed. Life sure looked different at twenty-eight than it did at eighteen!

The bishop cleared his throat. His voice was steady once more. Slowly, clearly, he read the names. "Mark Miller, Joseph Mullet, Amos Mast, William Yoder, Henry Graber, Dan Yoder." After a long pause, Bishop Ray said, "You may come up here on the front bench."

Six black books, each bound with a rubber band, were lying on the table in the front of the room. In one book was a slip of paper containing an appropriate Bible verse. The man who drew that book would be the one chosen by God.

Through a blur of tears, Sylvia Mullet saw the men take their places. Surely it would not be Joseph! How well she remembered her father's life. He had been a minister and had had such a burden to bear. How often he had been blamed for things he had left undone, or had done wrong. More than one night, she had awakened and knew by the light of the lamp in the kitchen that he was sitting at the kitchen table, with his Bible before him.

The knowledge that she was a preacher's daughter was always with her. There were many things she could not do that other girls did. Dear, dear Joseph. Must it be him? And what about herself? How unworthy and unfit she felt to be a preacher's wife. She twisted and untwisted the handkerchief in her hands.

Henry Graber sat with his head bowed. For months he had had this feeling. Perhaps God was sending him a warning that he would die soon. At night he would wake up, and the feeling was there. He reviewed his life. Was there something in his life that God was not pleased with?

Then the bishop had announced that a minister would be ordained, providing the congregation felt agreed and prepared. Was this what God was calling him to do? Henry tried to shrug the feeling off, but the thought persisted. "Prepare yourself. Prepare yourself." Over and over these words rang in his mind. At night he had wrestled with this feeling. Human eyes did not see the battles, the silent but real conflicts that raged within his breast.

The bishop was talking. He had laid the little black hymn books on the table. Only God knew which book had the slip of paper. God would lead and guide. He made no mistakes. The Lord would give grace and courage to the man he chose. "Let us kneel and pray," the bishop said.

There was a shuffling of feet, and then all was quiet as the people knelt. The bishop's voice had been steady and quiet, but now as he prayed it trembled.

Sylvia Mullet felt numb. She heard the bishop's voice, but to her shame she realized later that she had not heard a word of the prayer itself. Then the bishop was standing. "You may come and draw your books," he instructed.

Stand up, go over to the table, and pick up one little book. It seemed like such an easy thing in itself, but Dan Yoder had never realized how hard it could be to do such a small thing. He was a fearless man, unafraid to stand up for his beliefs. But now in this solemn moment, his courage and strength seemed to have left him.

William Yoder's blue eyes were dark and troubled. "Unworthy, unfit, unprepared," he thought. He lowered his head, and tears dropped on the small black book in his hands.

Henry Graber's face was very pale. "He is working too hard," the people said. And yet there was no one more willing to help others when the need arose. He often left his own work to help his neighbors.

Joseph Mullet looked very young as he drew his book. His brown eyes were clear and trusting. Joseph's mother tried to swallow the lump in her throat. Joseph had always been an obedient son. Tenderhearted, quiet-spoken Joseph.

More than one person had the feeling that the chosen one would be the bishop's son, Amos. Now his usual friendly look was replaced by a burdened look. How well he knew the load his father had to carry!

Mark Miller, his curly, bushy hair looking disorderly, picked up the last book. Only God knew the thoughts that went through the minds of the six men on the front bench. Only God knew which man held the book with the slip.

Now the time had come. How can a person describe the tension, the strain, and the silence that was felt at this time? For weeks this moment had been looming before them. It had been wondered about, prayed about, struggled with. Within a few short minutes, all wondering, all doubts, all questions would disappear. God's choice was about to be revealed. Yes, there was a strain that could be felt. But there was also a feeling that God was with them.

The bishop walked over to Mark Miller. Carefully the rubber band was taken off his book. Quietly, carefully, the bishop paged through the book. The rustling of the pages could be heard in the back of the room. The book was returned to Mark. He was not the one.

Next was Joseph Mullet, the youngest in the lot. He felt weak. His hand trembled so that he felt unable to give his book to the bishop. Sylvia sat with her head bowed. When she forced herself to glance toward Joseph, the book had been returned to him. He had not been chosen.

Next was Amos Mast, the bishop's son. Bishop Ray's hands trembled as he opened the book and paged through it. The slip was not there, so the book was returned.

Only three remained. The bishop's face was pale. He suffered with the men before him. How he could feel for them!

Would it be William Yoder? He was next. The slip was not found in William's book.

Now there were only two men, Henry Graber and Dan Yoder. Which one would it be? The bishop reached for Henry's book. How quiet the room was! The pages of the book rustled. The bishop cleared his throat, followed by another silence. "The Lord has chosen Henry Graber."

The congregation saw only the man with the bowed head. They did not see the turmoil of feelings inside. They did not know how relentlessly the good and evil had striven within his breast. They did not know how hard it had been for Henry to give up his own will and accept whatever it was that God had called him to do.

To preach the gospel, to help keep the church pure and unspotted, to visit the fatherless and widows, to help the sick and needy, to rebuke and admonish the sinners, to live a life that would be a shining example of the Gospel. Yes, it might mean to be blamed and misunderstood, to be accused of showing partiality and picking on certain members. It would undoubtedly mean spending sleepless nights and leaving his dear wife and children with lonely evenings, when his duty called him away from home.

One of the ministers was speaking. How well he knew the truth of the words uttered to the solemn, listening congregation. "You can help to make this a tiresome, heavy burden that God had placed upon our brother today, or you can help make it a great joy in his life."

A burden or a joy? Which would it be?

God had done the choosing, but now the answer to this question did not lie in God's hands alone, but in the hearts and lives of his people. A burden or a joy. Which would it be? (10-78)

Letter to a New Minister

I would like to write this letter to you while the scene from yesterday is still fresh in my mind. I am sure all of us will cherish for many days that experience when you were ordained as a fellow minister in our church district.

How short the day seemed. I know that many people in the world pity us when they hear that our services last for three hours. I wonder what they would say if they knew a service such as yesterday lasts up to eight or nine hours. While the outside world continued on its way, we met to worship, partake of communion, and to ordain a minister.

Today is another day. Today we go about our work. We milk the cows. We harness the horses. We fill the silo, haul the manure, or plow the soil. For most of us, life slips back into a familiar routine and goes on much the same as it did before.

For you it is different. You awoke this morning to a new world. The sun arose for the first time upon you as a minister of the gospel. Your life will never again be the same.

Many thoughts have gone through our minds since yesterday. Yesterday we spoke a few words to you, and wept a few tears with you.

But our tongues were too tied, our vocabulary too incomplete to be able to express the yearning in our hearts. How inadequate words seem at such a time. Mostly we could just sit and share the time with you in silence.

Yet words have their place. In the days to come, those words will return to you. You will recall comfort and support whispered to you that the rest of us didn't hear. You will remember that God has a purpose in each move he makes, a master plan he is seeking to fulfill. We often can't understand. Sometimes it doesn't even make sense to us. But God doesn't ask us to understand. He only asks us to believe, to trust, to accept, and to submit. "God is his own interpreter" [from the song "God Moves in a Mysterious Way," by William Cowper]. In his own time, he will explain when he is ready and, perhaps more importantly, when we are ready. You did not seek that calling. But I trust you will not shrink from it either.

In our humanness, we would have liked to come to you and comfort you by telling you that the task was not as great as it looks to you. But to do so would have been wrong. God does not want us to make the task smaller in order to make it bearable. But the Lord does want us to let his grace become greater in order to make the task possible.

Overnight, in fact in one hour, your responsibility has been greatly increased. You have been taken from the sheep and placed among the shepherds. You have been lifted from the residents of the city and set up as a watchman upon the walls. You must move fast enough, but not too fast. You must be firm enough, but not too stern. You must be patient, but not too patient with the wrong things. You must decide when to act and when to wait, when to speak and when to be silent.

Do not forget that your wife shares your calling with you. She cannot escape a share of the responsibility. At this time, she too needs to be comforted, needs someone to speak words of courage and strength to her. At a time when you need her to help you, you find she needs your help instead. It is often those in life who need the most help themselves who can be the greatest help to others. God's "strength is made perfect in weakness" [2 Cor. 12:9].

Satan will tell you it is not fair that you should be the one. He will try to make you rebel when you need to take a Saturday afternoon off to study or instruct applicants for baptism while your neighbor gets his oats cut. It will not seem fair that your neighbor can go ahead and get his chores done while you stand and explain some church decision to a member who questions the decision. The same is true when your neighbor eats a good warm bowl of soup after a hard day of work while you skip supper because the deacon came to take you with him on the thankless task of visiting an erring member.

To make matters worse, your neighbor will get up the next morning, rested and refreshed. It will not make it any easier to realize that some of the problems that kept you awake are the result of mistakes you yourself made along the way. These may be things you said but shouldn't have said, and things you didn't say but should have said.

In spite of such things, God is not a hard master. Not only is God fair, but you will find that members in the church will do their part, too. It is true that some may sleep while you preach, but others stay awake and listen. Some may cause you extra cares, but others will do their utmost to lighten the burden, showing their appreciation. I will never forget the neighbor who came over one afternoon to help me with my work, for no other reason than the simple explanation, "You often have to work when we don't."

Yesterday one of the ministers said to you, "Welcome." I can think of no word more fitting with which to finish this letter. Welcome into a new family. The ties in a family are formed by the trials the family faces together, by work they share, by joys experienced and difficulties surmounted. The ministry is such a family.

We know that you will not always agree with us. You will even discover that we do not always agree with each other. We try to live above our personalities, our petty grievances, our human weaknesses, and to work united by a common goal greater than ourselves— the welfare of the church. Often we fall short, but always we go back and try harder.

No one knows the weaknesses of other members of the family better than do the members themselves. But if the family is as it should be, each member still loves the other. We challenge you to lose yourself in a labor of love. Only then can you be truly worthy of the calling through which you were called.

There is work to do, challenges to be faced, mountains to be scaled, enemies to be conquered. God has been good to us all. *Welcome.*

(11-81)

8

Discipline and Shunning

The Amish Perspective

Few areas of the Amish faith are more misunderstood than those of discipline in the church, excommunication, and shunning. Newspaper stories focus on the tragic tales of those under "the ban," from the point of view of those being shunned. Hollywood movies find shunning great dramatic material, exaggerating it to incorrectly show the Amish refusing to talk or even look at shunned persons.

While shunning does indeed result in sad separations of family members, there is a reason behind it. The Amish themselves admit it is not always "properly applied." From the beginnings of the Amish faith in 1693 and right up to the present, shunning has played an integral part in preserving the Amish way of life.

Here then is a look at shunning, how it is carried out and why, from the Amish point of view and in their own words.

Church Discipline

Discipline in the Church

The teaching of excommunication (*Bann*) and shunning (*Meidung*) was an important point to our Anabaptist forebears. They saw that the state churches of their time, whether Catholic or Protestant, did not have a scriptural concept of a disciplined brotherhood. The Anabaptists believed that the true church of God must be a disciplined church, kept pure from sin and worldliness. The church should be made up only of sincere believers who live holy lives.

The Anabaptists felt that the state churches failed at both ends—in how they received new members (by infant baptism), and in not expelling those who failed to live holy lives. I believe most of the disunity today that is said to be about *Bann* and *Meidung* is about something else.

The present-day Old Order Amish churches can be divided into roughly two camps on the *Meidung* question, those with a policy of "*streng* (strict) *Meidung*," and those without it. By *streng Meidung*, we mean a policy of excommunicating and shunning a member who has joined a more-liberal group. (The exact line may vary as to how much more liberal [the joined group may be], but is usually drawn at the ownership of automobiles.) The rationale for this is usually that the member is breaking the baptismal vow, loves the things of the world, and shows a spirit of discontentment.

The Amish-Mennonite division of 1693 comes to mind. When Jacob Ammann and Hans Reist parted company, one of the points of contention concerned how *Meidung* should be observed. The Amish faction felt that expelled members should be shunned to the extent of not even eating an everyday meal together. The Mennonite factions felt that Paul's words, "With such an one, no not to eat" (1 Cor. 5:11), meant not to partake of communion with such a person.

This difference can still be found between the main groups of Old Order Mennonites and the Old Order Amish of today. Interestingly enough, the gap has narrowed over the years.

If a member has moved from a church without a *streng* policy, he would also usually find himself excommunicated and shunned [by his church of origin], and basically for the same reasons. The difference comes when the member has proved himself [as being built up in the faith] at his new church and is living in peace there. Then, providing the new church is basically the same in important points of doctrine, and also with regards to the working of the Old Order church to the extent of formally "lifting" the *Bann*, the erring member then ceases to be shunned by the Old Orders.

It should be pointed out that in each camp described above [strict shunning contrasted with milder discipline], there exists considerable variation.

This brings us to the crux of the matter: is there one true church, or are there many? That was the real issue in Jacob Ammann's time. Could the "true-hearted" find salvation in the state churches? Time has a way of bringing changes. It is now three hundred years since Reist and Ammann had their differences about the "true-hearted." Among the Amish, there are few groups today, if any, who believe in only one true church in the way Jacob Ammann did.

The issue between the *streng Meidung* camp and the others is not a question of *Meidung* as much as it is of whether we recognize those other churches as true or not. Of course, God is the final judge. But it is my understanding of the Scriptures that a church should excommunicate only those they feel will miss salvation unless they repent. Too many churches are playing with the *Bann*, treating it as though it were a light and trivial matter.

It is surely high time that we stop comparing ourselves with those in the opposite camp, which Paul says is not wise (2 Cor. 10:12). Instead, we should compare ourselves with the Word of God, and the standard set therein for the church. The place to begin is to make sure that we ourselves are what we should be so that the churches may be purged and renewed.   ("Views and Values," E. Stoll, 1-90)

Three Great Walls

Many worldly people, and perhaps some church members too, have mistaken the purpose of the *Bann* and avoidance (1 Cor. 5). The church is not to use the *Bann* as a wall to keep members from escaping. As in any discipline, some members, when they see what happens to those who err, may well fear to follow the same path. However, the primary function of the *Bann* is to keep the church pure.

The *Bann* punishes the evildoer not in the spirit of revenge, but to bring him to repentance. Used in this way, the *Bann* expresses in the strongest means possible the church's love and concern for the erring member's soul.   ("Fireside Chats," J. Stoll, 10-69)

One Church, Many Members

In a recent article, a writer stated that "willfully disobeying these small rules shows only one thing—pride." We have a duty and responsibility to help build the church of which we are a member. It is our obligation to submit to the church standards willingly. If we fail to do this, the church must discipline us. This is where the sometimes sad and unpleasant duty of the deacon and minister comes in.

One sister made the remark, "Many times a good sermon is spoiled when the bishop gets up after the services and tells about some rule that has been violated." This dear sister didn't realize that some lay member failed to do his duty, thus laying an extra burden on the bishop's already-heavy load.

Let us work for love, peace, and harmony among young and old. Only then can we have a church without spot or wrinkle. If the children know and feel their parents are giving the church their full support, it is only natural for them to want to do likewise. On the contrary, when parents rebel against the church and say, "Oh, they're just picking on us again," it works the other way.   (K. S., 9-68)

Touch Not Mine Anointed

[Title from 1 Chron. 16:22.] Criticism can be brought upon the ministers even by those who mean no harm. Even if we do not criticize them directly, we can be the cause that they must bear unjust judgment by others.

For example, a young man and his wife went to a store to buy linoleum. They had an old home with rough floors. They didn't have the money to spend on new flooring, so they decided some cheap linoleum would be all right. They were faithful church members and wanted a design that would be suitable for a plain home.

When the clerk showed them some brightly colored pieces, the young man shook his head.

"You're not allowed to have them?" asked the store clerk.

"No, the preachers won't allow it," the man answered, unthinkingly.

It is true that they didn't allow it. But answers like this make the ministers look like dictators. This may cause the church to be blasphemed by outsiders. How much better it would have been had the couple said, "*We* don't want that kind of linoleum," and leave the ministers out of it. But the sad part is too many people want the things they're not supposed to have, and so could not say this truthfully.   (Anon., 9-70)

Church Divisions

Five Reasons for Church Splits

1. Lack of teaching: the woeful lack of teaching against the evils of division.

2. Lack of humility: there are too many ambitious leaders and church members.

3. Lack of communication: there will be times when misunderstandings occur and people's feelings are hurt. These are wounds that need the sunshine of communication to heal quickly. Sometimes problems cannot be resolved between two church members. Then additional advice and counsel should be sought from brothers and sisters in the church. If the problem is still not solved, the entire church should be asked to help seek a solution that will lead to restored peace and harmony [Matt. 18:15-20].

Sometimes, of course, there are problems which a local congregation is unable to settle peacefully. In such cases, we have the recourse of calling in ordained men from sister congregations for an impartial settlement.

4. Lack of discipline: discipline is important anywhere people are to live together in peace, and especially so in the church.

5. Lack of personal peace: we cannot expect that peace will reign in our churches if we permit carnal members to be baptized and take communion year after year in our plain churches.

("Views and Values," E. Stoll, 2-82)

Nine Principles for Mending Broken Relationships

Two basic things can happen that cause broken relationships in a Christian community: someone sins against you, or you sin against someone else. Any sin, however small, that causes disharmony must be dealt with. Here are nine principles based on Scripture that will help us mend broken relationships:

1. Confess to the Lord.
2. Make the first move.
3. Do it quickly.
4. Meet the person face to face.
5. Go in genuine love.
6. Go in the spirit of peace and reconciliation.
7. Confess, apologize, and ask for forgiveness.
8. Let this end the matter.
9. Forgive your brother again and again.

(Sugarcreek, Ohio, 1-79)

Divisions and Discouragement

In our community, one church division seems to follow another. We have so many denominations that it indeed is a rare case where the parents, grandparents, and children are all in the same denomination. All this is apt to bring discord into what should be a sacred tie, resulting in married couples who can't agree.

Once Satan has succeeded in bringing division of opinion on such an important matter, the rest is easy. Frustrations follow, and confusions and discouragement, and in extreme cases, suicide. I'm afraid the church problem has to take the blame for at least some of the far-too-many suicide cases in our area the last few years.

("Letter," Holmes County, Ohio, 1-72)

Submitting to Each Other

Many splits in the past have been the result of people putting a lot of emphasis on certain points or doctrines. Many of these doctrines have been good and necessary in themselves. The danger resulted from promoting them so aggressively that a church split resulted.

We tend to forget that the Bible also teaches that we are to submit to each other, to esteem others more highly than ourselves, to walk in love and consideration for our brothers and sisters, and to be meek, patient, humble, and teachable.

("Staff Notes," D. Luthy, 2-82)

Sometimes mistakes are made and the wrong person is shunned. The following story of such a rare case is from an article about an Amish settlement a century ago.

Amish Factions in Union County, Pennsylvania

The years 1873-1880 were trying ones for the Buffalo Valley congregation. Disunity originating among the ministers, but soon spreading among the lay members, prevented communion services from being held. Since the people held grudges against one another, events that would have caused only a minor disturbance in other congregations, widened the gap between the factions in Union County.

One such event was a romantic letter sent unsigned to an unmarried Amish maiden. The unsigned letter became the center of a spiritual investigation. Since Bishop Riehl's son had previously sent a few such letters and had been disciplined for it, he was the obvious suspect. But he declared he was innocent this time.

The people did not let the matter drop. They sent away samples of a dozen young men's writing to a handwriting expert. He reported that none of them matched the anonymous letter's writing.

The matter surely should have been dropped by this point, but some people persisted in blaming Elias Riehl's son. He continued to deny that he had done it, and his father stood firmly beside him.

Many years later, long after the congregation had dissolved, the mystery was solved. The young woman confessed that she had written the letter to herself to impress her friends with her popularity!

(D. Luthy, 2-83)

Shunning: Examples and Discussion

The air was tense inside the courtroom at Wooster, Ohio, that November morning. It was the opening day of one of the most unusual trials in history. Andrew J. Yoder, a 33-year-old father of seven, was suing an Amish bishop and ministers for causing him to be "shunned." The three days of the Wayne County trial received wide attention and thorough coverage in local and national newspapers.

The trial opened on November 4, 1947, but Andrew Yoder's complaints dated back to five years earlier. At that time he had been a member of the North Valley (Helmuth) District Old Order Amish congregation of southeastern Wayne County, Ohio. But he became dissatisfied and decided to change membership to a more-liberal church. In July of 1942, he started attending services at the nearby Bunker Hill (Beachy) Church. Some weeks later he purchased a car.

His action brought him into conflict with his home church. After two decades, the details of the confrontation that followed are not clear, nor are they important to this article. Undoubtedly, mistakes occurred on both sides. It is enough to know that Andrew paid no heed to the voice of the church when he was asked to make amends.

The church put him under the *Bann*. In the years that followed, he was shunned as a disobedient and fallen member.

As grounds for his suit against the church leaders, Andrew Yoder claimed that the shunning or *Meidung* held against him caused him great financial loss, since he could no longer buy or sell with many of his neighbors. He claimed that shunning has the same effect as a boycott, and was therefore illegal and an infringement upon his rights. He also held that the shunning damaged his reputation.

In view of these grievances he had borne for five and a half years, he asked damages of $10,000 from each of the four defendants: John Helmuth (bishop), John Nisley and Isaac Miller (ministers), and Emanuel Wengard (deacon). Apparently Andrew Yoder did not consider the total of $40,000 sufficient to cover any future loss; he also asked the court to rule that the "shunning" be discontinued.

Andrew Yoder testified in court that his reason for the purchase of the automobile was so that he could take his infant crippled daughter, Lizzie, each week to the doctor in Wooster, a distance of sixteen miles. By this claim, Andrew won considerable public sympathy in spite of the fact that, as one of the ministers stated in his testimony, this reason had not been made clear at the time the automobile was purchased.

It hardly made sense, anyhow, since the Amish church did not forbid the hiring of an automobile when necessary. As one of the ministers testified in court, "He (Andrew) knows that if he needed transportation to take him and his child to the doctor, we would have helped him just like we do in lots of cases. We always help each other because that is what the Bible tells us to do. He knows that is true. So why does he say he could not take care of his child without owning an automobile?"

The church leaders did not hire a lawyer to defend their case. They came to court as summoned and answered the questions put to them. They repeatedly stated that the shunning was not a boycott since its purpose was not to harm Andrew, but to help him.

They pointed out that Andrew had voluntarily become a member of their church, with the full and clear knowledge that if he persisted in disobeying its rules, he would in time be banned and shunned.

Upon his knees, he had vowed to be faithful to God and the church. He knew it was a serious and lifetime contract. They explained that by his failure to remain faithful to his solemn agreement, he had brought the ban and subsequent shunning upon himself.

Nevertheless, the jury of nine men and three women ruled in favor of Andrew Yoder. But they awarded him only one-eighth of the damages he had asked for—a mere $5,000. Since the defendants did not voluntarily make the payment, a public auction at Bishop John Helmuth's farm was ordered to obtain the money. He did not resist the action.

Although the case was unusual, it was not the first of its kind. At least twice before a banned member had sued his church leaders for damages. Both previous cases occurred in Ohio.

The first such case occurred in 1878. A man named Joseph Liechty sued John Holdeman (founder of the Holdeman Mennonite Church) because Holdeman had excommunicated him from the Williams County congregation on the grounds of drunkenness.

The second case took place in Holmes County in 1919. Eli Gingerich sued Swartzentruber because he was banned after leaving an Old Order church and joining a more-liberal one. Both won their cases in court.

We should not be surprised that secular judges and juries fail to understand or sympathize with the Amish historic and present position on expelling and shunning unfaithful members. To the world, the practice of shunning seems like a harsh and unloving custom. It appears to them as both unfair and unreasonable.

It should not alarm us that the world does not understand the value of scriptural discipline in the church. What should alarm us is when we ourselves begin to question and doubt the practice of shunning unfaithful brethren. Let courts and judges rule as they like. It does not matter how often they decree that shunning is illegal or unkind. What does matter is that we ourselves are thoroughly grounded in the scriptural reasons for this vitally important practice in the church of Jesus Christ.

The following discussion of shunning is arranged in question-and-answer form. For many of the answers, we have quoted from the writings of our ancestors on this subject, especially from Menno Simons. Menno was the most outstanding leader among the persecuted Anabaptists in the Netherlands during the sixteenth century. He wrote much and traveled extensively, teaching and preaching.

• What is meant by *shunning*? The German term for shunning is *Meidung*. It refers to the practice of refusing to have social or business dealings with a person who has been expelled from one's church. It is applied to the extent of not eating with the person under the *Bann*. Another term for shunning is *avoidance*.

• Upon what Scriptures is the practice of shunning or avoidance based? There are a number of Scriptures which support shunning, but it should suffice to list here the five major ones:

1. Matthew 18:15-18. In these verses, Jesus explains the pattern to be followed in disciplining an erring brother. If the brother remains unrepentant, the matter must be made known to the church. "But if he neglect to hear the church, let him be unto you as an heathen man and a publican." Now the Jews to whom Jesus was speaking were totally separated from the "heathen and publicans." They had absolutely no dealings with them, did not eat with them, and in fact were reluctant to step inside their houses.

2. The second passage is the entire fifth chapter of 1 Corinthians. The report had reached Paul that the Corinthians left undisciplined a man who "had his father's wife." In this chapter, the apostle Paul earnestly commands them to "put away from among yourselves that wicked person." Once the church has "purged out" such a person, Paul explains further what their relationship should be toward him. "But now I have written unto you not to keep company, if any man that is called a brother be a fornicator, or covetous, or an idolater, or a railer, or a drunkard, or an extortioner; with such an one, no not eat."

3. Second Thessalonians 3:6. "Withdraw yourselves from every brother who walks disorderly, and not after the tradition which he received of us."

4. Titus 3:10. "A man that is an heretic, after the first and second admonition, reject."

5. Romans 16:17. "Now I beseech you, brethren, mark them

which cause divisions and offenses contrary to the doctrine which you have learned, and avoid them."

• Did our forebears believe in shunning? This question can best be answered by quoting from the Dordrecht Confession of Faith. This confession was drawn up in Dordrecht, Holland, in 1632, and was signed by 51 Mennonite ministers. It was adopted by [Swiss Anabaptist ministers in the Alsace in 1660, and kept by] the Amish [from their division of 1693]. Article 17 says:

"As regards the withdrawing from, or the shunning of, those who are expelled, we believe and confess that if any one, whether it be through a wicked life or perverse doctrine, is so far fallen as to be separated from God, and consequently rebuked by and expelled from the church, he must also, according to the doctrine of Christ and his apostles, be shunned and avoided by all the members of the church (particularly by those to whom his misdeeds are known), whether it be in eating or drinking or other such like social matters. In short, that we are to have nothing to do with him, so that we may not become defiled by conversation with him and partakers of his sins, but that he may be made ashamed, be affected in his mind, convinced in his conscience, and thereby induced to mend his ways."

• What is the purpose of shunning? Dirk Philips, a bishop and co-worker with Menno Simons, taught that the purpose of shunning is threefold:

"First, that the church may not become a partaker of the strange sins, and that the little leaven, leaven not the whole lump (2 John 1:11; Gal. 5:9; 1 Cor. 5:6). Second, that the person who has sinned may be ashamed and his flesh be mortified thereby, but his spirit saved in the day of the Lord Jesus (1 Cor. 5:5; 2 Thess. 3:14-15). Third, that the church of God be not evil spoken of on account of wicked members in it, and be not censurable on their account before the Lord (Ezek. 36:17-24; Josh. 7:20)."

Concerning the first of these three reasons, Menno Simons writes in greater detail: "The lepers were not allowed among the healthy in Israel. They had to stay in segregated places until cured. O brethren in the Lord, the leprosy of the soul is a leprosy above all leprosy, whether it be in doctrine or in life. It eats like a canker."

• Has not the question of shunning caused a lot of trouble in the churches? Shunning is a practice commanded and sanctioned by God for the protection of the church. The obeying of God's commandments brings a blessing to all involved, not trouble. But what has caused trouble in the church has been people who were no longer satisfied to accept what God has ordained.

The question of shunning has caused trouble in the church in the same way as have other Bible doctrines the worldly mind finds hard to accept: nonresistance, nonconformity, modesty in dress, prayer veiling, subjection of women, and foot washing. All of these and many others have been haggled over during splits and divisions because some members wanted a closer walk with the world. Shall we put the blame on the doctrine or on the worldly thinking that can no longer submit to it?

• Is it not true that shunning is done at times in a spirit of revenge and out of spite toward the person shunned? This is all too true in some cases and is to be deeply regretted. When the need arises to discipline an erring member in the church, the ministers and the members should pray earnestly that they might act out of love and concern, and never out of ill will or spite.

• Are not wayward members driven farther away from the church by shunning? If they remain unrepentant, it is well that they are driven far enough away so that their influence does not harm other members.

• Would many not repent sooner if they were not shunned? Evidently not, or God made a mistake when he commanded shunning as a means of bringing about repentance (2 Thess. 3:14). Sadly, today the reason shunning in certain cases is not more effective is the hypocritical way it is carried out. When the entire congregation stands united and consistently admonishes and rebukes the erring member with deep sorrow and love for his soul, it becomes a powerful force in moving him to repentance.

However, much of this power for good is lost when some of the members, although not actually eating with the banned member, seek every opportunity to be in his company and laugh and visit together as though nothing were wrong. It is a reproach to the church and a

mockery before God when members obey only the letter of a commandment, but disregard the spirit.

• Should shunning also be practiced between husbands and wives, and between parents and their children? Menno Simons answers:

First, the rule of the ban is a general rule and excepts none, neither husband nor wife, neither parent nor child. Second, we say that separation must be made by the church, and therefore the husband must consent with the church in the separation of his wife, and the wife to the separation of the husband. Third, we say that the ban was instituted to make ashamed unto betterment of life. . . . Spiritual love must be preferred to anything else. Fourth, we said the ban was given that we should not be leavened by the leaven of false doctrine or of impure life by the apostate. It is plain that none can corrupt and leaven us more than our own spouses, parents, etc.

Although Menno here advocates shunning between husband and wife, he also recognized that this matter was laden with great danger and needed to be handled with consideration.

• Are we allowed to show the banned persons needful services, love, and mercy? We are not only allowed, but commanded so to do. It is our duty to help anyone destitute and in need, even if they are our bitterest enemy. Menno Simons says, "The Scriptures do not forbid these, but they forbid common daily intimacy, conversation, society, and business. The ban is a work of divine love and not of . . . cruelty."

• When the Bible says, "Have no company with them," does that forbid a friendly greeting when we meet? Once again, we cannot improve upon the answer that Menno Simons penned over four hundred years ago. "Good manners, politeness, respectfulness, and friendliness to all people becomes all Christians. . . . How can such a one be convicted, led to repentance, and be moved to do better by such austerity? The ban is not given to destroy, but to build up."

• Should members ever be shunned before they are expelled from the church? Menno's answer is no. "It is not the custom or usage in Scripture to shun anyone as long as he is carried and tolerated in the church. Therefore, we should not shun anyone before excommunication, for if we do, we practice a ban neither known nor mentioned in the Scriptures."

• How serious should the ban be considered? Very serious indeed. Menno Simons said the ban is a death certificate of our souls. He wrote the following words only three years before his death: "I would rather allow myself to be cut into pieces until the day of judgment, if that were possible, than to allow myself to be excommunicated according to the Scriptures, by the servants of the Lord, from his church. O brethren, take this seriously."

We have already quoted so much from Menno Simons that we may as well let him add the summary to the article. After reviewing at length all the Scripture passages that teach shunning, Menno says, "I verily do not see how a God-fearing heart can oppose in regard to this matter. There are such good fruits and benefits contained in this shunning. But it seems that this vine must always have its harmful worm."

[Quotations from Dietrich Philip's *Handbook* (Pathway Publishers, 1966) and *The Complete Writings of Menno Simons* (Herald Press, 1956).]   (E. Stoll, 4-70)

Who Was Right?

In your article on shunning, I think you should have finished by telling what happened to the man who brought suit against the Amish church. He took his own life. I think that proves who was right.

("Letter," R. B., Mich.)

[Response:] We cannot agree with you that it proves who was right, for only the Bible does that. However, this tragic incident should give occasion for some serious thinking.

—*The Editors*   ("Answer," 6-70)

A preacher gives the following admonition to a man thinking of joining a "higher," more-liberal church:

Only One Step

Sometimes it does seem that we need a lot of rules. Have you ever given a thought as to why we need them? It's not because we hope to get to heaven by doing good and following the rules. The foundation of our faith is the saving blood of Jesus Christ. But we need guidelines, especially for the young people. Even after we are older, we still do not understand everything.

We need the counsel and guidance of the church and brotherhood to help us in our goal to deny the lusts of our flesh, and follow Jesus alone through a life of humble obedience and submission. If a man finds it hard to submit to the rules of the church, which after all are based on God's commands as expressed in the Bible, there may be something wrong with that man's faith. True faith in Christ brings humility and submission.

We don't claim that we are the only people who can be saved. But we do believe God asks each of his children to be faithful to the enlightenment that has been given to each. If you take a step in the direction of more liberality, you have taken a step toward the world, not away from it. Only one step, but so often that first step leads to another one.

The Bible says, "By their fruits ye shall know them." Do they follow direct biblical commands? Do the women wear coverings? What about Jesus' example of foot washing? Are humility and separation from the world represented in the way they clothe themselves?

I'd also suggest that we better not be too quick to label our whole church as thinking only about church *Ordnung* (rules), and not the gospel truth. Perhaps there are some among us who do, but basically our way of life is the fruit of our belief, our faith. Please, think about the future of your boys, too. What you do now may shape their future, for better or for worse.   (5-85)

Written to a person excommunicated and under the ban:

The Story of Demas

You have been admonished time and time again. But you have still chosen to forsake us and leave us for a closer walk with the world. The only course left for us was to excommunicate you from the church and now practice what scripturally follows that excommunication: the ban and avoidance, which goes with it.

The human nature in us does not want us to do so, but we have so much Scripture to support that doctrine that we cannot do anything else. Your way of life and your beliefs are no longer a help to us, but could even be deceiving to us and to others. We will therefore have to limit our dealings with you.

We know that some of you who have left us are saying that avoidance and separation are surely not the way of love. Our answer is that if we have a neighbor who is not even a churchgoer and who we know lives in gross sin, we will not hold the ban against him. We act this way because we are not to judge those who are without, but we are to judge those who are within (1 Cor. 5:12).

God knows that nobody can be more of a deceiver than someone "called a brother" who has fallen away and starts to live a life of sin (1 Cor. 5:11). That is why such a one is to be separated from the church, so that he does not have as much influence to mislead others. If you are one who has caused "divisions and offenses contrary to the doctrine which ye have learned," we must mark and avoid you (Rom. 16:17).

We did not first reject you. You have rejected us and the way of living that we value and hold dear. There is not to be a trace of hate in the practice of the ban. (11-83)

Comments by a woman whose husband left the Amish faith:

Our Life Is Different

We never discussed his leaving the church; he just went. What a shock it was! I am so ashamed to say that I did as Satan wanted me to do: I quit praying. There were no arguments between my husband and myself, but I was drifting right along with him, although I still went to our church. Then God held me back from taking that step [of leaving the Amish].

Our children have never known what a true Amish home life is like. They've never had their daddy in church. How much easier those first years could have been had he only had more love for us than for his worldly things. I have many faults and could so use the help of a Christian husband, but it's not to be. Some things are easier to live with as time goes on, but this isn't one of them. It seems so hopeless. Yet where there is life, there is hope. My husband says he wishes he could come back, as I wish he would, but adds, "I can't."

Roll a coal away from the fire, and it soon turns black and cold. The same happens to a person who leaves Christ's family. He turns cold. Life is too short to spend it in this way. We need to be together in love and harmony. How can God want us in his Home on High, if we can't get along down here?

Living like this often makes me feel unwanted, and I feel I'm not really a part of the church. We have never been able to hold church, though the children have often asked when we, too, can have church in our home.

If it would accomplish anything, I could sit and cry about it all, but life must go on. Crying helps, but brooding doesn't. Depression is something I have to work very hard against.

It also makes our children feel different. They often get pushed back. Not all people make us feel this way. We have many friends, probably more than we realize. But often on the holidays during the week, others will be invited somewhere for dinner and our children ask, "Why aren't we?"

In closing this article, my wish is that even though you don't know us, please pray for us. Without the prayers of others, we couldn't go on.   ("Letter," 7-87)

Response to an article about the difficulties of a woman named Esther, whose husband decided to leave the Amish faith:

Been There

How sad that no one visited them for six months when she need-ed the support of members most. How can anyone be a good influ-ence on him, the children, or her, if no one is there? Obviously Esther needed that influence herself, too, for her husband was enticing her to go elsewhere. What was she to think of her fellow church members for deserting her when trouble came?

At one time, we had the same situation in our home. It certainly was, oh, so lonely, and making doubts appear. In spite of our differ-ent feelings in church matters, my husband treated me kindly. With that and God's ever-present help, I was able to keep going.

In time, members of the church realized their mistake in not visit-ing us more and did differently. It has made an unbelievable differ-ence. The future is still uncertain, but now there is the good influence in our home of visiting church members. Such visits should be short at first, and they may be somewhat strained. But if they are done in love and kindness, most will feel the concern and respond to it.

Don't feel you can help anyone if you try to push or force erring members to return. Faultfinding will only widen the gap. They must return of their own convictions for it to be of any value to the church or to themselves.   ("Letter," 11-79)

Preparing for the Future

There is always a danger when churches have peace and prosperity. Children are born and raised in the church, but depth of belief and conviction may be lacking. Under such conditions, it is too easy to be a Christian, at least outwardly. Perhaps we should say it is too easy to be a church member.

Some fear that we may have such conditions today among our plain churches. We are increasing and growing in numbers as we have perhaps never grown before. But have we become more of a culture than a Bible-believing church?

Many of our communities are drifting in dress, as well as in other ways. When prayer veilings become smaller and smaller, what does that mean? Does it mean that children are growing up and being asked to dress in the *Ordnung*, but their hearts lack the real conviction that is necessary? They have agreed under social pressure and convenience to settle down, but have not been "born of the spirit."

When there are such things as drinking, foul language, shady jokes, tobacco, and low moral courtship among our young people, and when we have come to accept it as the norm—does that mean the problem extends back beyond the present generation?

("Views and Values," E. Stoll, 4-83)

The following is about a couple, Mary and Joe, who changed church districts to have some conveniences not allowed in the first district. Mary's mother sees more to it than that.

The Spirit That's Never Satisfied

"It'd be so much easier to get our work done if we'd have a Weed Eater and a power lawn mower. We can see no wrong in it," Mary said.

Mother sighed as she sank into a chair by the table. "No," she finally answered, "maybe having it isn't as wrong as wanting it."

"What do you mean by that?" Mary frowned.

"By having it, if allowed, a person needs some self-control. But by wanting it, it may show discontent that causes murmuring and takes away peace of mind and happiness. We need not live in a park to enjoy life. We can spend many hours making our home a showplace to satisfy our pride, and so have less hours to spend with the children and to teach them God's Word."

For a few years, Mary and Joe seemed to fit in quite well in the second district. Then one day Joe came home from a sale with a garden tractor.

"You don't intend on keeping it?" Mother asked softly.

"Oh, no," answered Joe quickly. "I can probably make a few dollars by selling it."

It wasn't long until Mother saw the tractor being used in the patch. His large tractor was also driven more on the road, instead of using horses.

"I can't see any difference whether we use a motor on the lawn, or in the field, or on the road. It looks the same to me," he tried to explain to the ministers.

Mother was aging fast. "Mary," she pleaded. "A person needs to get rid of the discontentment and disobedience in the heart. Only then can you be satisfied and happy."

"If they'd leave us alone, we would be satisfied and happy," Mary retorted.

"They're trying to warn you through love," Mother admonished her.

"Love!" scoffed Mary. "I can't see any love when people are against us."

"They're not against you. They are against the spirit of discontent and love for the world that they notice in your actions."

Mother's words did not seem to mean much to Joe and Mary any more. They found the church's restrictions on the use of material things more and more in their way. They changed churches this time, not just districts, and for a few years things seemed to go better. But then, once again, they were straining the line there, still longing and wishing for things that were just beyond the fence.

By this time, Mother was no longer living. Mary sometimes thought of what she would say: "Happiness does not lie in possessing more and more of the things of this world. Satan will always dangle one more attraction in front of you, just beyond your reach, to keep you unhappy and discontent. The only cure for that spirit is to stop feeding it."

Joe was ready to change churches once again. Mary pushed the doubts from her mind. Besides, maybe this time Joe would be satisfied and if not, well, they could always change churches again.

(8/9-85)

We Set the Example

We had scraped together enough to buy a farm of our very own. It was a large farm, and we were very busy. One day I came to the realization that things were not progressing as they should to make a go of it. What was to be done? I spent many sleepless hours pondering the problem. We simply had too much to do. If only we could have some of the laborsaving devices and equipment, we could get back on our feet. The farm was too large to be run the way the regulations of the church required.

A plan formed in my mind. I talked it over with my wife. At first she was aghast that I would consider joining a more-liberal church, but gradually I got her to see things my way. While I was trying to convince her, I was trying to justify myself.

The people dressed plainly in that church. They seemed very concerned to live a Christian life, and very sincere. They welcomed us warmly to their church services. The day came that we changed over.

Everything went as planned until our children joined church and wanted to be like the other young people. We found that the young people didn't dress as plainly as we'd thought, or else they'd changed. If our children wanted to have friends and mingle with the young folks, they had to dress like them. So we compromised a little.

Time went on. One by one the children married and left home. Sometimes when I saw how different their life was from what my youth had been, my conscience pricked me and I spent a restless night. But I pushed these thoughts aside.

Then one day the announcement came that made me see everything in its true light. It was a complete shock to me. Our second eldest son and his wife were leaving "our church" to join a still more liberal church, a church that allowed short skirts, television, small head coverings, and lately even divorces. My wife and I tried to talk them out of it. We pled as earnestly as we could, but they had made up their minds.

"Can't you see the pitfalls in such a liberal church?" my wife asked with tears in her eyes.

"Oh, we're not going to allow a TV set in our home," our son replied. "We and the children are going to dress the same as we always did. It's just that your church won't allow the long-distance trucking that is becoming a necessary part of my job. We feel we'll be able to serve the Lord more fully this way."

With that, they left.   (Anon., 3-83)

9

The Clothing
of the Faithful

When you're Amish, the whole world knows it. That is because of the unique plain dress. In some ways, this effort to show separation from the modern world and a lack of interest in worldly fashions has put the Amish into a fishbowl. Their nonconformity in dress attracts the interest and curiosity of those around them, especially in areas frequented by the touring public. Stories abound as to why the Amish dress as they do, and many of these are pure conjecture.

Ironically, the world sometimes finds the simplicity of Amish dress to be fashionable. In the early 1990s, *Vogue* magazine featured "Amish fashions" with slender, blond models photographed in Lancaster County. Several Amish saw the photo spread and were either shocked or amused by what they saw, not to mention the price tags!

Most Amish do not know much of the history behind why they wear what they wear. For them, their plain clothing is simply their way of doing things. Here are excerpts that provide some background and insight into the origins and importance of Amish clothing. They also relate fascinating experiences its wearers have had with their dress in the "outside world." These, then, are the words of the people who wear the clothes.

The Bible Talks About Dress

The Bible talks about dress from the fall of [humanity] to the end of time [Gen. 3; Rev. 19:8]. Sinful man continually designs fashions that are not pleasing to God. God designs clothes to cover the body, not display it. Men and women are to have different types of clothing. God's people in Old Testament times were to wear a peculiar and distinctive and uniform garb.

Nothing is to be worn for show or pride or vain display. The Christian woman is not to have her hair cut, or put up in worldly hairdos. The Christian man's hair is not to be long like a woman's. Combing the hair according to worldly styles comes under condemnation. Harlots' clothes are red and purple. Jewelry is forbidden.

The effectiveness of Christians' testimony depends upon their appearance. People with renewed minds do not walk as they formerly did. (6-74)

Living Our Faith

We believe our children should not wear fashionable clothes or cut their hair according to style, but do we explain to them why? How many of us realize that the rules and regulations of the plain churches are designed to protect us from the evils of the world?

To dress in simplicity will not necessarily put humility into the heart. But if our young people dress in plain and simple clothes, will they look right to walk into a theater, bowling alley, or like place? Would a man with a beard and black hat look right sitting in a tavern, taking strong drink?

We may have convictions against certain evils. But are we willing to teach our own children according to these convictions, if that would cause them to stand out from the crowd?

(Henry Hochstedler, Ill., 11-68)

The Accepted Pattern

I hope I wear my broad-brimmed hat as a protection against the weather and also because it has been the accepted pattern down through the ages among our people. But if I do these things, or drive my horse and buggy to show off, then there is pride in my heart, and I cannot expect a blessing from it. However, if I do it because I feel it is right and fitting for a nonconformed people, then I believe it can be a part of living my faith and living *by* faith.

("Now That I Think of It," D. Wagler, 11-90)

Reasons for Wearing Plain Clothing

There are several reasons for wearing the kind of clothes we do. The first reason, of course, is for modesty's sake, because we want to wear the kind of clothes the Bible says we should wear rather than what the styles and fashions of the world tell us.

Another reason is that we would rather be identified with the children of God than the children of this world. It seems right and proper to us that soldiers wear a uniform to show that they are a part of the army. Bus drivers wear a certain uniform, as well as many others, such as nurses, and so on. Why then should it be unusual for religious purposes?

Outward adornment is forbidden. Since jewelry serves no useful purpose, we believe it is forbidden. But the wearing of clothes does serve a useful and needful purpose; therefore, it is not forbidden. But adorning ourselves by the clothes we wear is what is forbidden.

Since women are not to cut their hair, it becomes necessary to do something with it, such as braiding or using some other method to keep it under control. Therefore, this serves a useful purpose. But we are not to adorn ourselves through plaiting the hair any more than we are to adorn ourselves by the clothes we wear. We believe it is the adornment that is forbidden, not the plaiting of hair. Even gold may be worn if it is for some useful purpose, such as dentistry work.

("Across the Editor's Desk," 12-74)

Judged by Our Clothing

We have a dress regulation or *Ordnung* in our plain churches. It is a call for a decent and discreet way of dress. It is scriptural to have such regulations on the way of dress. The epistles of Paul contain many of the regulations that needed to be mentioned in his time. It is also necessary to use church discipline for any member who weakens or attempts to wreck such guidelines by not being willing to support them.

One of the trends in today's styles is for a woman to wear the mode of dress that a man has. Deuteronomy 22:5 severely condemns this practice.

We know that *Demut* [humility], or plainness, is a command of the Lord. We are apt to think that the way people of the world around us dress is what is weakening the church *Ordnung*, but it isn't that. Really, the most dangerous decay comes from within the church itself, from members who will not support a Christian standard of dress. ("The Scriptures Have the Answers," 2-81)

Shoes

Some parents took their small children into a shoe store to buy some shoes. The clerk came with wedges, square toes, pointed shoes, and so on. Finally the mother asked, "Don't you have any shoes like they have on? Surely you know we prefer plain ones!"

"Yes, ma'am," the clerk replied rather sharply, "we do know some of you prefer the plain. But let me tell you, most of the Amish want something a little different, a little prettier. You know we have to satisfy our customers.

"The company sends us what we sell the most of and that, my dear lady, is why the plain ones are harder to get. We hardly sell enough that they are worth bothering with. The same thing goes for the dry goods we sell in the store, too. It's too plain! Most of your people want something a little prettier, and the plain materials are just gathering dust."

—*An Onlooker*   (Ind., 5-71)

Buttons: Why So Different?

Too often when we delve into the happenings of centuries past, we are not able to grasp the true meaning or significance of some of the events. What seems like a trifling incident to us may have been a serious problem at that time. Historians tell us that one of the clothes regulations among the Amish of long ago concerned the wearing of buttons. We do not know just when this occurred, but in time the Amish in some areas of Europe were given the nickname *Häftler* (hook-and-eyers), while the Mennonites were identified as *Knöpfler* (buttoners).

In our day, we Amish still use hooks and eyes on some of our clothing, but on other garments such as trousers, we use buttons. I have never seen a pair of trousers with hooks and eyes.

I used to be altogether unable to understand how such a small matter as hooks and eyes could play a part in a church disagreement. But after doing some research, I have come to the conclusion that the hook and eye issue may have had a greater significance than one would at first suppose. To understand the true issues beneath the surface, we need to know about the history of buttons. In *Encyclopedia International* we find the following information:

> The button as we know it today first became a permanent and important part of the costume in the Middle Ages. The ancient Greeks and Romans preferred removable pins for their flowing robes. Buttons gained acceptance only after the figure-hugging dresses became fashionable in the thirteenth century. In the seventeenth and eighteenth centuries, men showed their wealth by the number and size of their diamond buttons. Spectacular buttons became the mania with the Paris men of fashion. The finest craftsmen were engaged to carve ivory, to inlay tortoise shell, and to engrave mother-of-pearl for luxury buttons. Men wore buttons in sets of a dozen or more, and they were conversation pieces.

Apparently this was also the time when fancy and showy buttons became available to the common people. Not only did increased production make them available, but increased affluence made them affordable to many. Since Paris was going wild over buttons, they must have been at the top of fashion in Jacob Ammann's time.

The *World Book Encyclopedia* also gives buttons a military significance:

Buttons on men's clothes are sewn on the right side. On women's clothing, they are on the left side. At one time both men's and women's clothing had their buttons on the left side. Men's buttons were changed to the right side during the Middle Ages so a man could unbutton his coat quickly with his left hand and draw his sword with his right.

Many church leaders in Jacob Ammann's time, no doubt, could not understand why any Christian would want to adorn himself with costly, flashy, and showy buttons. Especially when something as convenient and practical as hooks and eyes was readily available.

There were likely differing opinions about what was suitable and proper for a Christian to wear. But the real issue went beyond clothes and reached into the underlying attitudes and spirit. The deeper issue was the whole question of church discipline. Does the church have the right and the responsibility to decide what is appropriate, and then to enforce that decision? The one side believed it did, the other did not [so believe]. The one group faithfully upheld the principles of simplicity, humility, separation from the world, and nonwearing of ornaments. In the other group, there was drift and accommodation to the fashions of the world.

Down through the centuries, clothing has been selected and worn for service. Most people in the old days could not afford many clothes, so they got what would last the longest. With the coming of new techniques in dyeing and weaving, clothes became cheaper and fancier. This made many styles and fashions of the world available to the plain people. Since that time, the world has followed Paris and New York into all kinds of dress and undress.

It seems that whatever is in style, that is what we have problems with in the church, no matter how unreasonable the style may be. Where there are large communities of our people today, there will always be some who are tempted to imitate the things of this world.

("Now That I Think of It," D. Wagler)

Head Coverings and Bonnets

The Anabaptists wrote little, if anything, about the women's head covering. The 18 Articles of Faith [Dordrecht, 1632] do not even mention it. The reason for this is not that they did not believe in it, but because they lived in a day and age when the head covering was not questioned. Until even a hundred years ago, no decent woman, let alone a godly one, would have appeared in public without a head covering.

Our historical library contains a clipping from a 1940 *National Geographic Magazine* showing an old woman in her home in rural France. No doubt she is Catholic, but her head covering looks so similar to an Amish cap that you would think she was Amish.

("From the Editors," 11-88)

Women's Veiling

The past seventy-five years have brought many changes in the practice of Christian women wearing a prayer veiling. One needn't look long through the pictures of old books to see numerous women wearing a white covering on their heads.

In chapter 11 of his first letter to the Corinthians, Paul treats the subject thoroughly: "Every woman who prays or prophesies with her head uncovered dishonors her head, for that is even all the same as if she were shaved" (11:5).

Therefore, a woman's head must be covered in public worship and at home when she prays or discusses Scripture. It is reasonable for a woman to wear her covering all the time, since she never knows when she will want to pray privately. Trying to find her veiling would often be awkward, inconvenient, or even impossible, depending upon circumstances.

Paul further writes, "For this cause ought the woman to have power on her head because of the angels" (11:10). This seems hard to understand. The American Bible Society's *Good News Bible* [interprets]: "On account of the angels, then, a woman should have a cov-

ering over her head to show that she is under her husband's authority" [supplying "husband's," which is not in the Greek text of 11:10.
Angels administer the divine order of creation, with women distinct
from men; see also Gen. 1:26-27; Acts 7:53; Gal. 3:19; Heb. 1:14].

Thus we can see that the veiling is more than a prayer covering. It
is also a symbol of subordination. By wearing it, a woman shows her
awareness and acceptance of her proper role in life—a helpmate to
man [Gen. 2:18].

The early Christian women left their hair hang loosely past their
shoulders, so they wore a long veil to cover their hair. One can't help
but think what these humble Christian women would think if they
saw some of the "coverings" of today. If they saw a girl with long
hair to her shoulders and a saucer-shaped piece of thin cloth perched
on the crown of her head, they would probably correctly ask, "What
is it covering?"

One can easily see the difference between an early Christian woman's lengthy veiling and a Catholic woman's stylish hat (or Mennonite girl's saucer-like "covering"). For a covering to qualify as a scriptural veiling, it would seem that certain requirements would have to
be met:

1. Does it cover as much of the hair as possible?

2. Is it made of plain material that is both inexpensive and practical?

3. Is the texture of the material thick enough that one cannot clearly see through it?

4. Is the design in keeping with the rulings of the congregation?

5. Does its design and appearance add to a woman's modesty and
shamefacedness, as mentioned in 1 Timothy 2:9?   (D. Luthy, 9-69)

Prayer Caps and Fads

Does it make any difference whether or not caps [head-coverings]
are tied? Since it's such a little thing, should we just stop worrying
about it and hope it doesn't lead to anything worse?

An old proverb I have often heard, "Cap strings flying loose on the
down road to hell," may sound rather strong. But the next step is to
eliminate strings altogether, and then the road is cleared for the

shrinking-cap trend. Such fads always start on a small scale and eventually wreak havoc if not checked.

[Many Mennonite women now wear no cap at all.]

(Liverpool, Pa., 6-75)

An eighteen-year-old girl with no mother asked if she should wear a prayer covering at night. Over three pages of replies were printed! Even more were sent in. Here is a typical answer.

Wearing a Prayer Covering at Night

First Corinthians 11:5-6 teaches that a woman while praying or prophesying is to have her head covered, covering her long hair. Worldly women display hair for sex appeal to the eyes of lustful men. With her covering, a woman signifies acceptance of her place in God's order, lest she dishonor her head (man), and in turn dishonor God, who gave this command.

A special promise for obedience to God's command is given to women in verses 10 and 15: power from God and glory in long uncut hair. My answer to the question is that God sees obedience to his commands both day and night.

("What Do You Think?" L. K., Va., 4-72)

Wearing a Prayer Covering in the Hospital

I was a patient in a hospital, and every day the nurses came to change the bed clothing. One day when they came into my room, I was still in bed and had my head covering hanging on the bedpost. One of the nurses remarked to the other, "She's got her religion hanging on the bedpost."

This brought shame to my face. I felt guilty for not having it on. From then on, I resolved that they would not see me again with my head covering anywhere but where it belonged.

Since then, I have been at the hospital a few times and have always kept my resolution. I have also been at the hospital to visit others. When I see their coverings lying on the bedstands, it brings back memories of the lesson I learned.

("Pathway Pen Pointettes," Mifflinburg, Pa., 12-72)

What Does a Bonnet Look Like?

[A woman wrote of her bus trip. During an overnight wait in Philadelphia, she couldn't sleep because passengers from arriving buses kept asking her to watch their suitcases for them.]

When I had time to think over my trip, I wondered why all the different people had singled me out from the crowd. I believe it was because of my plain clothes and bonnet. They never asked me if I was a Christian. They took that for granted.

Perhaps some girls or women will read this who are reluctant to wear plain clothes and a bonnet. Don't be ashamed of these things. The world trusts you and takes it as a sign of a Christian. Live up to their expectations, and then your bonnet will be beautiful indeed.

(Mrs. Wayne Miller, 2-68)

Do Bonnets Help?

Why should we be ashamed of our bonnets? Would it not be wise to take some precautions against the trend to drift toward the world?

It would look strange indeed to see a bonnet on the head of the wearer of a miniskirt. No one would think of making such a big change at one time, putting off the bonnet and putting on the miniskirt. It all comes one step at a time.

First we can go without bonnets, then the corners come off the caps [head-coverings], and then the strings. Dresses gradually get shorter and tighter, caps a bit smaller, and somewhere along the line we discard the cape. The apron, of course, has disappeared long before this.

Soon the only place to take anything away from is the dress, [leading to] bare arms, low necklines, tight bodices, and short skirts. This may not all come in one year or in one generation, but we have reason to believe that the passing of the bonnet will mean big changes are coming. Perhaps bonnets don't help, or do they?

—A Family Life *Reader*   (2-76)

Dresses

Only Yesterday

In general, a midcalf skirt is considered modest enough in most of our plain communities. Just take a look through a fashion magazine of fifty or sixty years ago and compare the length of the skirt with what most plain women are now wearing. There is quite a difference. Just think, if the average plain woman was transported back in time to 1910, she would be looked upon with great shock and amazement. "Look at how short her dress is," they might say, and she might even be arrested. And these would be "worldly" people who would condemn her.

The point is this: somehow over the years, plain women have been following after the world with regard to dress. They have lagged behind current styles, it is true, but have nonetheless been following along. Let us restore the modest, concealing attire worn by chaste women of old. Let us get rid of the signs of compromise which have crept into our plain garb almost unawares.

(S. S., Lancaster, Pa., 7-69)

Why Wear a Cape?

In our Old Order Mennonite churches, it is customary [for women] to wear a cape. But the practice is being questioned. I have heard mothers who were unable to explain why it should be worn.

I understand that some think it is an unnecessary article, just a hangover of tradition. But let's not miss the point. In 1 Timothy 2:8-9, Paul says, "I will . . . that women adorn themselves in modest apparel." Now the word "modest" is defined as chaste, decent, unpretentious.

Without a cape, we make an unnecessary show of our figures. Girls may not realize that they are tempting others to impure thoughts. The Bible teaches that the lusts of the people corrupt a nation.

By immodest dress, we are a hindrance to others. But by modest dress, we can be a help to each other to think pure and holy thoughts.

(I., Pa., 11-68)

Beards

The War of Whiskers

Let us take a look at beards in the Bible, in history, and among us today. There can be little doubt that in Bible times, God's people wore beards, not so much from religious convictions, perhaps, as for the same reason they wore eyebrows—simply because it was the natural thing to do. Yet in the Old Testament, we do find instructions forbidding the Israelites to shape and trim their beards according to heathen customs (Lev. 19:27).

During King David's time, it was considered a terrible shame and embarrassment not to have a beard (2 Sam. 10:4; 1 Chron. 19:5). Removing the beard in Bible times also carried a symbolic meaning, indicating a state of deep distress and shame, loss, and/or defeat (Isa. 7:20; 15:2; Jer. 48:37). Of the twenty times the word "beard" appears in the King James Version, in nineteen instances "beard" is translated from the Hebrew word *zaqan*, which included all the facial hair without making the modern-day distinction between the mustache and the rest of the beard.

We feel that Bible principles and common sense support a consistent wearing of the beard. First is the principle of sex distinction, the belief that the confusing and blurring of a clear line between man and woman is wrong. "The woman shall not wear what pertains to a man" (Deut. 22:5). Facial hair is a common mark of masculinity.

The second major biblical principle supporting the wearing of a beard is the teaching that the creature should be in subjection to the Creator. When a woman uses lipstick and eye shadow, we say she is not satisfied with the way God created her. Is not the man who shaves off his beard to make his face soft and womanish guilty of the same thing?

If we study history, we find that the beard was a point of contention in the 1690s between Jacob Ammann and Hans Reist, the leaders in the Amish-Mennonite split of 1693. Actually, not the beard, but merely the trimming of the beard was the point upon which they disagreed. The trimming and stylish shaping that Hans Reist permitted was the beginning of the end. Reist's followers eventually lost the beard entirely.

Today there is much reason to believe that the beard is once more threatened. There are still bishops living in some of our largest and oldest settlements who in their younger years required unmarried boys who were church members to wear beards. Today, no doubt many or perhaps most boys in those same communities think that unmarried Amish boys have always been smooth shaven.

Not only is the trend to wait until married or longer to let the beard grow, but Amish beards are shrinking in size and in length. The loss of the mustache brought with it Abraham Lincoln beards. Now the Lincoln beards are being replaced with neck beards. The next step will be no beards. What does being married have to do with wearing a beard? Or by the same token, when we give the right to shave off three-quarters of the area of our face where God causes hair to grow, why is it so wrong to take off the other quarter?

(E. Stoll, 8/9-83)

The Beard in 1779

At the Amish-Mennonite *Deiner-Versammlung* (ministers' meeting) at Essingen, Germany, in 1779, sixteen articles were adopted. Article 13 states, "All the young men who take off the beard with the razor shall be warned and admonished that, if they do not stop, they shall be punished with the ban, as likewise those who cut the hair of the head according to worldly styles."

("Letter," Enos Brandenburger Jr., New Haven, Ind., 12-83)

Be Careful! Your Symbols Are Showing

How can long hair and a beard be used to convey a certain impression when worn by the Amish, whereas the same thing can be a symbol of the very opposite when worn by a hippie?

In one way, the Amish are like the hippies. They do not conform to the world about them. They, too, have long hair and the beard. They are not concerned about the latest fashion in clothes, or in driving the latest model car.

However, here the similarity ends. Amish actions are based on religious convictions. They act as they do because they believe the Bible requires it. Morally, they are perhaps the strictest of all groups, and gross sins are punishable by excommunication.

In other words, the symbol they are carrying also denotes nonconformity. But since it is based on biblical reasons, it also denotes godliness, while the hippie's symbol denotes ungodliness.

In most of our communities, the size of the woman's veiling is set by local group practice. But those who wish to rebel, and have enough nerve to show it, wear a smaller covering, and it keeps moving further and further back on the head.

When a boy turns sixteen and feels like he is on top of the world, what symbols does he hoist to show it? Is it not too often shown in the way he combs his hair, and the angle at which he tilts his hat? Wearing his hat on a side denotes the attitude which is inside it.

Nor is this malady confined to the younger generation. In nearly every group, we find individuals who do not wish to conform to the accepted patterns. They show it by bringing questionable items into the church.

Nevertheless, there are also good symbols, persons who go a little farther than necessary to conform. Thus, the woman who is anxious to hoist a symbol of approval and cooperation will make a prayer veiling larger than the absolute minimum. The boy will be careful not to cut his hair too short.

Remember, it may be a very minor item, but still have significance. If you buy meat, it is a good idea to look for the government stamp of approval. It's just a little symbol, but it can mean the difference between buying nourishing food or something that will make you sick to your stomach. (D. Wagler, 11-68)

What Does Our Conduct Show?

Some years ago my wife and I, along with another couple, were traveling and came to a big city where we had to spend the night. As we walked up the sidewalks, we saw a man standing, weeping, with tears running down his cheeks.

He said to us, "When I saw your women, I had to think of my mother. She always wore a shawl and a bonnet, just like your women do."

As he talked, he was weeping. I had to think, "If our women had been dressed in the present-day garb with shorts or miniskirts, where would this man's thoughts have gone?" Never to his old mother. The garb of our women probably talked louder than the modern-day evangelists are talking.

Once when we wanted to get on a train, the conductor said the seats were all filled, except in the club car. He said we would either have to sit in the club car or wait for the next train. We did not know what a club car was, so we got on.

As we entered the car, people were drinking, smoking, playing cards, and what not. But the atmosphere soon changed. The seats in this car ran lengthwise along each side of the car. As we seated ourselves, there was a man on the opposite side who had a bottle in one hand and a cigarette in the other. He could not face us. He glanced first one way and then the other, and looked like he was going to faint. Soon he picked up his smoking stand and went to the other end of the car.

Soon a lady came to us and asked us what she must do to be saved. She was told to "believe on the Lord Jesus Christ, and you shall be saved" (Acts 16:31). Why did she come to us, since we were total strangers to her?

When she left, others came and asked questions concerning our faith. This went on from 7:00 p.m. until around midnight. We were busy answering questions out of the Bible. So the club car wasn't so bad after all.

However, we can also be a hindrance to people if our conduct is not according to our garb. A preacher once related that at one time he lived close to town. He learned that the town people called the plain people "the Pharisees." He could not understand this and decided at the first opportunity, he would ask the town people why.

As he was thinking this over, he remembered how some of the plain people were not always living an orderly life and were drinking and smoking. He finally decided, "If they don't say anything to me, I won't say anything to them about being called Pharisees."

May the Lord help us in our everyday conduct that the light of his presence may shine through us so that others can see that we are his followers.   (P. M. Y., Shipshewana, Ind., 5-70)

Heart and Conduct

Years ago someone said to one of our forefathers that if your heart is right, it doesn't matter how you dress.

Here is the answer he got: "Your heart is right? But can your heart be right if your conduct is all wrong? Just as the profane swearer might say, 'No matter what words I use, just so my heart is right.' No, your heart is not right if your conduct is wrong."

If our heart is right, we do not wish to follow the fashions of the world.

—Dad   (11-68)

The Blessings of Obedience

We wear plain clothes, but we know plain clothes do not save us. We give alms, but our good works cannot earn the grace of God. We partake in communion, but know that the emblems in themselves are just bread and wine, with no power to sanctify us. We pour water at baptism, and know the water cannot wash off a single sin. We obey because God said so. Is that not, after all, the best reason, the most important reason in all the world?

("Views and Values," E. Stoll, 8/9-81)

Clothes and Heaven

Clothes won't get us into heaven, but they can keep us out.

(1-75)

10
The World
Challenges and Changes

Some people are under the misconception that "the Amish live to-day the same way they did three hundred years ago." While their way of dress and "horse culture" may seem frozen in time to us, it is obvious that the Amish have changed a great deal. Anyone who has recently visited an Amish home in Lancaster County can attest to that. We see bottled-gas refrigerators and stoves, compressed-air food blenders. Some Amish businesses have answering machines or answering services when you call them by phone. Cellular phones and computers are now used by some Amish, but not with Internet connections.

Nevertheless, the Amish do not change as often or as much as the world around them. They attempt to limit and control change rather than have "progress" run away with them. It is sometimes a rocky road to travel, but in many ways they have been successful.

It has been said that the Amish are often as curious about us as we are about them. Here is a look at how the Amish view the modern world around them, and also how they are viewed by others.

A Baby to Pity

Freda Bender propped herself up on her elbow and surveyed the hospital room where she lay in bed. The only other occupant in the room was Mrs. White. Freda turned her head toward the door as a nurse called in with her baby boy. A second nurse followed the first with Mrs. White's baby.

The poor little boy! What kind of world would he be taken home to? How could a boy grow up surrounded by dancing pictures on the TV screen, a world of smoking and drinking, a world of gadgets and switches and concrete sidewalks? What chance did he have of grow-ing up and really amounting to something?

Suddenly Freda stopped, seized by a new thought. Was it possible that Mrs. White was also pitying Freda's little son? Was she saying to herself, "Poor little baby! He's doomed to grow up in that primitive way of life. All he'll ever have a chance of being is a common farmer, toiling with his hands, sweating all his life, deprived of so many enjoyments—no car, no TV, no chance to go to college, no chance that the poor fellow will amount to much."

There was no doubt that the two babies were born into homes that were different from each other. Baby White would grow up in a world that put a premium on good looks, brains, money, recognition, and pleasure. Baby Bender would grow up in a world that put a premium on character, conscience, morals, and serving others in love rather than trying to get on top.

("Views and Values," E. Stoll, 3-75)

Riding in the Caboose

Some churches have accepted material changes in part or in whole, believing these inventions can be used for good—cars, telephones, electricity, tractor farming, and so on. But if we look around us, we should be able to see by this time that these inventions have helped bring about the many harmful changes in the world.

Cars have put people on the roads, bringing easy travel and a way of life that has the emphasis on luxury and ease, rather than on self-denial. Electricity has brought television. Tractor farming and modern machinery have destroyed the idea of a family farm. Now most of the family can work in factories and away from home, even if living on a farm.

Surely we can see that the host of material inventions, although not evil in themselves, have brought with them an overwhelming influence that has swept the world in the wrong direction. Isn't it reasonable to think that these same inventions also have an influence on the church to whatever degree we accept them?

Recently a young man who grew up in an Amish home, but is now completely out in the world, made the statement, "All the Amish should be stuffed and put into museums. That's the only place in today's world they fit in."

It's true that we don't fit in today's world. Let us hope and pray we never will. ("Views and Values," E. Stoll, 11-72)

The Power of Suggestion

We are asked, "What! You don't have TV? What do you do in the evening?"

The first time I was asked that question, I was stumped. What *did* I do? I had never realized this was a problem. Yet this man made it sound as though there was nothing else to do except watch TV.

Once again, it would make more sense for us to reverse the question, and be asking, "What! You mean you have time to just sit and watch TV? Don't you have anything more challenging, more worthwhile than *that*? When do you get your work done? When do you visit your friends? When do you read good books? When do you tell the children a story, or help them play a game, or put a puzzle together?"

Instead of stammering around when asked how we can get along without TV, we might better be asking them how they can get along *with* TV? How do they cope with all that violence their children watch? How do they expect to teach their children good values? How do they hope their children will grow up and not have minds that are warped by all the immoral and trashy programs?

("Views and Values," E. Stoll, 5-77)

Many readers are familiar with school controversies in Pennsylvania, where Amishmen went to jail; and later incidents in Wisconsin leading to the 1972 U.S. Supreme Court ruling in support of Amish schools. Here is a lesser-known incident.

The Schooling of Amish Children in Jay County, Indiana

When the Amish first settled in Jay County, Indiana, they sent their children to the rural public schools, as was the practice in most Amish communities at that time. The state law required that children attend school until their sixteenth birthday. The Amish, of course, did not wish their children to go to high school, so they kept them at home after graduation from the eighth grade.

In 1948, the county school officials decided to press charges against one of the Amishmen, making a test case. Chester Gingerich, father of thirteen children, residing in Greene Township, was arrested for not sending his son Joseph, aged fourteen, to high school at Pennville, in neighboring Penn Township. A trial was held. Chester was found guilty, fined $200, and sentenced to the Indiana State Farm for sixty days, the maximum punishment for the offense.

Many local people felt this was too severe and appealed to the governor, Ralph F. Gates. One of the last things he did before being replaced by the new governor was to pardon Chester. He canceled the $200 fine and removed the sixty-day penal farm sentence. Chester had not yet started to serve his sentence, so he never was in jail more than the two and a half hours at his initial arrest.

The governor, in pardoning Chester Gingerich, had said his son should go to high school. So this put Chester again in conflict with the state laws. He was arrested again in March 1949. The judge convicted him and fined him $200 with no imprisonment. The decision was appealed to the Indiana Supreme Court. Meanwhile, Chester's brother Perry was arrested in April for keeping his son Daniel out of high school.

To the surprise of everyone, the Indiana Supreme Court ruled that the state school attendance law, which had been interpreted for fifty years to require attendance until the sixteenth birthday, could actually be interpreted to mean the fifteenth birthday. Since the Gingerich cousins were both past fifteen, the charges against their fathers were dismissed.

However, that was not the end of the school problems. All the public schools had been closed in Greene Township, where most of the Amish lived. Hence, the parents faced the decision of either sending their children to a consolidated school in the adjoining township, or building their own parochial schools. Private Amish schools were rare in 1950, but the Jay County parents decided to build their own on Perry I. Gingerich's farm. Of course, the county officials were upset by this and tried to have the school closed. In 1954, Chester Gingerich was again arrested. This time it was for sending his nine-year-old daughter, Katie Ann, to a noncertified school.

The United Press newspaper wire service picked up the story. In an attempt to work in harmony with the public officials, the Amish replaced their own teacher with a non-Amish woman. The only difference was that they owned the school and it had only Amish pupils. Otherwise, it was similar to the one-room schools of the previous era.

The Jay County school problems caused some of the Amish settlers to consider moving elsewhere. Tension in the church about other matters also influenced some in looking for new homes.

(D. Luthy, 6-81)

Court Ruling Recognizes Amish Way of Life

[A well-written article quoted the 1972 U.S. Supreme Court decision, "The state does not have the authority to force Amish parents to send their children to high school," and commented:]

The court saw the religion of the Amish as a "way of life," and that their everyday living is regulated by what they believe. This is in direct opposition to the popular churches, many of whom believe that their religion is something to be lived on Sunday. Naturally, it presents a challenge to us to live the kind of life as set forth in the opinion of the court. Are we really worthy of such an opinion?

We have no guarantee that, if a similar case were brought before the court within several years' time, the opinion would be favorable. Nor do we need to depend on the opinion of the Supreme Court or any other court. Our Anabaptist forebears suffered persecution and even martyrdom rather than going against their understanding of the Bible.

If the Supreme Court would have ruled against the Amish in this case, then it is doubtful whether the decision would have influenced many Amish parents to send their children to high school. True, they may have had to accept the consequences, and be branded as criminals, or had their property confiscated. Or they may have migrated to other states that are more favorable.

In short, we are thankful for a favorable decision, and we should strive to live up to the opinion of the court as far as our educational standards are concerned. Yet we should not allow it to influence us in becoming slack in our standards. What we do, we should do to serve God, not man. We should be diligent in providing a satisfactory education for our children because we believe it is the right thing to do, and to train them and bring them up as the Bible teaches, in the "nurture and admonition of the Lord" [Eph. 6:4].   (8/9-72)

Fighting for Freedom?

Recently my wife and I were waiting in a depot to board our bus. We noticed a man with a large emblem on his coat: "U.S. Marine Corps." He was soon joined in conversation by another man, who asked him how long he'd served in the Marines. For a few minutes the two discussed their involvement in Vietnam. Then the Marine said, "I think everyone should be willing to serve their country and fight when necessary."

The other man agreed, but then commented, "Yet war is a bad thing and not right."

"Of course war isn't right," the Marine agreed. "But it's our duty to fight to preserve our freedom when an invasion comes. The trouble with our country is that we have too many cowards, too many draft dodgers, even people who want to be religious. They dress differently and look down on those who go to war to fight for our freedom. They think they serve the good Lord by not fighting."

I was now beginning to realize this man was really speaking to me.

"By refusing to fight, these people weaken the very structure of our country. If they don't want to fight for our country, they should all be thrown out. Junk is what I call them."

I was somewhat aghast at this man's vehemence as he expressed himself. I was still thinking about him as we boarded our bus. Is it really true that the strength of the nation lies in having the biggest guns and the bravest soldiers? Or does it not lie in the Christian homes and churches? Is the nation free because of huge arms and defenses, or is the nation free because God in his goodness has chosen to bless the nation with freedom? In one day God could take that freedom in spite of all the arms in America.

America has freedom, yes, and it is something we should daily thank God for. Yet Jesus, when he was here on earth, taught his followers not to fight. He never talked about becoming free from the oppression of cruel or bad governments here on earth. But he did talk about becoming free from a spiritual kingdom—that of Satan.

Is America then free, with a moral disintegration of society, the rise of corruption with divorce and remarriage, fornication, drinking, drug abuse, theft, murders, hate, strife? The list could go on. No, America is not free. Yet Jesus spoke of being free from sin. He has the answer: "If the Son therefore shall make you free, ye shall be free indeed" (John 8:36).   (David Bender, Aylmer, Ont., 2-90)

Doing Good on the Wrong Side of the Globe

[In an article about Secretary of State Henry Kissinger, the author was at first impressed by his peacemaking diplomacy. But then he discovered Kissinger was divorced in 1964 and had two children living with their mother.]

Isn't that something? Kissinger is supposed to be so great because he can charm into friendliness the Chinese, the Russians, the Arabs, the Israelis, and the Vietnamese. But all the while, he cannot get along with his wife. While he is patching up other people's problems, he can't solve his own. While he is coaxing others to stop fighting, he seemingly can't end the strife in his own household. While he works to bring peace to nations, there is no peace between himself and his wife, whom he promised to love, cherish, and remain faithful to.

What good does Kissinger's greatness do on the other side of the globe while he is such a dismal failure at home? If he is indeed a peacemaker, he goes to the wrong side of the globe to be one.

To work on problems in the community without solving the problems in the home, from which the community problems stem, will get us nowhere. The world makes a hero of those who can make a great show and do great things, but in the end their greatness isn't genuine. We must learn to see where true greatness lies—not in pomp and show and pride and publicity, but in warmth and love and closeness and kindness at home, on the family level.

I would rather spend five minutes visiting with the lowliest man who has the love and respect of his family, than to be counted the closest friend of a famous person who neglects his family.

Jesus asked the question, "What shall it profit a man if he shall gain the whole world and lose his own soul?" (Mark 8:36). We could reword it to ask, "What shall it profit a man if he gain the whole world and lose his own family?" The answer would surely be the same to either question, on any side of the globe.

("Views and Values," E. Stoll, 6-74)

The American Family in the Past Century

Since 1910 there have been three main items that have had more than ordinary influence on the families of the nation. These are the automobile, the movie theater, and television. Without the automobile, the theater would never have come into importance. The coming of the auto also hastened the movement from farm to city.

Among the plain people, there may not be much temptation to go to a theater, or bring home a television set for the living room, or buy a car. But we are faced with many pressures to conform to the ways of the world in thoughts and actions.

We can rest assured that anything building up the strength of family, builds up the church. And anything that tears down the family, tears down the church. If we don't want to end up where the world is, let's be careful not to travel the same road that took it there.

(D. Wagler, 4-71)

Permissiveness

The attitudes and values, or lack thereof, in American society are bound to have their influence on children of the plain churches. When you see a seventeen-year-old boy drive out of the farm lane early Saturday evening, sitting in his $500 buggy, pulled by his $300 horse, and hanging next to him a $90 store-made suit, then you see the result of permissive [Amish] parents. When you see an eighteen-year-old boy pull away from a drive-in restaurant in his $3000 car (yes, it may even be black), there is a product of [non-Amish] parental permissiveness.

Permissiveness has really only recently become large scale in some plain churches. It is too soon to see what effect it will have upon crime. But there is little hope to think that "plain permissiveness" will lead to anything milder than "American permissiveness."

(D. Luthy, 3-68)

Anchored to the Book

The man in the Cadillac laughs when you ask him about nonconformity to the world. His wife says dress and conduct don't matter. It's what's inside that counts with God.

The man in the buggy says he agrees that the heart is what counts with God. "But," he continues, "I figure what is inside comes out."

Somehow, when people want to do so, they can ignore or reason away Scripture passages that teach separation from the world. (Here we can all be on our guard!) Some Scriptures that are shrugged off as nonessential are the following:

• The words of Paul in 1 Corinthians 11, teaching veiling of women, and that it is a shame for women to cut their hair.

• The instructions of both Paul and Peter concerning modest apparel, and forbidding the wearing of jewelry.

• The warning against the unequal yoke with unbelievers.

• The commands against divorce and remarriage, against violence and revenge, against going to law.

• The practicing of the holy kiss, foot washing, and a banning and shunning of apostates.

There are others, of course. In his Sermon on the Mount, Jesus said, "Strait is the gate and narrow is the way that leads to life, and few there be that find it."

Has the gate been remodeled into a four-lane highway, to keep in touch with the times? Hardly. A Christian doesn't take his orders from the times. Not if he is anchored to the Book.

("Fireside Chats," J. Stoll, Guaimaca, Honduras, 4-70)

Testimony in Words or Life?

Soon after a man had changed his church for one he felt was more spiritual, he was doing some trucking for an Old Order man. All the way, he was talking of spiritual matters, giving a testimony about how he was born again, and the many things he did different than before. He said he used to do things that were good [before he shifted membership], but he did them for the wrong reasons. The other man didn't say much.

When they neared home, the man who had changed churches

asked, "Well, what do you think of my testimony?"

"Well," answered the other man, "there was an old deacon who used to say that if you roll an empty barrel, it makes a lot of noise. A full one doesn't."   ("Pathway Pen Points," Pa., 2-77)

Thoughtless Zeal

I suppose we've all been guilty of being more zealous than thoughtful. There's an old story that I understand is true, illustrating what I'm trying to say. It proves that no matter how right or how righteous we may be, if we use faulty thinking to support our position, we're not going to be very convincing. This is the way I remember hearing it:

An Amish brother was walking along the road toward town. A car came along, slowed down, and stopped. "Want a ride into town?"

"Sure thing."

The car was soon on its way again. The driver was a stranger to the Amish, and he was curious. Between puffs of the cigarette he was smoking, he began asking questions. He found his passenger friendly and talkative. Before long, the driver reached for another cigarette. He held the pack to the man seated beside him. "Here, want a smoke?" he offered.

"Uh, no, I don't smoke. I don't believe in smoking," the brother answered. Then he laughed a little self-consciously and continued. "You see, I figure God didn't intend that man should smoke. If he had, he would have built him a chimney."

The driver didn't say anything for a moment. Then he braked the car and brought it to a stop.

"I'm sorry, sir," he said. "You can get out here. I suppose if God had intended that man should drive, he would have put him on wheels."

This may sound like a joke, but it really is not. There's a deep principle here. We must be careful to base our faith on the Word of God and not on human reasoning.   ("Fireside Chats," J. Stoll, 2-69)

We, the Keys of Death

War has slain its thousands,
We, our tens of thousands.
      Mightier than rumbling tanks,
      Deadlier than soldiers' ranks—
The twisted steel,
  The crumpled wheel,
    The sudden crash,
      The fatal gash,
        The wrenching thud,
          The pool of blood.
All is still;
Thus we kill.
We, the keys of death,
Of violent death.

Divorce has slain its thousands,
We, our tens of thousands.
      Not by courts and laws
      Granted marital flaws.
Our success is owing
  To the ease of going.
    Constantly driving,
      Leaving and arriving,
        No time to be together,
          Away in all weather.
What once was meant
  To bring content
    And fellowship deep,
      Is but a place to sleep.
        The urge to roam
          Has broken the home.
Thus family ties of goodwill,
We break down, destroy, and kill.
We, the keys of death,
Of subtle death.

Hollywood has slain its thousands,
We, our tens of thousands.
          More alluring than the lighted screen,
          More dangerous than the lustful scene.
A young boy and girl,
   No appearance of peril,
      Just a ride
         Through the countryside.
            But aloneness brings
               With it baser things.
Their parents say
   It's just a way
      Of going to town,
         Of getting around.
But the sober truth
   For many youth
      Is we've unlocked the door
         To plenty more.
Thus we continue still,
Virtue to kill.
We, the keys of death,
Of tragic death.

We,
the keys of death:
Of physical death,
Of family death,
Of spiritual death.   (E. Stoll, 3-70)

Outsiders, Tourists, and "Seekers"

Seeing Beyond Culture

My wife read to me your article on tourism in Lancaster County,
Pennsylvania. I listened with interest but also with sadness. The sadness that comes to me is because so many tourists are seeing the
Amish [merely] as a culture. I do not believe the Amish could have
endured as they have for three hundred years if there were not a

deeper reason for not changing with the world.

This is especially true in a place like Lancaster County, where the Amish are encircled by the industrial complex. Their prosperity itself would long ago have exterminated their culture. In other American groups, the German dialect, or any other dialect, failed to survive much shorter periods than this, due to the pressure of the society about them.

What then makes the Amish click? It is their faith in God. Of course, we know that the Amish are not perfect in all their practices, and they have room for improvement. But their sustaining power is their belief and understanding of Scriptures concerning nonresistance, nonconformity, divorce and remarriage, worldly education, separation of church and state, non-joining with worldly churches, and their theology. These are the things that have kept the Amish from drifting and becoming swallowed up by the worldly culture around them.

("Letter," 1-81)

"I Don't Mean to Be Nosy, but . . ."

What did this [inquiring tourist] think our religion was—just a quaint game, a novelty, a museum? Did the man actually learn anything by talking with us? Did he know more when he drove away than he did when he came? Did we answer his questions, or did we evade them? Shouldn't we somehow have left him with a challenge to look below the surface, to consider what the true values of life are?

What is our religion—just buggies, beards, and broad-rimmed hats? Couldn't we somehow have given him a glimpse of the New Testament pattern—a nonconformed church; a strong, close-knit brotherhood of believers, living together in fellowship and love, helping each other along the way?

I guess I'm like the stranger from Texas. I have a bunch of questions I would like to have answers to. But I don't think stopping someone at the end of his lane for five minutes is the best way to get them answered. (4-69)

Telling About the Faith

A man said that he had always thought the Amish people were not friendly. But now that he had met some, he didn't find it that way at all. It is true that when we are driving down the road and someone tries to take our picture, it is hard to be friendly. So many people are interested more in our customs and culture than in what we believe. Because of our dress, we attract attention. Instead of rushing away, we have a good chance to tell them about the faith that is within us [cf. 1 Pet. 3:15].

("Letter," Monroe Beachy, Sugarcreek, Ohio, 1-73)

How I Tried to Get Rid of the Rude

The most unpleasant experience I ever had with photo hunters was several years ago. I had my horse hitched to the surrey and had four or five of the children with me. We were going to my sister's house. My nerves were tense as I turned north, for I always dreaded this one mile on a U.S. highway.

At first it wasn't too bad. We had gone about half the distance when a car passed me. "Tourists," I said when I saw how they looked back and watched us. Then they turned around and approached us slowly from the rear. I saw they had a camera ready. "Put your heads down," I told the children on the front seat, and I also put mine down.

They stopped beside the road in front of us. We passed them, and I urged my horse on. I watched for the car to pass us again, but they stayed behind us until the highway was clear from both directions. Suddenly the horse jumped, and I saw they were passing us on the wrong side. When they were in front of us, they suddenly pulled across the road in front of us. I pulled the lines up tight, hoping none of the children would slide off the seat because of my sudden stop.

Suddenly I realized they had us where they wanted us. I couldn't put my head down because I had to control my horse, and the children were too curious to see what was going on. I felt anger rising up inside me and, before I knew what was happening, I was yelling at them, "The nerve of some people!" I don't know if I shook my fist or not, but at least I almost felt like it.

Of course, just at that moment the camera clicked, and I could see they greatly enjoyed my annoyance. Right away I felt ashamed of myself. I checked both ways for traffic and drove past without looking at them. They soon went around us again, and this time they were laughing and waving their hands mockingly as they sped away.

What kind of witness had I been to these people? Would it make them respect the Amish more? And what did God think of me? Just because they were rude didn't make it right for me to be the same. Maybe God lets things like this happen to try us out. I have also found out that not all tourists are rude and disrespectful.

Several years ago one evening, my husband and I were at the sale of a friend of ours in town. A man and a woman came out, and the woman asked, "Would you mind if we took your pictures standing beside your rig?"

"We'd rather not," answered my husband.

"Thank you," said the lady. "We just didn't know."

We looked the other way and started walking toward the alley. My husband said to me, "They'll probably get us anyway."

I couldn't resist a glance backward and was surprised to see them walking away. They had respected our wishes and didn't take any pictures.

Human nature being what it is, I suppose we will always have the politely interested, the curious, and the rude people. But I hope, with the help of God, I will never again lose my temper when I meet the latter kind. ("Pathway Pen Points," Ind., 6-73)

Letters from Non-Amish Readers of *Family Life*

My husband and I visited Lancaster, Pennsylvania, for a small, three-day vacation. Also, to look at the Amish and Mennonite people. What first was a sightseeing trip turned into a spiritual awakening! When you don't need God's help every day, you get out of the habit of needing him at all. (N.Y.)

I am neither Amish nor Mennonite. But this does not mean that I disagree with what you believe, nor does it mean that I regard your faith as "simple and primitive." It simply means that I was born into a family of another affiliation and have not as yet changed.

I read *Family Life* because I enjoy learning about the people I believe are closer to Jesus than any other people on earth. There are a great number of "outsiders" who admire you for the fortitude and courage displayed in living your lives for Christ.

As a child in Lancaster County, I often saw the "strange people" in the little black buggies. As I grew older, I began to wonder, "What makes these people give up the luxuries of life to pursue a life of humility and hard work?"

Often I asked questions about the Amish, but those I asked knew no more about you than I did. So I began reading books about the Anabaptist movement and about the development of the Anabaptist faith. However, these books were written by scholars whom I felt did not reflect the true nature of the Amish people.

At this point I began to realize that I did not really want to know *about* you; I wanted to *know* you, a people who would voluntarily choose to become members of the Christian community. I wanted to know people who would not give up merely one hour on Sunday to worship God, but would devote their whole lives to being Christians.

So I subscribed to *The Budget* to learn what I felt would give me values to base my own life upon. Through *The Budget,* I learned of *Family Life.* Now I feel I understand basically what you believe in, and at least in my mind I am able to share and enjoy a magazine that I feel helps me to be a better Christian.

So you see, sir, there are many of us outside your faith who believe yours is the way of Christ, and we want to know about your faith so that we, too, might become better Christians. We want to learn about you so that our lives might resemble your lives, our families might resemble your families, and our love of Christ might resemble your love of Christ.   (Ronald Vassally, N.J., 2-70)

I'm fifteen, male, and live in the "outside world." I'm not Amish or Mennonite. I'm Protestant. I live in a development near Philadelphia. I would jump at a chance to work on a farm. I have some experience. I sent for a booklet on Amish doctrine, have read it, and believe if I am to achieve eternal life through the glorification of God, I am going to have to become Amish. But how? I need more training in your ways and beliefs.

I pray to God each night and have dreams of becoming Amish. The more I pray, the more God calls me to the plain people. Please help me. I need to know if I can become Amish. If it be for just room, board, and the true teachings of God, I would gladly work my summer on a farm. I guess I was born into the wrong faith.

("Staff Notes," Warrington, Pa., 11-79)

I am a convert to the Amish, and I would like to write a few lines to those people who "didn't have enough time to stop and answer some unbelievers' questions."

I am glad someone took the time to "talk" with me. At first they did not have to say one word; their lives did the "talking." I feel this is the main way in which God called me out of the world into his kingdom.

("Letter," Von der Englishe, Ohio, 7-75)

"Outsiders" Joining the Old Orders

One of our local ministers said recently he was having a conversation with an Old Order Mennonite about their experiences with "outsiders" wanting to join the church. Later, when the newness wore off, they tended to leave again. When the Amish minister learned that this Old Order Mennonite group uses English in their church services, he commented how they don't have the language barrier like the Amish do. But the Old Order Mennonite man shook his head and said, "If they're sincere, they'll learn the language."

I think most Amish are willing to speak English any other time a group includes somebody who does not understand the German.

I have a good friend who some years ago was an "outsider" and then made the changeover to the Amish church. It was a struggle for him, but I think he is now fairly well adapted to his present way of life, and he has been an inspiration to me.

Don't ask us to be like the people mentioned in Revelation 2:14-15, conforming to the world in order to win it. I think this is quite popular nowadays, and God hates it. To all outsiders, if you see good works from the Amish and your heart is yearning to know more, go and visit a minister or anybody [Amish] you know. They should be able to help you a lot, even if you can't understand German, if they can talk with you personally.

("Letter," Daniel L. Hershberger, Millersburg, Ohio, 11-82)

The Power of Language

For the safety of our church, I think we need to keep the German language. I don't know of a place where they changed from German to English that they didn't start drifting. It seems that in North America, the English language is style, since that is what the worldly people use. If we aren't careful, the styles of this world can draw more people than what the ministers preach.

For example, when the boys wanted to cut their hair too short, the church had lots of problems until the hippie style came. Then they could change and go to the other extreme. Now the name *Amish* isn't what gets us to heaven. But disobedience, drifting, and following the styles of this world will surely keep us out.

I think it's a big change to be raised in the world and then join an Amish church. I like the advice our bishop gave, that they should come and live the way we do at least one whole year before they start joining the church. This way they could prove themselves to the church, and also see if they really want to change for the rest of their lives.

("Letter," Mahlon Yoder, Dixon, Mo., 11-82)

What Others Think of the Amish

"Are you Amish?" asked the taxi driver. We told him we were. He asked us about horses, and we told him we have a few.

"Well," he said, "you stick to horses. You can make more money if you farm with horses. You just can't make money with this modern machinery unless you farm over eighty acres. It's too expensive—can't get your money out again."

I had to wonder, how many of us agree with him? Many of us want more modern machinery. Isn't it just because it looks bigger and because the world has it?

The taxi driver went on talking about the Amish people, how he likes them and can trust them. We didn't know what to think about it. Did he really mean what he said, or did he want to hear what we would say? This man seemed to think the Amish are all honest and nice people. If the Amish people would be as honest as he thought, they would of course be better than they are.

—*A Reader*   (Mifflintown, Pa., 10-68)

Hypocrites?

It is a sobering thought to think that the only members of our congregation that many worldly people come into contact with are those who are not living the faith. The logical conclusion is for the world to decide that if these are hypocrites, then we are all hypocrites.

("Across the Editor's Desk," 2-70)

Envying the Plain People

Today there are people in the world who are tired of their sinful living. Perhaps they envy the plain people for their simple living and try to imitate them in many ways. They will plant their own gardens, sew their own clothes, heat their home with a wood-burning stove, and may even go to live in a cabin in the woods.

However, all these things without the true faith in God are but clinking cymbals and empty shells. We all know what happens to the hippie type of commune started by the people of this world, in an attempt to live together in love on their own strength.

When people of this world want to join our groups, we ought to be careful to explain to them that the plain and simple life in itself merits us nothing. We should emphasize that the way of faith is the way of the cross, of self-denial, obedience, and self-discipline.

It is true that we are promised many blessings in this life. We are promised food for our bodies, clean air to breathe, clothing to cover our nakedness.

Yet these are only fringe benefits. The real reason for serving our Master is because he has loved us with an everlasting love and called us to be children of the Most High. The promise he has given us is that through sorrow we can have the peace of God in our hearts, even in this life, and after this life we can be partakers of his glory in eternity. ("Pathway Pen Points," 7-87)

Amish in Magazines

Today it is not at all unusual to pick up a magazine and discover an article featuring the Amish. As the gap widens between the simple Amish way of life and the push-button American society, more and more attention is focused on the Amish. Americans likely view the

Amish with much the same regard they are showing high-priced antiques, as something that contains part of their own past, a heritage they have left for modern living, yet cannot help admiring.   (2-75)

Living Up to Our Reputation

Has there ever been a time in the history of the plain people when we have received so much favorable publicity as today?

We know that many of the things they are saying about us are not really true, at least not for many of us. They say we put God first and do not live for worldly pleasures, yet you and I know we fall short in this. The pursuit for the dollar and things money can buy is much too common. They say how peace-loving we are, how gentle, kind, and forgiving. You and I know there is too much ill will and gossip, too much strife and backbiting and hate, and too many church splits. They say we lead clean lives, yet in some communities the sins that should not once be named among us (Eph. 5:3) have become much too common.

They say we are farmers and people of the land, and yet we have entire church districts where hardly a farmer can be found. They say we are careful with the soil, conscientious conservationists. Yet when it comes to drenching the earth with poisonous sprays, some of us keep up with our non-Amish neighbors. They say we have no juvenile delinquency. Yet in entire communities, the majority of the young people spend their weekends in drinking and rowdy living, so that at times police have had to be called in to restore order.

Against such a dark picture, lest we despair, we need to remember that there are entire communities where most of these evils are unknown.

A group of Amish men were working together, repairing their schoolhouse, when a newspaper man stopped in. He asked for permission to take some pictures. When the men declined, he insisted a bit.

"But what about all the bad things people are writing about you that aren't true?"

"The bad things people say about us that aren't true won't hurt us," the Amish man replied. "It's not in our place to worry about that.

Our task is to just make sure the bad things they say *aren't* true!"

("Views and Values," E. Stoll, 6-88)

The Messiah Syndrome

Is the latest craze to adore the Amish, to idolize the plain people? There is no doubt about it. The plain people are in the news today and in public favor to an extent that they probably never were before. The Amish turn up in movies and television shows. Book after book is written. Stories and pictures fill newspapers and magazines. Tourists flock to our communities by the millions.

Now even the president of the USA has come to visit the plain people! It is certainly evidence of the plain people's popularity among the public when the president wishes to be so visibly identified with them. A reader in Lancaster County, Pennsylvania, sent us some clippings about President Bush's visit and his meeting with leaders of various plain groups. A letter accompanied the clippings saying:

"It seems the big event in Lancaster County for 1989 is the first ever visit of the president of the United States to a two-room school to hear how the plain people manage to protect their young from the temptation of drugs. In the discussion with the president, it was agreed that a strong family life and a sound teaching and training from youth are the best safeguard against the evils of the world.

"Besides drugs and drinking, part of the problem is the increasing number of broken homes in the world's society. It is interesting to note that a certain bishop who sat at the table with President Bush has performed over a thousand marriages since 1944, and only three of these couple have separated."

How should we respond to all this favorable publicity? How should we feel about it?

• *We should be concerned to lead lives consistent with what we profess.* But how many people in the world have looked to the plain people for an example of Christian living and have been disappointed? How many have been turned aside by our many splits and divisions? How many people have been surprised that in some communities, young people do use drugs, in spite of what President Bush may have been led to believe? How often has our testimony to the world been ruined by our inconsistencies, our empty formalism, our hypocrisy, our self-righteousness, and our spiritual coldness?

• *We need to be careful to give all honor to whom it belongs.* The world is desperate for something to satisfy its hunger, some answer to its search for meaning in life, wanting something external to base faith upon, something to see and touch and handle. While they focus upon our beards and buggies and bonnets, they miss entirely what our faith is all about.

• *We should be more concerned to share with others the values we hold dear.* For many years now, we plain people have been saying that although we do not send missionaries to Africa, we do believe in letting our lights shine where we are. It is true that many of the people who are fascinated by the Amish are probably driven by idle curiosity and are really not genuinely interested in matters of faith. But here and there among the teeming tourists are sincere and seeking souls who honestly long for better things. They are asking for bread. Will they be given a stone?

Several years ago, a young couple of Catholic background became interested in learning more about the Amish. So they drove six hundred miles to a large Amish community. For over a week, they watched for an opportunity to talk with an Amish person who would and could tell them what the Amish believe, and whether it was possible for outsiders to join. They waited and watched in vain. Finally, the last day of their visit arrived, and they went home deeply disappointed.

They had tried to start conversations that went deeper than the wind and the weather. They had gone to myriads of tourist places, where all kinds of knickknacks and souvenirs of the Amish are sold. But what they were really seeking for, they had been unable to find: just one person who had the time and the interest to sit down and discuss with them the things that really matter in life.

Every year more people are wanting to come and join plain churches. Too often in the past, our response has been one of hesitance and reluctance and uncertainty. Too often we have taken the position of wait-and-see. We wait and see if they can make it before we will become involved in offering real support and help.

("Views and Values," E. Stoll, 7-89)

11

Old Age, Illness, and Death

Every society and religion must deal with illness, aging, and death. The way each handles these can tell us much about that culture, its beliefs and values. In the Amish faith, the separation of church and state is clear; they traditionally accept no Social Security benefits and take care of the older folks themselves. Sometimes the grandparents live in a separate section, added onto the home.

Living with in-laws and grandchildren has its joys and challenges. Sometimes brothers and sisters take turns caring for an ill parent. Communities often rally to help pay a friend's costly medical bills. Times of trial can make people stronger, or destroy them. Death is the ultimate test of faith. It may be awaited with fear, or a calm acceptance. The Amish deal with all of this within the framework of their family, the community, and their belief in a life yet to come.

When the Young Grow Old

When late autumn strips the leaves from the trees around us, we can see the distant regions that were hidden from us all summer. In the same way, old age may rob men and women of earlier enjoyments, but it is only to enlarge the prospect of eternity. Old age is a threshold.

Listing some of the problems and discussing them may help our older brethren and sisters to be better understood and appreciated:

- We are still tempted.
- We don't have anything to do.
- We don't feel needed.
- No one takes our advice anymore.
- We get blamed for spoiling the grandchildren.
- With only ourselves to care for, it's so easy to become selfish.

(J. Stoll, 8-68)

Widows

A Note to Family and Friends

First of all, a few words of appreciation for the care you have given me during the past months. Lying here in bed, unable to do much more than think, I realize it must take much patience on your part to leave your families for your turn on duty here for a day and a night.

It was not by choice that I have been a helpless bed patient. My wish would have been to follow my wife when she died peacefully after only a brief illness. But God has a purpose in this, even though it is hidden from us. It may be a test of our faith.

I feel thankful that my family and neighbors have enough concern to care for me here at home. It would be heartbreaking to have to live out these last days in an old people's home. Those have their places, too, but one hopes the plain churches may hold what they have kept through the years and continue to give tender loving care at home to their aged. If at times the way seems hard, just remember that some day you, too, may be disabled, and then you will appreciate the care you receive from the next generation.

Surely if your labor is done in a loving spirit, you shall not be unrewarded. And the King shall say unto them, "Verily, I say unto you, Inasmuch as you have done it unto one of the least of these my brethren, you have done it unto me" [Matt. 25:40].

—*Your Aged Father*   (2-83)

This Lonely Road

Since I have been a widow, I have become aware of how little thought or regard is given to the widow, and this probably holds true for the singles, too. I do not want to leave the impression that no one in our church does anything for the widow. There are some who do plenty and regret it that they can't do more, but the majority are like myself before I walked this lonely road. They have their own troubles and their own work to do, and don't bother to think of others like they should.

—*A Widow from the East*   (3-76)

Widowhood—a Life of Loneliness

In many larger communities, there are many widows and numerous activities for them. Widows' quiltings and comforter knottings are not uncommon. Widows are often invited to other people's homes for meals. There they meet others who, like themselves, have outlived their companions. They can share their trials and problems with each other, and give each other encouragement. These gatherings serve a worthwhile purpose, as long as they are not overdone.

Ask any widow who has experienced it, however, and she will tell you that being invited to eat with a family does not bring the satisfaction that being invited to *help* does. With all the help we neighbors can give the widows around us, their lives still contain moments of loneliness, of sighing, of tribulation, and of grief. It is certainly our duty to do what we can to lighten their burden as much as possible by helping them, praying for them, visiting them, and doing what we can to make them feel like useful and needed members of our society.

(Anon., 1-78)

Sharing the Company Meal

An elderly friend of mine lives with her son and daughter-in-law. Being a widow, she doesn't often bother to cook for herself. Many times the young people have had visitors for meals, cooking big meals, usually having leftovers, yet never offering the mother a single bite! So while they are enjoying their delicious meal, she is in her part of the house, eating a cold lunch. I know of several occasions when she even helped her daughter-in-law prepare the meal for their company and again did not get a bite to eat. I simply can't understand how anyone could be so inconsiderate.

If the woman has so little love for her mother-in-law, the least the son could do for his mother would be to bring her a plate of leftovers. After all, she has done a lot for him already. She has always tried to be good to her children and worked hard for them. In return, she is being treated like this and has no partner to share her trouble with. *Wake up, young people!* Some day it may be too late to bring your mother a plate of food. (Anon., 3-76)

In-Laws

Living with In-Laws

People who live with in-laws can perhaps be classed in three categories:

- Those who say it is impossible to live in peace with in-laws.
- Those who say it can be done with sincere effort.
- Those who find it a joy to share a farm with their partner's parents.

Most of the people who wrote us fit in the second category, those who feel it is possible, but it takes effort on both sides.

When we stop and think about the people who don't get along with their in-laws, and don't make any effort to keep it a secret that they don't, we often realize that the problem doesn't stop there. When they get done telling you about the faults of their in-laws, they will start complaining about other people—the neighbors, the ministers, the school teacher, sometimes even their own husbands.

Over the years they apparently have trained themselves so well to look for other people's faults that they can't help but see them [and mull over them]. I feel sorry for people like that. Think of the many friends they fail to enjoy.

When I hear a young woman talk about her mother-in-law, I can't help but think ahead. In a few short years, she will probably have some married sons. Then she will be in the mother-in-law's shoes. Will she be able to get along with her daughters-in-law? Human nature does not seem to improve over the generations. Unless she comes to realize that the biggest problem is within herself, she has little chance of getting along with her future daughters-in-law, or with anyone else, for that matter.   (7-77)

Golden Alphabet for Older People Living with a Younger Family

Always remember that you are the "extra" one.

Be willing to fit into family arrangements.

Cultivate some separate ideas.

Don't expect to share too many family outings.

Early to bed is probably a good rule now.

Find some areas in which you can make your contribution to the work in the home.

Give careful consideration to the children in the home.

Have respect for your in-law. Show your appreciation.

Imperfect humans are everywhere. Remember, there is even one
    standing in your shoes.

Join in family activities, but withdraw sometimes.

Keep a sense of balance between present and past.

Learn to cooperate the best you can.

Make every effort to get along.

Never offer advice; wait until it is asked for.

Open your heart; close your eyes to the mistakes of others.

Pray for guidance in meeting new situations.

Quarrelsome people make life difficult for everyone. Don't be
    bad-tempered.

Resolve not to let your sadness spread through the home.

Start a new interest, a fresh hobby.

Talk only when you have something worthwhile to say.

Undo promptly the mistakes you make.

Value the comforts you enjoy, particularly freedom from
    loneliness.

Wish the best for those who have opened their home to you.

Xpress the appreciation you feel.

Your youth may seem a century ago, but . . .

Zing! Try to keep some of its spirit!

—*Great-Grandparents Living with Their Son and Six Children*

(4-85)

View from the Other End

When we moved in at one end of the house with my husband's parents, my husband and I always had a few children, and we made guidelines for ourselves.

1. Do not expect the grandparents to take care of our children while we do the chores. My husband always said that they had taken care of their own children, so why bother them with ours.

2. Don't expect Grandpa to come out and help with the field work.

3. If Grandpa and Grandma want a few chores yet, as long as they are able, cooperate with them. So we had the chickens and hogs fifty-fifty. We always tried to do the heaviest part of the work.

4. Never get aggravated at Grandparents if they give us advice on

how to be saving more. They started up farming in the early 1900s, and we in the early 1940s.

5. Always pay our rent when due, as we know that's what they depend on for their living.

6. Never interfere with their plans if they want to go somewhere.

7. Never expect them to care for your children so you can both go to the field.

8. Always be very appreciative if Grandma comes over and wants to help with the work.

9. If the grandparents ask you to do something for them, small tasks that they can't do anymore, always do them willingly.

10. Never go to your brothers and sisters and complain about Grandma or Grandpa, especially after one is left alone. Try to work these things out between you in a nice way.

11. Realize that it costs Grandparents something to live, and if Grandma has taken in quilting or quilt piecing to supplement their income, take an interest in her work and respect her for it, even though you don't have time to help. (She doesn't expect it.) Just let her know you care and love her.

—A Widow   ("Letter," Kan., 1-85)

Alone in the House

Once upon a time our house was filled with tears and laughter, quarrels and noisy play, the patter of little feet as in and out they went, the lisping of a baby making some first words. When washday came, it was a pleasure to whisk those dirty clothes into the washing machine and watch the clean things come out. The wash line was then filled and oftentimes the fence beside it, too.

When mealtime came, the table was stretched out long and filled with simple foods. What a pleasure to watch it disappear! With hearty appetites, it took a lot of cooking and baking.

On school days after four o'clock, we'd listen for the sound of feet marching across the porch. On wintry days they would be stomping and sweeping snow off boots before they'd all file in.

There was always a lot of sewing and also the altering of passed-down things. Every time I did it, I would have to marvel at the length of each new dress. The children were growing so fast.

In our family, grandparents also had their place. They took care of themselves and their rooms for many years. Through the busy summer months, they'd come and help us slice pears and apples, clean the beans and berries, and shell the peas. What a time we had, sitting on the porch, grandparents, half a dozen children, the hired girls and myself, each with a dish of peas. Sometimes while working we would sing or play some thinking game.

Now the grandparents are gone. They are laid to rest in the graveyard yonder. Their house is empty. Nothing remains with us but memories. Some are very dear to the heart, but there are also memories of sickness and suffering, patience, and many lonely hours. Did we appreciate them enough while we had them? Those are the thoughts that came to me as I walk through the empty rooms, my footsteps echoing and reechoing.

Only now do I realize how good it was to have the house so full of people, even if I was knee-deep in work. Now I often think of those homes where there are young folks and old folks who are hoping and dreaming of better days to come. Please let me remind you that all too soon those children will grow up and be gone, and the old folks will be laid to rest. Then you may find yourself in a quiet and orderly home—yes, but in a lonely one.

I know. I too have yearned for those things, and now I have them. But something far more precious is gone, and for me never more to return. Now I am all alone in the house.   (Anon., 10-73)

The Handicapped

The Voice of a Least One

You may not be interested in my story, but I will try to explain a few of my troubles and frustrations from trying to live with people who are so much smarter than I. My Christian name is not important. People usually know me as the "retarded child."

Other children think they have troubles, my brothers and sisters, for instance. They often think I am a bother, and don't want me trailing along. I can't run or climb as they can. Then when I become frustrated and cry, they call me "crybaby." I get pushed around, and sometimes they sneak off without me. They let me know in many ways that I'm not wanted, and this makes me feel bad. So I get even.

When Mother and my sisters are working, I want to help. But so often they say, "Oh, you can't do this, and you can't do that." I know I often don't do things right, but I'd like to feel needed, too, sometimes.

My sisters get cross with me at times. They say they would have more friends if it weren't for me. Sometimes I think nobody likes me. Well, I suppose Mother does, but I heard her say that I'm really a trial. I'm not sure what she means, but she sounded a bit discouraged.

I wonder why God makes children like me, anyhow, if we aren't good for anything. It would be nice to feel that other people really liked me, instead of just tolerating me when I go to visit or they come here. Is there anything I can do to make people like me?

("A Page for Shut-Ins," Anon., 6-73)

A Day to Remember

It was quite a day, June 14, 1969. One we will not soon forget, nor wish to. This was the day the annual Gathering for the Handicapped was held at the Berlin School in Ohio.

"I sure wonder what it will be like," I said to my husband as we made the twelve-mile trip by horse and buggy.

"Look," I exclaimed, "there are some people from Lancaster, Pennsylvania. You can tell by the way they're dressed."

As we entered the hall, I could not believe my eyes. Both sides of the large hall were lined with chairs and wheelchairs, with people seated on them as far as we could see—the maimed, the crippled, blind, deaf, dwarfed, and those deformed from disease—come together to spend a day of fellowship.

Behind every such person are days of trials, sorrow, and possibly tears. First comes the shock of reality that it really is so, then the struggle to learn to live with it, the joy of knowing it is God's will, and next comes humble submission.

An aged Amish bishop was asked to speak briefly before prayer, giving thanks for the noon meal. "Friends," he began, before we all bowed our heads, "it is indeed a happy privilege to be here today. I cannot help but almost weep as I look over this crowd of handicapped people. I am encouraged to see everyone in such good spirits, and would like to say one more thing. All of you that are physically crippled or sick are much better off than all those people out in the world who have healthy bodies and minds, and don't use them to the honor and glory of God."

Each one of the handicapped who lacked in one area of perfection sought to bestow his energy on the strength he had left. Each had his own talents.   ("A Page for Shut-Ins," Mrs. Monroe Kuhns, Apple Creek, Ohio, 8-69)

Memories

Twenty-four years ago this month, the first issue of *Family Life* (Jan. 1968) was published. Its cover, as many future ones, was drawn by Sarah M. Weaver, who had begun working at Pathway the previous summer. Besides doing artwork and editing, she wrote poems, songs, short stories, and books. When Sarah died at the age of seventy on November 9, 1991, she was residing at her sister Mary's home in the Doughty Valley of Holmes County, Ohio, where she lived for many years. With her passing, Amish society lost a unique and memorable person.

People who visited Pathway during 1967-1976 will remember Sarah, who throughout much of her adult life was confined to a wheelchair because of muscular dystrophy. She was a ready conversationalist with a kind word and an interesting story for all who visited her.

Children were always fascinated with the "elevator" especially constructed to lower her from her upstairs bedroom-office to the main floor of Pathway. Built under the eaves with a short door opening into her room, it was operated with a hand-cranked winch. Sarah would roll her wheelchair into the boxlike "elevator," and one of us would slowly release the handle that lowered the cable. Sometimes we let the cable out too quickly and would try to slow it down, resulting in a jerky descent for Sarah.

She had a fear of being lowered too quickly and crashing onto the cement floor below. However, she survived hundreds of rides in it with a few tense moments, but with many chuckles, too. The "elevator" is still part of the Pathway scenery and is now used to transport heavy cartons of books to the upstairs for storage.

Another unusual item that was installed for Sarah was a two-inch-wide speaking tube. It stretched from her room upstairs to two different locations downstairs. Through it she could converse with workers without them having to climb the stairs to her room. It, too, was popular with visiting children, who took turns talking through it, then switching ends, as if it was more fun to talk from one end than the other.

Sometime after Sarah moved back to Ohio, the speaking tube was removed, but its memory lingers on. Visitors can still see the wide holes drilled in the ceiling, floor, and walls to allow it to pass through.

These are but a few of the many memories we have of Sarah's years at Pathway. In special memory of her, we are reprinting in this issue her poem, "Winter Has Come," from the first issue of *Family Life*, nearly a quarter century ago.

Winter Has Come
Sarah M. Weaver

Winter has come in our life today—
    The heart is heavy that the frost so soon
    Deadened the flowers that bloomed in June,
And blue skies turned to gray.

Winter has come in our life today,
    Winds whine through the black trees tall;
    Barren vines cling to the garden wall;
The songs of summer passed away.

Winter has come in our life today,
    But summer in hearts may yet remain—
    The past, sunny days in memory retain—
Then winter is sweet as May.

Winter has come in our life today;
   Let storms rage in fury outside;
   There's peace in the heart, where God does abide;
The shriek of storm cannot dismay.

Winter may be with us today;
   But God's love blooms still warm and bright,
   Guiding the wanderer through the cold night;
Winter soon passes away.

("Staff Notes," D. Luthy, 1-92)

Family Life has printed many moving letters and articles by those who lost loved ones to illness or accident. Here are a few:

Illness and Death

Explaining the World

[From a family with three diabetic children, one named Susan, who died at the age of thirty-one.]

In later years she talked much of things that would happen to the church. For hours she could explain and tell why the world is doing like it is. She said, "The people of the church reach out and grab little handfuls of the world at a time. These can be easily consumed without choking." (9-69)

Our Time of Testing

[From a mother whose sixteen-month-old daughter, Naomi, recovered from an illness.]

Many thoughts raced through our minds as we sat by her bedside. We would rather see her die peacefully than to continue suffering as she was. We knew little children were promised the kingdom of heaven. We would sooner see her called home now than to grow up, fall into sin, and be lost forever. But I hope we will not forget the lesson we had needed so badly—to be able to give ourselves up and pray, "Thy will be done." (Mrs. Eli E. Miller Jr., 1-69)

Why

[From a mother whose baby died soon after birth.]

Of course, all the time the question "Why?" comes to our minds. But we should not expect to be able to understand everything in this life, and should never put a question mark where God has put a period.

(Ontario mother, 10-76)

A Memoriam for a Child Who Died of Cerebral Palsy

LaMar Lynn Diener at five years old,
Left this world to join God's fold.
He was one of God's chosen few—
Temptation to evil he never knew.

He left this earth in heaven to sing,
The rest of us closer to Jesus to bring.
Though parents and sisters miss him so—
We're glad for LaMar that he could go.

(Jake Diener, 10-68)

That Dreaded Sickness—Cancer

Who knows? Who will be the next one? Always someone has cancer, and always it was someone else until it happened to our daughter. She seemed to be a healthy, active girl, and we did not realize what cancer was or is until it was in our own family. Oh, the trials and headaches and sorrow that were to be ours within that year. But God knows best, and we feel it was his way of calling us closer to him.

Magdalena was going on sixteen when she started with a slight limp. On January sixth, we took her to a chiropractor. He took X-rays and told us she had strained the muscles in her knee. But the treatments didn't help. He told us he thought she might have rheumatic fever and sent us to our medical doctor. The medical doctor gave her a shot, what he called an arthritis shot, and told us to come back in two weeks if she was no better.

We hoped and prayed this would make her better, but always every morning it was just the same. We thought of cancer but pushed that

thought aside. When the two weeks were up, we took her to the doctor and then to the hospital for X-rays.

Two days later the doctor told us she had a cancer of the bone and
there was only one thing to do: amputate her leg high above the knee.
This would leave her a cripple the rest of her life.

Oh, the sorrow that was ours, and the questions! Why must such
a young, cheerful girl go through all this?

We asked her if she would like to be baptized before going to the
hospital, and she said she would. Our bishop baptized her before she
left for the hospital, and told her if she would be able to come to
church that summer, she could get her instruction then.

We would not let them operate without telling Magdalena what
she had to go through, and if she wanted to live the rest of her life a
cripple. She cried when the doctor told her, but said she would be
willing to go through with the operation.

On February 11, her leg was amputated, and she stood the operation well. Her nurse was a big help, for she explained to Magdalena
how it would feel and what she would have to go through.

Magdalena improved fast, and we got her an artificial limb. She
learned to walk again and only with a slight limp. She was always
singing and never complained in all her afflictions. We feel she was a
living testimony to the rest of us.

She was able to attend church every Sunday and took her place for
instruction with the other young folks, including her oldest brother.
The last Sunday she attended church, the other young folks were baptized and she got to see her brother baptized, which was a joy for all
of us. We feel God had it all planned to be this way.

The last of September, she started with a cough. We took her to the
doctor the first week in October. The doctor told us she had a tumor
in her chest. It was growing inward and pressing on her windpipe,
and there was nothing to do. It was hard to accept, but when we finally gave ourselves up completely to God's will, the load was not so
heavy. It seemed all we could pray was "Thy will, and not ours, be
done."

She had to suffer so much, but was always happy and had a smile
for everyone. Oh, that we could be more like her! Her coughing and

breathing got worse all the time, and it was so hard to see her suffer. But God's ways are not our ways, no matter how hard it is to understand. She was in the hospital three weeks, and two weeks of this time she spent under the respirator.

She had a vision a week before she died. She told us she saw a bright light. Such a bright light she had never seen before. All at once something held her up under her arms and lifted her up, up until she was way up in the clouds, and always this bright light was before her. All at once she saw a beautiful place. She had never seen such a beautiful place before. Then all at once it was gone, and she saw only her father standing beside her.

She was so different that last week. She suffered much, but it seemed she was looking forward to the time God would come to take her home. When the time came, she closed her eyes and went to sleep, never to wake up in this world again.

Magdalena walked to the hospital, and in three weeks the undertaker carried her out. We feel God sent this sickness for our own good. We always think of these words, "The Lord has given; the Lord has taken; blessed be the name of the Lord." We feel we do not have to mourn as do those who have no hope.

It is eight years now since Magdalena died, but she is still missed and always will be. We hope our loss is her eternal gain. Her favorite song was "Where the Soul of Man Never Dies." We have hopes that she is there now. She is a big step ahead of us, and will never return to us. We who are left want to try and live such a life that when our time comes, we can go to be with her.   (2-76)

Who'll Be Next?

"Did you hear that Aaron Riehl drowned?"

"Aaron Riehl?" I said with a shocked tone.

"Yes, on Sunday evening. He and some of the other boys were swimming, and he drowned."

Next morning we walked across the field to the Riehls, since Aaron was single and at home yet. Neighbors were cleaning out the barn for the funeral service. Inside, women were helping, too. Mrs. Riehl greeted us and also the rest of the family that was there.

"Do you want to see Aaron?" she asked.

"Yes," I replied. They took us into the next room, where he lay. To me it looked like he was sleeping, so healthy and strong he looked. I thought I should say something to comfort the brokenhearted mother. But it seemed I couldn't say anything. Since the funeral was the next day, I helped a little to get ready.

The next day I was over to help with the horses, and then went up to the barn for the funeral. Two ministers preached. Sometimes they wept a little, and it seemed to me like a touching service. But I did see some people fall asleep. After a prayer, we viewed the body, and then he was carried to the graveyard.

There the coffin was opened for the final time. After we filed past again, the family gathered to look upon his face for the last time. Something like that is very touching, and I can't see how one can keep from shedding tears. I watched while they looked and wept. Then he was let down into the newly dug grave and covered with fresh earth. I had to wonder how the family felt, as it seemed to rend my heart.

Just recently I stopped at the graveyard and walked to look where he lay. It wondered me, if he could come back and talk to me, what he would say. Would he tell me to lead a more concerned and Christian life? Would he tell me not to think so much of the worry and cares of the world? Would he tell me to think more of the hereafter, of things above and not of things below?

But isn't that what he did tell us by leaving us so suddenly? Wasn't it to get me to think on things like that? But alas, how soon that is forgotten. Who'll be next—the next one to remind me?

(David W. Oberholtzer, Leola, Pa., 1-69)

12
Amish
Controversies

It should come as no surprise to the reader by now that not all of the Amish agree on everything. Indeed, the variety and differences in Amish lifestyle and religious interpretation across North America is surprising. The spectrum runs the gamut, from conservative to liberal, yet all within the scope of the Old Order faith. Naturally, the pages of *Family Life* can become a forum where these different views, opinions, and perspectives may be aired, even if agreement remains elusive.

Changing situations in the modern world often bring on these debates, and such is the case with insurance of different kinds. Some Amish accept liability insurance, but most do not accept commercial life, accident, or health insurance. Thus, the problem of paying large medical bills resulted in the idea of an Amish Aid Plan, and other internal plans that some communities now have. Many saw this as a way for church members to help each other, rather than being "unequally yoked" (2 Cor. 6:14) to an outside, worldly insurance company. Others saw it as insurance in just another form.

Insurance

What About the Aid Plan?

With medical and hospital bills rising steadily over the years, some of our people feel that something should be done to ease this financial burden. I believe it is out of good intentions that some of our people are advocating an Amish Aid Plan. Although it may seem like a good plan, we want to be careful that we do not turn away from what the Bible teaches us: "Trust in the Lord with all your heart, and lean not upon your own understanding" (Prov. 3:5).

Some people feel that the alms are not always used where most needed, but that under the new plan, this will be taken care of. This may be true, but if I understand the aid plan, then it will enable the well-to-do man to collect the same as the poorer man.

The Bible teaches us to give alms and aid the needy, but nowhere can I find that it teaches to help those that don't need it. In Proverbs 22:16, Solomon says, "He that oppresses the poor to increase his riches, and he that gives to the rich, shall surely come to want."

Some people say that the aid plan will help to do away with our people having hospitalization. It may not be as bad as being involved in a worldly company, but yet if it is not scriptural, it cannot be justified.

In the sixth chapter of Matthew, Jesus teaches us how to give alms. If done in secret, our heavenly Father will reward us openly. Under the aid plan, the need to give alms will be lessened. Since each person is expected to pay the same and anyone can collect, we can hardly expect a blessing to be in store for us.

Perhaps at times some of our people think they are not being helped as they should be, but maybe it is God's way of teaching patience.

Suppose God would let everything be taken away from us. I'm afraid any kind of insurance would fail us then. If God would let something like that befall us, it might help us to see our need of putting our complete trust in him. "Humble yourselves therefore under the mighty hand of God, that he may exalt you in due time; casting all your care upon him, for he cares for you" (1 Pet. 5:6-7).

(I. B., Pa., 5-70)

Hospital Aid Plans

The biblical way is to support our poor and needy by giving alms. Insurance plans are the ways of the world. Our giving of alms must be freewill, spontaneous, generous, and in secret (Matt. 5:42; 6:1-4; Luke 12:33; 2 Cor. 9:6-7; Gal. 2:10; 1 Tim. 6:18; Heb. 13:16).

Alms are to help the needy, not to restore the possessions of the well-to-do.   ("Views and Values," E. Stoll, 12-89)

Fire Insurance Plans

Fire insurance plans are pretty well all through the plain people. They have paved the way for two other kinds of insurance that have come in more recently, liability insurance and hospital insurance. Yes, at least two of the three largest Amish communities have their own liability plans, too. Plus, both of these permit liability insurance with commercial companies, too, which will go to court on your behalf.

("Staff Notes," 12-89)

Old Order Mennonites and Insurance

On the insurance issue, the Old Order Mennonites come out clear and strong. We have received letter after letter confirming that they take a consistent stand against all forms of insurance, whether with worldly companies or church plans. They care for their poor and needy, and fire and storm losses, and hospital bills, doing so entirely by freewill alms given to the deacon. ("Staff Notes," 2-90)

Whom Do We Trust: God or Insurance?

Many people are telling us it is no longer safe to live without insurance of some kind. Are we afraid that we will be sued? Do we have insurance to protect us from this? If we do, how is that consistent with what Jesus said, "If any man sue you at the law and take away your coat, let him have your cloak also" (Matt. 5:40).

But you say times have changed. You say that today the world people are merciless and would sue for more than is right, making it dangerous to be on the road [with a horse and buggy].

We agree that times have indeed changed. Four hundred years ago it was even dangerous for God's people to stay at home. Our forebears were inhumanely treated in many ways: their bodies stretched on the rack, their legs broken, their fingers cut off, and their tongues burned out. They were buried alive, roasted, stoned, crucified, drowned, beheaded, left in the cold to freeze, had molten lead poured down their throats, and left in filthy dungeons for years with no companions but the vermin. Yes, times have changed.

Our forebears had no insurance except the protection of God. But today we think we have to have insurance because "it isn't safe to go on the roads." We cannot deny that times have changed, but which period of time would we rather have lived in?

Man wants to do things the human way. He wants to be his own savior. Or he relies on his good works for salvation. All this is trusting in man rather than exercising faith in God.

In today's world, insurance policies are taken for granted as a part of life. This is not surprising for the world does not have faith and does not trust God. They do not have the living God of heaven and earth to rely on for their protection. They do not believe that God will do what he says in the Bible.

Is insurance then limited to nonreligious people? Sadly, the answer is no. Protestants and Catholics alike consider it no sin to protect their belongings, and even their lives, through insurance. The people of this world insure themselves in large companies for protection against loss of property. This may be all right for those who do not know God. But God promises in his Word that he will care for his children, in his own way; the world naturally does not believe this.

Nowadays people say they are afraid they will be sued for all they are worth. They don't want to lose all that they have worked so hard to get. It's too dangerous to be without insurance. Yes, times have changed! But God is the same.   (Monroe D. Hochstetler, 7-69, 6-72)

Should a Christian Sue?

The past days I have again been told of several cases where plain people, yes, Christ-professing people, are suing for damages. There were two cases where there were accidents and the people hurt want to sue the drivers. Is this the way our Lord and Master taught?

Matthew 5:38-42 gives us Christ's teachings on what to do if someone sues us. It would seem that suing others should "not be once named among" us [Eph. 5:3]. In 1 Corinthians 6:1-8, Paul writes about Christians going to law, and says it is not to be.

Romans 12:17-19 says, "Recompense to no man evil for evil. Provide things honest in the sight of all men. If it be possible, as much as lies in you, live peaceably with all men. Dearly beloved, avenge not yourselves, but rather give place unto wrath: for it is written, Vengeance is mine; I will repay, says the Lord!"

In Leviticus 19:18 we find, "You shall not avenge nor bear any grudge against the children of your people, but you shall love your neighbor as yourself: I am the Lord." These words are very clear, and there is more to be found. May we strengthen one another.

("Points to Ponder," Pa., 10-86)

Is Insurance Right or Wrong?

I trust we have been working for treasures and values that cannot be taken away by any court of this land. I trust the court cannot seize your faith in God. I trust they cannot mortgage your love for your fellowman. I trust they cannot seize your hope of a home in heaven.

A lot of people make a difference between liability insurance and other types of insurance. "I don't have anything to cover myself, just for the other person." That makes it sound as though we are willing to take a loss, but we don't want the other person to have to take one. I believe most people have liability insurance to protect themselves. If we have an accident and no insurance, we fear that *we* might have to bear the cost.

That brings us to another common view of insurance—that it is only wrong when it is connected with the world. Frequently, when someone is asked "Do you have insurance?" the answer will be "Not with a worldly company. Our church has its own insurance plan."

The Bible does speak of an unequal yoke (2 Cor. 6:14), but is the "unequal yoke" the *only* scriptural objection to insurance?

We believe that God still wants us to put our trust in him in every way, including the security of our earthly possessions. We believe that holding an insurance policy of any kind detracts from a simple, childlike trust in our heavenly Father.

All insurance plans are based on a worldly sense of fairness, that everyone is equally entitled to keep what he has. This sounds just and fair to the natural man, but it falls short of the standard the Bible teaches. The Bible teaches that there should be a voluntary sharing and equality, none of the believers having too little and none having too much (2 Cor. 8:12-15; Acts 2:44-45). The Bible plan is to help according to the need of our brethren, not according to loss.

Charity should begin at home. If someone has a loss or hospital bill, he should pay what he can himself. Beyond that, his relatives are responsible to help. If the need is still not met, the local congregation will be willing to help. If the need is exceptionally great, sister congregations will be willing to help. If the people have the right love for each other and are willing to share the blessings God has given them, such a plan will work.

Most of us know the Jacob Hochstetler story, that ancestor of many of us who lived in the Northkill Amish settlement of Pennsylvania. Toward dawn one fall morning of 1757, the Hochstetlers awakened to the sound of the dog barking. The house was surrounded by hostile Indians.

The Hochststler family included two grown sons, both of them expert marksmen. The two sons now grabbed their rifles to fend off the Indian attack. But Jacob put a restraining hand on his sons. "No," he said. "We won't shoot. That is not the Bible way. We will trust in God for our protection."

We know the story, how the Indians set the cabin on fire. The Hochstetlers fled to the cellar, where they held out as long as they could by splashing apple cider onto the beams overhead. Finally, they ventured from the cabin unhurt, only to have the Indians murder three of them and take three more captive [see chapter 2, above].

We profess to be children of the martyrs and descendants of the Hochstetlers, and say we will not defend our lives or our loved ones should thieves or other evil men threaten us. It seems strange indeed to me that we can trust our lives and the lives of our loved ones so readily to God's hands, but feel we need some way to make our earthly possessions more secure.   (E. Stoll, 4-84)

Politics

Voting and Propaganda

Almost without fail, come election time in the United States every fourth year, someone will send us a picture or two of Amish at a polling booth.

One of my earliest recollections of a national election was in 1960, when John F. Kennedy was elected. A study published in 1968 showed that in one of our oldest and largest Amish communities, nearly 40 percent of the eligible Amish male population went to the polls in November 1960 and voted against Kennedy. This is hard to believe, as that number must be close to the national average of active voters. To keep a Catholic out of the White House was definitely seen by some as their moral duty.

In some Amish communities, if asked about voting, the following answer is likely to be given: "We don't vote in national elections, but we do vote locally, such as for township officials or on school issues. We consider that different."

When we really stop to analyze it, what reason can we give for not supporting the federal government if we are involved in the civil government on a municipal level?

We have absolutely no business in politics, whether locally or nationally, because politics and propaganda go hand in hand. Propaganda is to give people information in a slanted way, to make people believe the way you want them to believe.

There is hardly a better place to find a good example of this than to return once again to the 1960 presidential election. Those who were anti-Kennedy said he was a Catholic. From an assortment of facts, they implied that if John Kennedy was elected to the White House, he would start persecuting all non-Catholics. And that, of course, was a ridiculous untruth.

Kennedy's foes might have pointed out that at the time Catholics were persecuting our forebears, the Protestants were, too. Martin Luther persecuted Anabaptists, as did the other Protestant Reformers. The only American colony that had full and complete religious and political liberty was the Catholic colony of Maryland, founded in 1634!

The Bible tells us that our duty is to pray for our governments. Our duty is to pay our taxes cheerfully, willingly, and thankfully, yes, even when they are higher than we wish they were.

How strange that back in 1960 people were so frightened the government would interfere with the affairs of the church that, to prevent it, they themselves forgot the principle of separation of church and government, and tried to run the affairs of government.

In conclusion then, the Bible lists four duties for a Christian with regard to government:
- Honor (1 Pet. 2:17)
- Prayer (1 Tim. 2:1-3)
- Payment of taxes (Rom. 13:6-7)
- Obedience (Rom. 13:1-5)

If we do these four, and we do them well, we will have neither time nor need for any more.   ("Views and Values," E. Stoll, 1/2-89)

Alcohol and Buggies

Why do we drive buggies? Is it because cars are wrong in themselves, machines that are evil? Of course not. If the car were wrong in itself, we should not ride in it at any time, not even in an ambulance when deathly ill. Especially not when deathly ill, for who would want to do something wrong when in danger of dying?

But, of course, none of us have ever claimed to be opposed to the ownership of automobiles because they are evil in themselves. We have only said that the misuse of them is wrong. And we have gone on to say that if the use of them is not restricted somehow, history shows that on a community and church-wide basis they invariably do become misused and overused, and turn into a harmful influence.

We drive buggies because we feel that the unrestricted use and ownership of cars becomes a temptation so overwhelming and so great that people do suffer spiritual harm.

Why do we not take the same stand with alcohol as we take with automobiles? God honored in a special way the Rechabites, who refused to drink wine. (Read this little-known story in Jeremiah 35.)

My experience has been that any community allowing the drinking of alcoholic beverages in the homes and neighborhood gatherings will have many problems with strong drink. Such problems might be spared if a consistent and concerted stand were taken against all alcoholic beverages.

That is why I am so puzzled that people who drive buggies to avoid temptation insist on keeping alcoholic beverages around under the excuse that it is not wrong to drink in moderation.

("Views and Values," E. Stoll, 5-86)

Tobacco

As a Mortgage Lifter?

We have often heard of the evils of tobacco, although the use of it is still common among our plain people in some areas. "Wherefore do you spend money for that which is not bread?" (Isa. 55:2). This leaves no room for spending money for the lust of the flesh. Some people are opposed to the use of cigarettes and chewing and call it worldly, but cigars are considered all right. Is it not all a lust of the flesh? Can we read anywhere in the Bible of a worldly "lust of the flesh" and a plain "lust of the flesh"? No, it is all the same, and those who are guilty will not inherit everlasting life.

We hear of famine and starvation in the world, innocent children crying for food, yet we are using God's good farmland for growing tobacco! Beloved brethren, shall we continue to grow tobacco to get rid of the mortgage, or would it be better to get rid of the tobacco first? (Norman Zimmerman, Fleetwood, Pa., 9-68)

A Burning Issue

In our plain churches today, there are few issues more discussed and disputed than tobacco. Although more and more people have a conscience against its use, there are still many who see no harm in tobacco, or attach little importance to it.

We find three lines of thought: (1) Those people who are opposed to the use of tobacco. (2) Those who see no harm in tobacco. (3) Those who are neither for nor against it, but would leave the matter up to the individual conscience.

We will first, in all fairness, consider the common arguments *in favor of* tobacco. There are perhaps four main points upon which tobacco users justify their position.

• God created tobacco, so he must have intended it to be used. Has man a right to pass judgment on the creation of God?

• Our forefathers used it. By condemning tobacco, we condemn them as well. Are we setting ourselves up as holier and better than they?

• Tobacco is nowhere mentioned in the Scriptures. If we set up rulings against it, are we not adding to the Word of God?

• Those who are against tobacco often go to "higher," more-liberal churches. If this is the trend, we are afraid of it.

In stating the case *against* the use of tobacco, the four objections above must be satisfactorily explained.

• *God created tobacco.* Condemning the misuse of tobacco is not condemning God's creation any more than forbidding the eating of poisonous mushrooms would be condemning it.

• *Our forefathers used tobacco.* It is true that many of our immediate forefathers used tobacco, but there probably was a reason. Some of our older people today tell us that in their youth tobacco was thought to kill disease germs in the mouth and digestive tract. Doctors sometimes prescribed it for certain ills. Today, though, hardly anyone lays claim to using tobacco for health's sake.

• *The Bible does not even mention tobacco.* This is true. Neither does it mention movies, television, lipstick, and other modern evils. Tobacco was unknown in Bible times, and first discovered by white men when America was being explored.

• *The "higher" churches are against tobacco, and look where they're going.* What a mistake, this regrettable custom of denominations measuring themselves among themselves instead of with the Word of God!

Of the four points listed in defense of tobacco, this fourth one is perhaps the most difficult. Our Amish churches are constantly being pressured and almost ridiculed by the "higher churches" on the tobacco question. Because of the tension that exists in many cases, this pressuring does more harm than good. Human nature being human nature, the common reaction to any writing from outside the church is one of resentment, and perhaps even a determination *not* to give in on the point in question.

If our churches were free of tobacco and strong drink, and of certain worldly courtship standards (all of which were prohibited in years gone by), we would at once remove the stumbling blocks that are sincerely used by many as excuses to join more-liberal churches. At the same time, we would improve our witness to those churches as a whole, and they might better realize where worldly dress and worldly ways are leading them.

• *What does the world think of our smoking?* Many people have been shocked and disgusted when they first saw an Amish person smoking. They no more expected it of the Amish than they did cheating or stealing. To most people who have heard or read of us, we are serious-minded Christians who have nothing to do with the luxuries and pleasures of the world.

In summary, there have always been members of our churches with strong convictions against tobacco. At times they may have been overly zealous or were not as respectful as they should have been toward those who disagreed with them. This is regretful, for people are seldom persuaded by heated words.

In a number of Amish districts, the use of tobacco is now wholly unknown. In other communities, the practice is gradually being thinned out. In the majority of churches, it is discouraged. This reflects a trend that was not noticeable even a few years ago.

The putting away of tobacco, however, is not a magic cure-all or remedy for lukewarm spiritual conditions. No one really claims as much. But if our bodies are to be temples of the Holy Ghost, as Paul writes in his first letter to the Corinthians [1 Cor. 6:19], then we will want to keep that temple clean, and not willfully harm it for what appears to be mere pleasure.   (J. Stoll, 8-69)

Feeling Trapped

We heartily agree to all you have said, but what can we do? We grow the dirty stuff. It's like this: we live on a small farm in Lancaster County, and I'm sure you know the price of land here. We have no dairy nor the money to put one in. Our lane is too long and washed out for a milkman to come in, and we have no money to pave it.

Shall we buy another farm? Where? With what? Go to another state? We have six small children and want them to attend church with us regularly. We do not want to go away from our church.

What shall we do? Go on farming it against our conscience? But that's what we are doing. To us it is not only a bad habit, but it is bread and shoes. Even with the tobacco check, we only broke even in our first year of farming. What can we do?   (10-69)

Growing Strawberries Instead of Tobacco

We also grew tobacco against our better knowledge, but I could not ask the Lord to bless a crop that was harmful to my fellowmen. Instead of farming tobacco, I planted one-half acre of strawberries in the spring. One year later that patch yielded about $1,600 worth of berries. This was better than the average but, even so, strawberries do pay well, and we can ask the blessing of the Lord upon it.

(Luke Martin, Pa., 12-69)

Working Together

There are a number of communities of Amish churches who are very strict and plain, where the use of tobacco is not only discouraged, but forbidden under penalty of discipline. In our own particular churches, we don't hear much about the subject. I know from experience that many members are opposed to the use and farming of tobacco. But they are afraid to voice their opinions because of the ridicule they would receive from their friends and relatives. They know they would be blamed for wanting to cause an uproar and to leave the church, so they would sooner remain quiet, feeling it is useless to say anything, for "one man can do nothing."

It's time to face the facts and realize that using tobacco is a lust of the flesh, a harm to your health, and a waste of your money. Why don't we work together to get this evil out of our churches? Maybe if we band together, we can do something. Let's see what we can do to use our influence against this evil. (2-76)

Faith in Tobacco?

Though many of our church people both raise and use tobacco, there are also many with growing convictions against it. Many times I have heard the remark, "Without the money tobacco brings in, it would be impossible to stay on the farms." Our faith, it would appear, is in tobacco or our own good management. We are not willing any more to be poor for Christ's sake. Satan must be highly pleased with his work among us. ("Letter," Mr. & Mrs. D. H., Pa., 7-77)

Fighting Bad Habits

I had at one time been a user of tobacco myself. I'm trying to overcome it, and it is a battle not yet quite won. But what gets me is some women complain about their husbands wasting money for tobacco. Yet at the same time they waste money for fancy things to set around in the house, and say this is their "tobacco money." I know of one woman who, according to this, must be "smoking" about six to eight packs a day, and she does not try to keep herself in the *Ordnung* [rules] of the church. This to me looks to be as hard on the soul as smoking is to the health. ("Letter," Pa., 7-77)

Produce Farming Instead of Tobacco

In Lancaster County, with the high price of land plus high taxes, farmers have to have a cash crop. In the years past, tobacco filled that role, and no one worried if nearly every farmer had from two to ten acres. Because it is now known that tobacco is the single greatest health menace in the United States, many want to get away from it. Produce farming is enabling them to do so.

Doctors are finding that vegetables such as carrots and the cole crops (cabbage, broccoli, and cauliflower) give added protection against cancer. People are starting to change their eating habits. This will increase vegetable consumption. Produce farming is the wave of the future for the plain people if they want to stay on the farm and work with their children. ("Letter," Pa., 10-85)

Smoke Hiding Light

Someone, sometime, is going to have to give account for all the seeking souls who turned back to the world when they could not see the light because it was hidden behind too much smoke.

("Staff Notes," E. Stoll, 1-88)

Tourism

Not for Sale

The women in our area are so busy making things for the tourist trade. Yes, it gives them extra money to spend. Of course, even the men are busy. "It pays better than farming," some are saying. Things are being made to cash in on the tourist trade that we would not approve of having ourselves, such as a lot of lawn ornaments and decorations.

Should we not try to make our living by growing or building something that is useful to mankind? Is it any wonder our roads are heavy with the tourists when our own people are joining in to attract them? Some young women don't even have time to sew for their families. What is happening to us? ("The Problem Corner," 7-90)

A Quilting Mother

In our area there is a great demand for handmade quilts. There are several younger and older women who spend some time in the long winter hours to make some quilts to sell. Most of us are not so well-to-do, and every available income is used to help along with average family expenses.

Often the quilt money is needed promptly to help make one payment or another. My husband is grateful to me whenever I sign that quilt check and hand it to him. (He fully supports me in my quilting hobby.) As I think of the hours I labored and the fingers I pricked until they bled, I feel it is a great reward when the quilt is sold and another debt can be paid.

It is not an unusual scene in our home in the winter months to find me engrossed at one side of a quilt, with my preschool youngsters seated on a bench on the other side, eyes sparkling, their faces lit up with bright smiles, eagerly waiting for their mother to begin to tell stories—Bible stories, stories of her childhood, or to teach them to count or play games involving colors and numbers.

In the summer months, you will find me in the fields, laboring at my husband's side, struggling to keep up with the housework, child-care, canning, and all the numerous jobs the average mother and housewife must attend to.   ("Letter," Ont., 6-86)

What Businesses Build Community?

Sam Miller felt a twang of guilt as he put the "For Sale" sign up on his front lawn, surrounded by lawn ornaments. He had felt this way before, like last year when he had introduced his line of wind chimes and designer flowerpots. But was it any worse than Joe across the road, with his trampoline business; or Petes, with their "quilt factory"; or Amos and his exotic animals? It seems that in these times, everybody needs a little extra income. "If the tourists are going to come here anyway, we might as well sell them something," Sam reassured himself.

Sam's problem is not unlike what is happening to many Amish families and indeed whole communities across America. Is it good or all bad? What effect does it have on the plain churches?

Just a few decades ago, these plain people who produced or sold things not used by the church would have been considered wayward or not very conscientious. Thirty years ago, 90 percent of the Amish in Lancaster County farmed. While never a quick way to wealth, farming provided ample income to live on and to buy more farms for the next generation.

By the early 1960s, prices of farmland and inputs had risen to the point that small dairy herds no longer made enough income. The fifty-cow herd became the norm, and included such things as bulk milk tanks, milking machines, and specialized buildings and machinery. But in 1965, a farmer could still jump in and have his farm paid off in fifteen to twenty years.

By the 1980s, the situation had changed. Interest rates hit 18 percent, and farmland in Lancaster County sold for $5,000 to $10,000 per acre. Farms were split until they became too small to split again.

This is coupled with the fact that the Amish population is doubling every twenty years, and half of our people are now under eighteen years of age. Obviously, the problem will not go away. There are too many people and too few acres.

Initially, many farmers began sideline industries to help pay for their farms. The 1977 *Old Order Shop and Service Directory* listed 135 in Lancaster County. An updated 1987 version would likely contain 400-500, a quadrupling in ten years. Many of the shops have turned from sidelines into full-time employment, with 50-70 percent of the workforce now employed off the farm. Many laborers are working in Amish shops or construction to earn enough money to someday buy a farm. Many have given up their dream of farming.

One farmer with a sideline shop and several teenage sons said, "Basically, we're trying to keep the family together. I don't know what will happen when these chaps get married. They'll probably keep right on working here. They'll have the business, and I'll do the farming. We're working out of sheer fright. We've got a forty-acre farm with an eighty-acre mortgage."

At the same time that the economic woes began to beset the Amish, another force was at work. Tourists discovered the Amish. While Lancaster was discovered first, the last twenty years have also seen an upsurge in tourism in almost all plain communities. Millions of tourists jam the roads, attractions, and flea markets. Sleepy farm towns have become thriving "handicraft" and "country-look" centers.

While we would like to blame such activity on outsiders, it is becoming evident that some Amish have welcomed and even encouraged the tourist trade. A very conservative Amish group in a new settlement in Minnesota began allowing car and bus tours of their homes and shops. The tours made a real hit, and today 10,000 visitors a year file through Amish homes there, buying the wares they have for sale. This system is apparently being repeated in other small Midwestern settlements of plain people.

Most of the tourists are anxious to see the plain people. Many are only interested in the nostalgic "country image," and the Amish just happen to be there, like a convenient backdrop or prop. All the tourists have a lot of money to spend. Some want to indulge in food or recreation while there. Some would like a keepsake from the Amish. Others see us as a source of quality country craftsmanship. Others will settle for junk. Literally anything you want to sell will find a willing buyer in the more heavily traveled areas.

While they may be somewhat tied together, we can perhaps divide our discussion into two separate questions.

First, to what extent should we encourage the tourists? The problem lies in the fact that tourist trickles tend to become streams, and streams become torrents. While there is certainly nothing wrong with answering a few well-thought-out questions from a passerby, or selling some baked goods or pieces of furniture to someone outside our own circles, there comes a point when the involvement goes deeper. As tourist numbers swell, we find it brings changes to our families and communities, and these changes are rarely for the good.

We can no longer go out to make hay without an audience. There are always cars stopped on the road in front of our church meetings. Often it is not safe for our children to walk to school or our girls to go to the neighbors. We find that the fabric of our culture is coming apart and we are no longer "the quiet in the land."

Along with the tourists come the developers. They buy up land for attractions and shopping malls. Many visitors decide they would like to live permanently in such a "quaint setting." So lots are bought, and oftentimes Amish crews are hired to build rows of luxury homes. Land prices spiral upward so that farms are neither affordable nor available. Demand for "services" increases. Where does it all stop?

The process is nearing completion in some of the older settlements, most notably Lancaster County. But other settlements, such as [the counties of] Holmes [Ohio] and LaGrange [Ind.], are also well on the way. Perhaps it can't be stopped, but will have to result in the migration of concerned plain people to new settlements. For those communities where tourism has not become a problem, don't start it. We don't need tourist dollars that bad. Let us work quietly and with dignity on our farms and leave the public contact and high-visibility jobs to other people.

There is a second question. To what extent should we be making or selling things we would not use ourselves? Most of us would not be able to imagine an Amishman operating a used-car dealership or opening a jewelry store. But how much different is that really from selling Rototillers or other items not used by our church? And what is the difference between jewelry to adorn someone else's body, and lawn ornaments or patio furniture to adorn someone else's house and yard?

A similar dilemma lies in the very production of nonessential or nonuseful items. The plain people have long been known as practitioners of basic industry and craftsmanship. Not so long ago, this was still true. Our farmers produced staple foods, our welders and blacksmiths produced wagons, tools, and machinery. Our woodworkers produced lumber, furniture, houses, and barns. Today, we often find ourselves producing decorations and playthings for an increasingly sick, decadent society.

When we consider this subject, two Scriptures immediately come to mind. In James 4:4 we read, "Don't you know that the friendship of the world is enmity with God? Whosoever therefore will be a friend of the world is the enemy of God." How close a relationship dare we have with the world before we become its friend? Friends are those who help us and encourage us. If we encourage the world by helping supply the items they desire for the wanton, extravagant lifestyles, are we not then their friends?

In Romans 1:32 we read, "Who knowing the judgment of God, that they which commit such things are worthy of death, not only do the same, but have pleasure in them that do them." Yes, have pleasure in them. Do we enjoy the company of well-dressed society high-rollers with their flattering talk and sophisticated airs? Are we pleased that our knickknacks and quilts are going to New York or Chicago, or perhaps becoming decorations or wall hangings at a fashionable restaurant?

If we truly see the dangers in the modern lifestyle and all that goes with it, how could we encourage someone else to indulge in it? What are we really telling our children? Is our light shining as bright as we think it is? Or have we possibly become like the Pharisees of old, with one foot in the world and the other in the church?

What can we do about it? Well, for one thing, we should look honestly at our income-producing sidelines and ask ourselves why we are involved. Do we need the money to make ends meet on the farm? If so, off-farm income doesn't have to mean working away or selling questionable items. There are many useful, community-minded businesses we can pursue right from the home or farm. If we really don't need the money, then why dabble in something that is questionable? If engaged in a small business for a living, ask yourself again, "Is it a community-building occupation? How big is the business really becoming? Am I living a lifestyle that is higher, easier, or more luxurious than the farmers in our church?"

One builder of mini-barns who sells over a thousand a year said, "The off-farm jobs are a bad thing for the Amish. Prosperity was never good for Christians. Too much money is not good for anybody. Money is the root of all evil. Too much prosperity is no good."

(Robert Alexander, 10-90)

Profiting from the Amish Label

Do we stand alone? What do others think about using the Amish name to make money, such as advertising "Amish quilts," or "Amish girl wants housework," or "We serve dinners in our Amish home"? Is there any wonder some settlements are overrun by tourists? What do others think about this? I would like to know.   (Anon.)

Misusing the Amish Name

No, you do not stand alone. We also feel it is wrong to use the Amish name to sell something. Here in Lancaster County, the tourist bureau and many local businesses advertise, using the Amish name to increase their trade. This is bad enough without us ourselves doing it.

Our Anabaptist forefathers suffered persecution for their faith. Nowadays the Amish name is being exalted far too much, and I don't believe it is for our good. Even if we feel we are selling an exceptional product, God should be given all the glory, who gave us our talents.

I feel also that it is wrong to make or sell Amish dolls to shops and stores that are frequented by tourists. We do not dress the way we do just to put on a show, so why should we put dolls out for the tourist public? May we strive to be a more humble people.

(Lancaster Co., Pa.)

Others Advertising the Amish Name

We live in a settlement where lots of tourists come through every year. I don't know of any Amish people using the name Amish to advertise. Rather, it is the English people using our name so they can make extra dollars by selling Amish eggs, Amish cooking, etc., even though no Amish are involved. (Holmes Co., Ohio)

Using Religion to Sell Products

No, you do not stand alone in your beliefs about using the Amish name to make money. I am afraid the Amish name is held too high by some of our own people. We are to be on the quiet side, and withdrawn from the activities of the world. Yet when you pick up the paper and see the word *Amish* being published by our own people, it looks like they are using their religion to sell their product.

(Tourist City, Pa.)

Pleasing the Lord?

Lo and behold, lots of the Amish-made quilts are not plain anymore, but are made to suit the worldly people. Now the Amish are also using them in their own homes. Yes, it about breaks the heart to see some of these Amish-made crafts, which I feel are mostly idols.

Let us not do anything we would not want to be doing when the Lord comes. We see ads of Amish girls wanting housework, and yet some of these girls are not even dressed Amish, except for a little cap.

("The Problem Corner," Miller, Ohio, 7-92)

Tourists May Strengthen Our Faith

Coming in contact with tourists every day may have a detrimental effect on some of our people, but there is another effect on many of us. Over and over they tell us we have something worth keeping. This has a strengthening effect on us.

("Letter," R. J. Y., Millersburg, Ohio, 12-91)

Giving an Answer for Our Hope

There is a difference between the tourist who is out seeking sights and the traveler who is genuinely interested in the beliefs of a religious group. The latter type deserves our attention and a fair answer.

The idea of being viewed like some specimen on display in a museum is not exactly to our liking. Also, being in the spotlight of the public eye is an undesirable situation.

It does seem strange that we, as Amish people, are suddenly objects of great interest to many people. This is such a contrast to the times of our Anabaptist forebears, who were ridiculed and persecuted as an unwanted people. Now, as the world struggles under the pressure and tension of modern living, there is much interest in us. For some, the interest goes deeper than just our lifestyle, for they can see that it is only a part of our precious faith. We certainly have the responsibility to give such people an answer for "the hope within us" [1 Pet. 3:15].   ("Insights and Ideals," Cephas Kauffman, 1-91)

Our Greatest Danger

What is the greatest danger facing the plain people today? This is the question asked in the January 1979 issue of Family Life. *We received more than fifty answers. Judging from the letters we received, the greatest threat is prosperity—too-much and too-easy money.*

Money Drawing Us from Spiritual Things

With money, so many things are possible, and these things tend to draw the mind away from spiritual things. Most of us don't feel that we have a lot of money, especially when we are just trying to keep up with those around us. But if we just stop and think what all we have, what comforts, yes, what luxuries we enjoy, and then think how our grandparents and their grandparents lived—we see that we could get along with a lot less money. We see so many fancy new houses, and those who do not have new ones must remodel theirs.

(Belleville, Pa.)

The Second Greatest Danger Is for the Young Folks

So many are working in factories and worldly homes, and I am afraid that is where some of the trouble lies. The trend of the world today is for higher wages and less work.

—*Hoping for a Change* (Pa.)

Young Folks and the Worldly Lifestyle

I feel that in this community, the worldly style of life among the young folks is the greatest danger facing the church today. Around the age of sixteen or seventeen, the majority dress differently, and many of the boys get cars if they can afford one. Those who do not follow this are suspected of being queer. The fashionable clothes, hippie hair, and cars are used to freely mingle with the world at fairs, carnivals, movies, ball games, or just to hang around at public places.

(Pa.)

Young Folks Needed to Carry on the Faith

I am a young person and I feel the greatest danger the churches face is *us*. Naturally, if our churches are to prosper, we are the ones who will have to carry on the faith. The young people are watching you older ones to see where you stand, and to see what we can get away with. (Ind.)

The Third Greatest Danger Is Lukewarmness

One of the greatest dangers facing our churches is being too self-satisfied and complacent with ourselves and our churches just as they are. Life can be compared to rowing across a swift stream. We must unceasingly continue our efforts of paddling against the current, or we shall drift downstream to the rocks and rapids and not reach the other shore. (Pa.)

A Cure for Empty Lives?

Some lukewarm members can trace their problem back to when they were young. Several years later they found these times to be empty and degrading, but where do they turn? Instead of repenting and living fully for God, these lukewarm members go to some more-liberal church, and then later proclaim how they had lived such cold, carnal lives, how ungodly they were then and how godly and righteous they now are. Is this the true Spirit of Christ, or is it the "old man" striking out in a new suit of clothes?

—*A Fellow Pilgrim*

13
To Be Nonviolent

As described at the beginning of this book, the early Anabaptists suffered torture and death for their beliefs, yet met their fate with quiet resignation. They resisted with words but not with physical violence. They showed their faith and changed other people's lives by their examples, not by force. This heritage of nonresistance continues and has put some of the Amish to their most severe personal tests in the twentieth century.

We read the horrible stories of intolerance from hundreds of years ago and feel that we are so much more "civilized" today. Yet it is sobering to be reminded that humanity's greatest atrocities toward his fellow humans occurred just a few decades ago, in our own lifetime.

The Revolutionary War, Civil War, World Wars I and II through to the Vietnam War—these violent times created challenges for Amish, Mennonites, and others who believed in nonviolence and Jesus' call to love the enemy. Those who refuse to take up arms to defend their country are often viewed with suspicion, even hatred.

These stories are a lesson in how societies respond to those who are "different," and in the power of faith during adversity. Regardless of what your personal feelings may be in these matters, you will come away pondering the issue of religious freedom in an increasingly violent and intolerant world.

The Revolutionary War

In 1776, when the American colonies declared their independence from England, all the colonists were expected to help fight the English. Naturally the Amish, being nonresistant, refused to do this. Because they refused to be drafted into the army, some Berks County [Pa.] Amishmen were arrested. These men were placed in prison. After a speedy trial, the Amish prisoners were sentenced to death and the date of execution was set.

The death penalty, however, was never put into effect. A minister in the local German Reformed church pleaded with the authorities to release the Amish prisoners. He said they had fled Europe to avoid military service and that they shouldn't be expected to do in America what their consciences had told them was wrong in Europe. He also testified that the Amish are quiet and unassuming people, doing harm to no one. Because of his testimony, the government freed the men, but not without fining them and making them pay a tax for hiring a substitute.   ("Yesterdays and Years," 11-71)

Amish Settlers and the Civil War

It was the time of the Civil War, in the land bordering on the Mason-Dixon Line and the western tip of Maryland. Daniel Beachy, the Amish bishop in that region, and his people had heard rumors of the war in the East and South, and they knew the danger of being caught in destructive border skirmishes.

A quiet and peace-loving people, Daniel and his followers prepared for such an emergency, not by loading their muskets, but by planning escape routes for their families and hideouts for the livestock. Daniel's wife, Elizabeth, packed a set of clothing for each of their eight children in a bedsheet, which she planned to hide in a nearby cave if the need arose. This took more than a trip to town to buy extra clothing. It meant countless hours of spinning, weaving, knitting, and sewing by hand.

It turned out that no actual battles were fought in their part of the Alleghenies, near the village of Aurora, West Virginia. But to the north of them lay the B & O Railroad, coveted by the Confederates. And through their area passed the main turnpike (now U.S. 50), also a prized possession.

Daniel Beachy realized early in the war that this land could well become an easy target for the Confederate raiders. As bishop of the Gortner-Aurora congregation, he went about encouraging his flock to put their trust in God, but not to ignore any warnings that might reach them.

From their farm nestled in a valley just northwest of Aurora, the Beachys saw many troops of both Union and Confederate soldiers, marching on the turnpike. In fact, one troop of Union soldiers, apparently stationed to guard the pike, camped for several weeks on the Beachy farm. Although they were of a friendly nature, the soldiers did take some of the Beachys' supplies. When the troops left, the young Beachys swarmed the campsite and enjoyed some hardtack candy the soldiers left behind.

The time passed peacefully for the Amish until Crist Petersheim, a neighbor of the Beachys and a member of his church, was captured by the gray coats (Southerners). Mrs. Petersheim, having no clue as to what had become of her husband, spent a week of anxiety alone with six small children. After forcing Mr. Petersheim to haul supplies for them with his team and wagon for a week, the soldiers permitted him to return to his home.

To add to this, in March 1863 the Federal Conscription Act was passed; it made no provision for conscientious objectors. News of this law reached into the larger Amish settlement in northern Garrett County, Maryland, and Somerset County, Pennsylvania. The law did permit, however, the hiring of substitutes or the payment of a $300 tax instead of subscription [signing up to serve in the army].

How did the Amish respond to this law? Records show that the Amish Mennonite churches of Garrett and Somerset Counties raised a sum of $16,000 to pay the taxes of their drafted members. Apparently drafted men reported personally to headquarters and paid these dues. But this was all a part of the wartime, and they took it in stride.

Daniel Beachy apparently escaped being drafted, but his brother-in-law, John V. Tice of Bittinger, Maryland, was called. He left his wife (Daniel's sister) alone with three small children to care for the farm when he went to fulfill his obligations. No word was heard from him until he returned during the night three weeks later. Aroused from sleep, Mother Tice rushed out of bed to open the door for him. Then, overcome with joy, she dropped helpless to the floor, and John half carried her back to bed.

In spite of impending dangers, the Gortner-Aurora Amish continued to hold church services every two weeks in their scattered homes. Always aware of the danger of being captured, Bishop Beachy regularly made the long trips about this community by horseback to minister to his flock.

Then came the raid led by General William Jones in the spring of 1863. Jones's primary purpose was to destroy the bridges on the turnpike and cripple the B & O Railroad. His second objective was to collect horses, cattle, and supplies. He was forced to do this by the sea blockade which had caused a serious shortage of many items in the South. Wild inflation made the price of a pair of shoes to soar to $400 and a barrel of flour sold for $1,000.

Unlike the destructive raid that General Sheridan led into the South, General Jones's orders were to seize cattle, horses, and supplies indiscriminately, but to respect other private property at all times. So the Amish escaped the destructive loss that some communities suffered.

The uncertainties and horrors of war, however, did tax the nerves of the Amish people. Anxiety erased some of the sparkle from Daniel Beachy's courageous eyes. It is said that an elderly Amishman became emotionally disturbed, supposedly from worry. Seeing danger in everything, he insisted that his sons should restack a pile of logs that lay with ends facing his home, lest they explode like cannons and shoot his family.

On April 26, 1863, a beautiful Sunday morning after days of heavy rains, Daniel Beachy mounted his dainty mare, Baldy, and set out for Gortner to preach at the Joseph Slabach farm. Riding along the turnpike, he was joined by two of his members, Crist Petersheim and Peter Schrock. As the three men traveled eastward, they met Confederate soldiers straggling along the muddy road. Approaching the Maryland state line from the west, they rode squarely into the main force of General Jones's army.

The men drew their horses up on the road bank to let the soldiers pass. But a trooper, evidently in a jovial mood, approached Mr. Beachy, jerked off his hat, and clapped his own officer's cap on him. At the same time, he put Beachy's broad-brimmed hat on his own head. After a round of loud guffaws about the joke, he again changed hats as well as his manner, gruffly demanding that Mr. Beachy dismount and give up his horse.

Daniel remained calmly seated. His blue eyes were fearless as he replied, "Sir, I cannot give up my horse. I need it for farming."

The trooper stared in disbelief at this man who refused to obey his orders. Clearing his throat, he said roughly, "Sir, if you don't get off that horse, I'll put you off." Profanity rattled about like hailstones as he began to unbuckle the saddle girths.

Still Mr. Beachy remained seated. Crist Petersheim spoke up: "Sir, we are on our way to church, and this man is our preacher. How shall he get there if you take his horse?"

Instantly the trooper stopped, glancing about uneasily for the officer in command. "Why didn't you tell me sooner?" Quickly rebuckling the saddle girths, he sent the men on their way.

Urging their horses into a brisk trot, they hastened on to the Maryland state line and turned north on the Oakland Road, which was clear. Arriving at the Slabach farm, Daniel Beachy and a fellow minister held a short church and prayer service.

After church they learned that Colonel Harmon, with a detachment of a thousand men, had captured the Union troops on guard at Oakland and had invaded the town. The soldiers were now destroying bridges, crippling the railroad, and scouring the countryside for cattle, horses, and supplies.

Men hurriedly drove their cattle and horses into hiding. Daniel Beachy and his companions retreated to a deep woods and stayed under cover until dusk, when they set out through the forest for their homes. They forded treacherous streams, swollen by heavy rains. Finally, Daniel tied his horse in the forest near his home and walked home, carrying the heavy saddle.

Meanwhile, Elizabeth Beachy, at home with her eight children, was alarmed at the sight of hundreds of soldiers carrying the Confederate flag, marching westward on the turnpike. But where was her husband? Quickly she went to the loft and got several pieces of cured meat. Taking them out in front of the house, she dropped them into a hole between some rocks and covered them with sticks and stones. Then she instructed her two older sons, ten and thirteen years old, to drive the cattle and horses back of the barn, beyond the lime quarry and into the forest. They left only one old horse in the stable.

While the soldiers stopped in Aurora to raid David Ridenhour's store of everything eatable or wearable, the boys made a fast getaway with the livestock. Mother Beachy's alarm grew as a group of the men in gray turned in at the Beachy lane. Horrible stories about Confederate raids raced through her mind. With frightened children clinging to her skirts, she clasped baby Lena to her breast and watched them approach. But the men went past the little one-room log house and rode on to the stable.

The soldiers wanted cattle and horses and forage for their horses. They fed their horses and left, taking the Beachy's old horse and leaving a worn-out horse in its stead. Three times during the day, small groups of soldiers came in to the farm to feed their horses, each time exchanging a worn-out horse for the one that had rested in the stable. The horse that they left there at last was worthless.

As the long afternoon wore on and Daniel did not return, Elizabeth Beachy became more uneasy. At twilight, when the coast was clear of soldiers, she slipped back to the forest with the boys to help milk the cows. Returning to the house, she took care of the milk, washed up, smoothed her brown hair under her white covering, and tried to eat a bit of the supper that twelve-year-old Mary had prepared.

When the dishes were washed and the moon had climbed high above Backbone Mountain, she sent the older children to bed in the loft. Mechanically, she tucked two small girls into the trundle bed, put the six-month-old into the cradle, and rocked her to sleep. Then she sank into a chair to wait and pray for her husband. Weariness overtook her and she dozed.

Suddenly she woke with a start. Clutching wildly at her throat, she listened. "Soldiers," she gasped, "and they are surely coming to the house." In the candlelight, she glanced at the children, asleep in the corner of the room. Desperate, she sprang up and pushed a heavy wooden chest against the door.

The loud clatter as Daniel Beachy dropped the saddle on the porch terrified her. Then Daniel spoke her name. A strange weakness overtook her. No longer spurred on by fear, she could not move the chest but had to call her sons from the loft to come help let their father in.

During this time, the Jacob Swartzentruber family, who had moved from Pennsylvania to Redhouse, Maryland, became the victims of numerous raids. We do not know the exact date of the one that forced them to move back to Pennsylvania, but probably it was this same Jones's raiding party on April 26, 1863.

At dawn, the Swartzentrubers were routed from sleep by hundreds of starving soldiers, demanding food. When the bread supply was exhausted, they ordered Mrs. Swartzentruber to make buckwheat cakes. The starving rebels crowded into the kitchen, eating batter from the bowl, or pouring it directly onto the stove and devouring the half-baked cakes. They swarmed around the spring like thirsty cattle and drank up all the water. They raided the pantry and cellar of all that was eatable. Some jerked a setting hen from her nest and ate her eggs, raw, unhatched chicks and all. Others milked the cows and slaughtered one, roasting the meat over open fires on the lawn.

When the soldiers left, they took bedding, clothing, Mr. Swartzentruber's watch, and all that could be carried along. They drove their cattle and horses ahead of them. (Undoubtedly these were among the 1,000 cattle and 1,200 horses that General Jones reported having sent South after his raid.) This was a hard blow to the Swartzentrubers, who had lost their first two infants to death in the preceding two years.

When the congregation shepherded by Daniel Beachy heard of their plight, it came to their rescue. An aunt who lived there took them into her home until arrangements could be made to move them back to Pennsylvania.

Even after these episodes, the little Amish colony refused to be dismayed. Bishop Daniel Beachy continued to lead his flock in love and unity. Every two weeks they gathered to hear his admonitions.

Although lines of anxiety did show in Elizabeth Beachy's kindly face, her hands were never idle. In spite of her many duties, she found time to be neighborly. Committing herself into God's care, she walked miles to carry a nourishing dish or offer a helping hand to a sick neighbor.

Besides the anxiety of war, there were the family crises that they went through together. Unaided by a doctor, Daniel and Elizabeth ushered three new babies into their home during this time. And their three-month-old Susie had been laid to rest beside her little brother in the graveyard on the hillside.

Undoubtedly the Beachys rejoiced when the end of the war was announced. No longer would Father need to be on the lookout for raiders as he went about his work. No longer would Mother need to defy danger to make her neighborly calls.

Today, as one drives through the settlement at Gortner, there are no scars to show what took place there a century ago. Old Backbone Mountain is mute to what happened here in his shadow. But the Amish descendants tell us these fragments of the past.

(Mary Elizabeth Yoder, 3-71)

World War I and the Arrest of an Amish Bishop

The United States entered World War I on April 6, 1917, and had as its main opponent Germany. To support its war efforts, the U.S. government issued a series of five war bonds known as Liberty or Victory Bonds. These were not taxes but requests by the government that the American citizens loan money to help wage the war. The buyer of a bond received from 3½ to 4¾ percent interest. The American people loaned their government nearly 21 billion dollars by purchasing war bonds.

Since purchasing war bonds was to be voluntary, the Amish, Mennonites, and other nonresistant Americans should not have been affected. But the bonds were voluntary in name only. Each community was assigned a quota and had a committee of local citizens to see that the quota was reached. This meant that the local people put pressure on their fellow citizens to buy war bonds. It was a classic example of high-pressure salesmanship. Anyone who hesitated to buy a war bond was labeled a "second-class citizen," "traitor," or "friend of the enemy."

Since the war was being waged with Germany, all American citizens of German background were naturally suspected by their neighbors as being possible traitors. One way to test them was to ask them to buy war bonds. This anti-German sentiment was felt by all Americans of German descent. Since the Amish and Mennonites were "Germans" too, in the public's opinion, they felt the pressure quite a bit. But the pressure differed from area to area.

Following are five statements by present-day elderly Amishmen who remember what the pressure was like at the time the war bonds were being urged upon all Americans:

War Bonds in—
Lancaster County, Pennsylvania

The first airplanes I ever saw in flight passed over us in the fall of 1918. They were dropping leaflets urging purchase of bonds. I did not hear of much pressure but heard several ministers, one a bishop, had been somehow pressured to buy, but were able to back out again. It seems we here in Lancaster County have had lenient draft boards and a good feeling between us and "outsiders."

LaGrange County, Indiana

I remember there was something about buying war bonds, but I don't remember if the Amish bought any or not. I think it was to each individual as he felt about it. I know I didn't buy any. There was some violence going on, like painting buggies or houses with yellow paint.

Johnston County, Iowa

I got married the summer of 1918. My wife and I worked for Dan Fisher, a Mennonite minister. One day as I was plowing, there came a row of cars. I first wondered if there was a funeral, but soon saw them parking at Dan's farm buildings. My first thought was to go in, since it was almost time for dinner and the women were alone. Then I thought maybe they were better off without me being there. They did no violence, but the women heard them making remarks about Dan not having purchased war bonds. They might have been there for an hour.

I once was called with two others to appear before some men and took them to be officers. They said we should buy war bonds. They let us go for that time and said we should appear later, but we got no call.

We were watched about our German talking, and some who were caught at it were given some "rich" talking.

Mayes County, Oklahoma

We have two Amish women here who remember a little about the time of war bonds, but don't think their parents bought any. They remember the time they went to meet their mothers and one horse fell, breaking the tongue of the spring wagon. A man helped them by letting them use his wagon. Then he happened to hear them talking Pennsylvania German, which made him mad. He said all "Dutch" [German] people should be hung. This scared the girls pretty badly.

This was at Couteau, and it seems the people did not give the Amish much trouble. But we have people here, Russian Mennonites, and most of their addresses were Inola. They had a lot of trouble. One church was just on the edge of town, and it was burned. They had church in a barn, and it was also burned. They spoke all German at that time.

Reno County, Kansas

Yes, I remember well of some of the pressure and also the hard feeling it gave at that time. I was a young man and was just ordained to the ministry a year before. Of course, they thought I just took up the ministry to get exempted from the draft, and said I had to get an affidavit to show I was ordained by lot. Then, since my dad was bishop, he made up a writing and got a few signatures, so that settled that.

They then came and said every member over twenty-one has to buy a war or liberty bond. The Amish didn't want to buy any because we felt it would be helping the war. Well, we had a real nice banker here in our little town of Yoder. He helped us all he could. So our people, just to try and keep peace, went and bought bonds and gave them to the banker as a present and never asked for the money back.

Since we were married a few years, we were very hard up at the time. But there was no other way. So we had to borrow $75 to buy a bond. So we just did like most of the others. But I remember a few older men who refused to buy any. One day some officers came to Noah Beachey's, knocked at the door, and asked Mrs. Beachy where Mr. Beachy was. She said she didn't know where he was. But they didn't believe her and opened the door and went in and hunted in every room, closets, under beds, and everywhere.

Mr. Beachy had seen them come and had hidden outside somewhere. So when they couldn't find him, they told her if he didn't buy a bond by such a time, they would tar and feather him. They were in much fear for a few days and then went and bought one.

Then the officers went over to Mr. Kaufman. They warned him the same way, then also went to a Mr. Bontrager. So I think after it was all over with, everybody did the same and just turned the bonds over to the banker.

Conscientious Objection to War

War bonds were a new type of test for the Amish churches. Should they or could they in conscience purchase the bonds? The ministers felt their members should not purchase any, for by doing so they would be helping to wage the war. But some churches, such as the Reno County (Kan.) church, experienced such pressure that they reluctantly purchased bonds, but refused to accept them back after the war was over. To some people this seemed a solution, and to others a compromise. Those who felt it was wrong to purchase bonds, even under severe pressure, compared the situation to that of Amish boys who were being drafted.

The United States made few provisions for conscientious objectors when war was declared on April 6, 1917. The only provision was that they must go to the army and wear the uniform, but could perform noncombatant work. So the Amish boys were drafted, sent to the army camps, and expected by their home churches to remain steadfast under mockery, persecution, and severe pressure. But now back home, members were going partway and reluctantly purchasing the war bonds. This went down hard with many Amish people, for they wondered how their boys could be expected to bear the test in the army camps if they heard that the people back home were compromising.

With such thoughts in mind, one person decided something should be said about the situation. Manasses E. Bontrager, bishop of the now extinct Amish church at Dodge City, Kansas, put his letter in an envelope, sealed and stamped it, and mailed it to *The Budget* office in Ohio, which printed it for May 15, 1918:

Letter from Dodge City, Kansas, April 24, 1918

A greeting in our Savior's name. People are all well, excepting some colds. The weather is cool again. We're having more rain than usual this spring. Oat fields are nice and green. Much more barley is being put out this spring than usual on account of the wheat failing. A few farmers think they have some wheat that will be harvested. Some corn is planted.

We are living in a time when the gospel is preached over a wider area than ever before, but in what state of affairs the world is in! A world war! Never since the time of Julius Caesar was so large a portion of the civilized nations at war, never were such destructive weapons used to destroy life, never were the nonresistant people put to a more trying test in our country. How are we meeting the general problems confronting us? Shall we weaken under the test, or are we willing to put all our trust in our dear Savior? Are we willing to follow his footsteps?

Our young brethren in camp were tested first; let us take a lesson from their faithfulness. They sought exemption on the ground that they belonged to a church that forbids its members the bearing of arms or participating in war in any form.

Now we are asked to buy Liberty Bonds, the form in which the government has to carry on the war. I am sorry to learn that some Mennonites have yielded and bought the bonds. What would become of our nonresistant faith if our young brethren in camp would yield? From letters I received from brethren in camp, I believe they would be willing to die for Jesus rather than betray him. Let us profit by the example they have set for us so far, and pray that God may strengthen them in the future.

Many people can't understand why we don't want to defend our country. Christ said, "Render unto Caesar that which belongs to Caesar, and to God that which belongs to God." Caesar protects our property, for which we should willingly pay our taxes as Christ asked us to. The money, its denomination, and value is estimated and made by the authority of civil government. But our coming in this world, our intellects, our physical powers—these do not belong to Caesar. If he claims them to defend him, Christ's laws strictly forbid our yielding to such a claim.

How many of our brethren have gone to the ballot box, giving their choice who should govern our country? Will the same brethren respond to the call of the men whom they helped put in office? Paul says, "Be ye not unequally yoked with unbelievers." Are we pilgrims and strangers? Or do we think we must use our right of citizenship at the ballot box? Christ said, "My kingdom is not of this world." If we claim citizenship in Christ's kingdom, can we serve two masters? Christ said, "Ye cannot serve God and mammon." We cannot have citizenship in two earthly kingdoms at one time. Much less, I think, can we claim one in a heavenly kingdom and one in an earthly kingdom.

Self-defense is the first law of nature, it is often said. Did Christ appeal to self-defense? No. When the chief priests and captains of the temple and the elders came to him, Jesus said to Judas, "Betrayest thou the Son of man with a kiss?" Christ did not defend himself, but Simon Peter drew the sword, smote the high priest's servant, and cut off his right ear. Here is an act of the first law of nature; the cause seemed to Peter to demand it. Did Jesus justify it? No.

Instead, Jesus showed his sympathy for humanity, healed the wounded man, and said to Peter, "Put up your sword into its place, for all who take the sword shall perish with the sword." He did not say *should* perish *by* the sword, but *with* it. So all who used the sword or other weapons of carnal warfare and have not repented must perish, and all the weapons of our warfare will perish with them.

On April 21 I attended two funerals. One a mile north from us was for an old man nearly eighty years old, a good neighbor, but who never belonged to church. I took a great lesson as the minister in his sermon called him brother. Oh, how can we call such a person a brother? Is it any wonder that the people are satisfied to live without confessing Christ? I heard much of heaven in their sermons, but never a mention was made of hell. They often brought forth the name of Christ, but the name of Satan was never mentioned. The same Jesus who told us about heaven also told us about hell. If we fear God, we need not fear Satan; as we have sown, so we shall reap.

If people are deceived through preaching, is it any wonder they go to war with one another and call it right? I must often wonder that there is so much strife and misunderstanding in some localities among the nonresistant people. I was in hopes this terrible war would bring all church members closer together. A house divided against itself cannot stand.

—*M. E. Bontrager*

Violation of the Espionage Act?

Several months passed. A U.S. marshal arrived at the peaceful Kansas farm of fifty-year-old Manasses Bontrager and arrested him. The marshal said that Bontrager had written a letter to an Ohio newspaper. Part of the letter was in violation of Section 3, Title I, Espionage Act of June 15, 1917. He along with *The Budget* editor, S. H. Miller, would have to appear before a judge in federal court in Cleveland, Ohio, the federal district in which *The Budget* was published.

Manasses's second son remembers when the marshal took his father away: "The way I remember it, the U.S. officer treated father with all consideration possible. He did not mistreat father or use any harsh words. When they went to the depot in Dodge City, he bought a ticket and gave it to father so that nobody on the train could know he was under arrest. I think father stayed in a hotel room while in Cleveland."

On August 5, the trial of Manasses Bontrager and S. H. Miller was held. Following is an account of the trial as reported on page one of Cleveland's largest newspaper, *The Plain Dealer*, on August 6, 1918:

The Trial of Manasses Borntrager and S. H. Miller

Federal Judge Westenhaver yesterday imposed a fine of $500 on Rev. Manasses E. Bontrager of Dodge City, Kansas, a bishop in the Amish Mennonite church, after Bontrager had entered a plea of guilty to violation of the espionage act.

The bishop, a man with long whiskers, which nearly hid his face, and flowing hair, listened as the judge denounced activities of conscientious objectors who try to convert others to their antiwar views.

With the bishop was his brother, Levi Bontrager, also a leader in the Mennonite church, hundreds of members of which, called to cantonments by the draft, have refused even to perform noncombatant service.

Both men wore dark clothes, blue shirts, and the broad-brimmed felt hats characteristic of the attire of members of their faith.

Bontrager was indicted in Cleveland for writing a letter to the weekly *Budget*, a Mennonite paper published in Tuscarawas County, in which he deplored the purchase of Liberty bonds by Mennonites. The paper has a large circulation in the Mennonite colony in Holmes and

Tuscarawas Counties, from which many conscientious objectors have been sent to Camp Sherman. The editor of the paper, S. H. Miller, is under indictment for publishing the letter.

"When the country is at war," Judge Westenhaver told the bishop, "you and all who benefit by its powers are equally bound to bear the burden. Religious liberty such as you enjoy was not gained by non-resistance. No persons in this country regret the war more than those not of your faith.

"No man, no matter how rich he may be, can buy exemption; no man may furnish a substitute. But out of consideration for your religious belief, there has been granted to your young men exemption from combatant service."

The bishop announced in court that he would henceforth leave the matter of bond buying and military service to the individual consciences of members of his church.

"I made a mistake by writing that letter," he confessed. "I did wrong. I thank Mr. Kavanagh and the judge for showing me my error."

As an individual, Bishop Bontrager declared he was "still opposed to killing Germans."

"But I want Germany beaten," he added. "I shall pray that they may be. Perhaps the Lord will destroy them as he destroyed the Egyptians."

The bishop produced affidavits to show that he has conducted vigorous campaigns in Kansas in behalf of the Red Cross and the army YMCA.

Other conscientious objectors who come before the court, the judge indicated, may receive much severer sentences.

Judge Westenhaver sentenced Bert Bonen of Gallon to four months at Warrenville for pro-German talk. Bonen declared he was drunk at the time he made the remark.

Stanislaus Dangel, editor of the *Polish Daily News* of Cleveland, was fined $50 by the judge for a technical violation of the trading-with-the-enemy act.

Was the Penalty Fair?

Manasses Bontrager paid his $500 fine immediately and returned to Kansas. He had received offers from prominent people in Dodge

City to help pay his fine, but he paid it himself.

How could a person be fined for advising others not to buy something that wasn't legally required of them in the first place? The newspapers do not supply us with the real reason for his arrest and fining. The answer is found in File No. 186400-18 at the Department of Justice in Washington, D.C.

In one letter the U.S. Attorney General asked the U.S. Attorney of the federal district of Cleveland to explain why Bontrager and Miller were fined. In his letter of response, the Cleveland U.S. attorney made no mention of war bonds. He gave the reason for their arrest and fining as "for inciting and attempting to incite subordination, disloyalty, and refusal of duty in the military and naval forces of the United States."

Bontrager had written, "What would become of our nonresistant faith if our young brethren in camp would yield?" The government considered this sentence as encouraging COs not to obey the commands of their army officers to perform military duty. Such an attitude and statement, the Cleveland U.S. attorney pointed out, was in violation of the 1917 Espionage Act.

The event is now a part of Amish history. We need not take pride in it, but should feel no shame either. An Amish bishop unknowingly wrote a letter in a public paper [advocating what] was not legally supposed to be done. But morally he was not guilty. In fact, his letter undoubtedly was a good moral influence on the lives of many people who saw it in *The Budget* in 1918. Who knows but that it may have helped many readers not to compromise their consciences.

("Yesterdays and Years," D. Luthy, 3-72)

Excerpts from one of four accounts by Amish of their experiences as conscientious objectors in World War I army camps:

Amish Army Camp Experiences
Camp Taylor, Kentucky

One day we were taken to a room where the bunk beds were set up. We were told to pile them up in a neat stack. When we had finished, we were ordered to put them back again like they were. This kept on for quite some time.

On Sunday I was given some work, and when I refused, I was sent to the guardhouse. One of the guards became angry and struck me across the breast with the bayonet of his gun, nearly knocking me down. The same guard also struck one of the Ohio boys, knocking him down and stabbing him with his bayonet. He made a cut in his pants and a gash in his hip about two inches long.

On July 11, we were released from the guardhouse and sent back to our company, where we met more trials. We were taken to the latrine and given orders that it must be cleaned. But we refused to obey the orders, so the commander got a broomstick and beat me across the legs till he broke his stick. I had streaks and swellings on my legs.

Then we were taken back to the orderly room and told that we would be tried by a special board of inquiry and, if we were found sincere, we could be let out on farm furlough.

But our trials started again, and July 28 was one of my hardest days. It was a Sunday, and they were determined that we must work. They ordered us to pick up all the cigarette stubs that lay on the parking lot grounds, and when we refused, we were thrown on the ground. We were kicked and knocked around, and finally I was taken to a building where the company commander said he would teach me to fight. He began hitting me in the face with his hands until I began going down. Then he would quit for a moment. Another fellow helped him, and they kept on till I started to fall, and one of the men would catch me so I would not fall down.

Finally, one of my partners and I were ordered to carry a can of sweepings, which we did. Then we were taken around to see what was done to the other partner. He was out on the public road with his face and head well marked with blue bumps and marks, and a sign hanging on him that read, "I refuse to fight for my country." Then we were sent back to our barracks.

The next morning the first lieutenant asked us, "Are you now willing to wear uniforms?"

When we said we weren't, he had the government overalls taken off us, which we were wearing, and said we should wear the clothes that God gave us. We were compelled to stand naked till noon the next day.

On August 10, the major of the camp heard of how we were being used. We were called upon to witness in a court-martial against our officers.

About September 6, we were again called upon to witness, and when we refused, we were put under guard. The reason the officials were court-martialed was for disobeying military law in striking anyone on the camp grounds. We felt that we could not conscientiously testify against them, for it would be helping to punish them.

On November 1, we met the special board of inquiry and were passed for farm furloughs.

—*Menno A. Deiner, Arthur, Illinois*

Before their release, one man's wife died. The war ended November 11, 1918. One Amishman reported abuse at another camp, such as being hung by the neck until unconscious. Another finished his letter about Fort Oglethorpe, Georgia, this way:

What a Blessing!

On January 23, 1919, I was given a green discharge paper that read: "This man is a conscientious objector and has done no military duty whatsoever. He has refused to wear a uniform and is not recommended for re-enlistment." What a blessing!

—*Levi S. Yoder, Belleville, Pennsylvania*   (12-70)

World War II
Amish COs in CPS Camps

During the war years of 1941-1945, Amish boys and other conscientious objectors in the U.S. were not drafted into the army. Instead, they were assigned to jobs that were in the interest of the public's good. The program under which they worked was called Civilian Public Service, or simply CPS. While soldiers were stationed at army camps, the COs lived at separate CPS camps.

Some of the 441 Amish boys who served in CPS were given employment at mental hospitals; some served as firefighters in the forests of the far West; some volunteered to become human "guinea pigs" at hospitals where tests were being made for the prevention of various diseases. Others worked in forestry projects or were involved in studying better farming methods and soil conservation.

Altogether, there were 138 CPS camps scattered across the U.S. Not all of them had Amish, but many did. One unit, the Boonsboro Camp in Maryland, was made up entirely of Amish boys. But generally the camps contained boys from various religious backgrounds. Two camps with a high percentage of Amish COs were Grottoes and Luray in Virginia.   ("Yesterdays and Years," 10-74)

The Way of Love

[Based on a World War II incident, from *The Story of Amish in Civilian Public Service*, by Bishop Ira Nissley.]

The man's knuckles shone white as he gripped the razor blade and slashed wildly through the air around him.

The scene took place during World War II when many Amish young men were in CPS camps and hospitals. The man with the razor blade was a patient in a mental hospital where some Amish conscientious objectors were serving their time until the war ended. The regular attendant, who was not a CO, had come upon the patient, but had quickly backed away and locked the door behind him. Even with four or five strong men to help him wrestle the patient down, there would still be a chance of someone getting injured. Yet something had to be done.

"Get those Amish boys who just believe in love and peace," someone suggested, with a bit of mockery in his voice. "Let them handle him. This is a good job for them."

Three COs were called in and told to get the razor blade from the insane man. They sensed at once the importance of the test to which they were being put. The other attendants were watching them to see what they would do.

With a prayer in their hearts, the three consulted together for a few seconds. Then two of them sent off to get a mattress, and the third unlocked the door for them when they came. The mattress appeared to be more than they could handle in the narrow doorway. They heaved and fumbled and pulled. Finally, they looked up at the insane man and said, "Maybe you could give us a hand with this mattress?"

The patient forgot all about his anger and violent intentions. He dropped the razor blade and grabbed the mattress. In that instant the third CO, with a flick of his hand, had the sharp blade and slipped out of the room and down the hall with it.

Everyone breathed easier. The battle had been won without violence. The regular attendants were surprised and a bit beaten out to see with what ease the COs had solved the problem.

Although cases might arise where it would not be wrong to wrestle an insane person to keep him from harming himself or others, these three COs were still far ahead to try and find a more peaceful solution. In so doing, they left a good example for the attendants watching them.

In the same way, in the problems and frustrations of our daily lives, we do well to seek peaceful means to settle disputes and difficulties. No matter how trifling or how great the problem, a solution based on gentleness, kindness, and love will surely prove to have been the better way in the end.   ("Views and Values," E. Stoll, 8/9-74)

The Vietnam Years

Where to, I-W?

During the last year of World War I, many conscientious objectors found themselves in prison or army camps. Much has been written of their trials and sufferings. Most of the brethren proved steadfast in the faith and would have been willing to face the firing squad rather than go against their convictions.

As a result of this, provisions were made during the Second World War so that the COs did not need to go to the army camps. They were given work without pay, under civilian directions, something they could conscientiously do. The program was financed and operated by the churches. But when the war was over, the camps were closed.

A few years later the draft was resumed, but the churches were not interested in going to the bother of opening more camps. It seemed much easier to turn the matter over to the government. This resulted in the I-W program of working in the hospitals.

"The Amish would never be able to operate their own camps," it has been said. Apparently many people have forgotten that the Amish did operate their own camp during World War II at Boonsboro, Maryland. The churches of Pennsylvania were responsible for this camp, and they did an excellent job. What about the need for a better place to send our I-W boys? (10-68)

Behind Prison Walls

"In case of doubt, I feel it is best for Christians to choose the course that goes hardest against his nature or desires."

This bit of advice I heard when I was a boy. It was branded on my conscience. When I was called to report for I-W service, I decided it would indeed be easiest to go with the group. But my conscience would not allow it.

I was arrested for violating the Universal Military Service and Training Act. I was sentenced to prison for two years. But because my friends and customers (I am a blacksmith) interceded for me, my sentence was reduced to one year. My case received quite a bit of publicity over radio, TV, and by newspaper, which brought much sympathy from unknown friends in many states. But there were others who felt I should be dealt with more harshly.

On my arrival at the Federal Penitentiary, Lewisburg, Pennsylvania, one of my first trials was the barber chair. The barber, who was an inmate, was ordered to give me a shave and a haircut. Four officers stood by in case of trouble.

The barber explained to me several different styles of haircuts. Then he asked, "Which style do you prefer?"

"I do not want any other kind except the one I have," I answered.

He kept insisting that I pick one of the styles, but I steadfastly answered, "I will not choose any of the styles which you have to offer."

He sympathized with me and finally suggested that he could take off just enough to satisfy the officers. When he had finished, he put on enough grease so the hair would lay over in modern style. By the next morning my hair had returned to its normal position.

On the way to the mess hall, I was called aside and told to report to the barber shop again after breakfast. This time I was given a short crew cut, the style in which my hair was kept until I had served my time.

The first night I did not sleep very well. I dreamed that one of my younger brothers opened my cell door and came to stay with me so I would not be so lonesome. I thanked him, then begged him to go home because I did not feel it was a very nice place for such a young boy. I woke up with tears in my eyes. Now, four years later, this same brother is working out a two-year sentence on the same charge.

The next few days seemed long to me, alone in a cell without anything to read and no watch to see what time it was. Later they gave me my Testament.

From there I was transferred to an honor camp at Allenwood, Pennsylvania, where my job was shoeing horses and repairing gates, feed bunks, buildings, etc. The second week some of us were called in and asked to volunteer to be moved to a new institution just finished by contractors. I told them I would rather not, and they said I wouldn't have to if I didn't want to. They couldn't get enough volunteers, so they placed about twenty of us on a list.

The next morning, I told the authorities I would prefer not to go by plane. They told me that was not my worry, but theirs. When the time came, they sent two guards to put me on the plane. I did not struggle when they took hold of me.

Once on the plane, we met ten more prisoners from another group. The first 2½ hours on the plane was a smooth ride, flying at 14,000 feet. The last half hour was a very rough ride. The plane would drop 200 feet at a time, then rise at a steep angle. At times it wouldn't more than get back up when it would drop again.

I was very sick, lying on the floor of the aisle, and straining to vomit till I was completely worn out. Most of the prisoners were sick. We landed at Terre Haute, Indiana, and were held over at the federal institution.

The next morning, we left in a prison bus for Marion, Illinois. There were two extra guards on the bus besides the driver. One was with the driver. A steel door and partition kept us apart, the door being locked. The other guard was locked in a cage in the rear of the bus.

A few busloads had arrived ahead of us and got bunks and lockers ready for us. It was a dirty place, for the building was newly built with steel and concrete, and the walls had not yet been finished and covered.

The officer's prediction that I would be rejected proved just the opposite. The fellow inmates came to see if they could help me. Finally they were more insistent than the officers in trying to be on my side. Many times they advised me what to do, and they would stand back of me. It was coming to the place where I was worried about hurting their feelings, and still I felt I could not do some of the things without permission from the officers.

I was there only a few days till they demanded I change clothes. At the honor camp, my clothing was changed to make it a little more plain for me. But at the new place they refused to do so.

After a couple of days on an outside detail, I was called inside and locked in a five-by-seven foot room with two of the biggest officers there. They ordered me to take off my clothes, which I did. Next they told me to put on the clean clothes. I refused to put them on. One of the officers hit me with the palm of his hand. Then they put them on me. Then I went back to my job.

One time the inmates decided to take me to the movies. That evening some of the men came to persuade me to go along. I did not go, so the next time a group of them planned to take me by force. They claimed if I would go once, I would like it and would want to go again.

"You can lead an ox to the water, but you cannot make him drink," I told them.

They were going to take me anyway. A little before the time I expected them to pick me up, I decided I could take a shower. When they came, I was taking a shower, so they gave it up and didn't ask me to go any time later.

While I was in the gym one day, watching others play a game of shuffleboard, an inmate came over and slapped me across the face. It took me by surprise, and I didn't know why it was done. At once, the prisoner was ashamed of himself. We had always been friends. He told me some of them were betting that I would strike back, so they decided to test me. Actually, I was too much surprised to strike back. There were other times when they tried out my faith by betting with each other. It made me feel quite small.

I have been asked why I chose prison instead of serving in I-W. It was a hard decision to make, but I tried to go according to my understanding of the Scriptures.

Most of us are probably acquainted with Titus 3:1, 1 Peter 2:13, and Romans 13:1, "To be subject to the principalities and powers, to obey magistrates. For there is no power but of God." But we are bound to obey only as long as it is in accordance with the Scriptures.

In Matthew 5:39-44 Jesus says, "Whosoever shall smite you on your right cheek, turn to him the other also. . . . Love your enemies, bless them that curse you, do good to them that hate you, and pray for them which despitefully use you and persecute you."

The soldiers asked John the Baptist, "What shall we do?" and he said to them, "Do violence to no man." That leaves no room for war.

If war is wrong in the eyes of God, how far can we go along with the law to register? I feel I could not sign my name on their papers again, although I did when I became eighteen years old.

When I refused to accept a job in the hospital, I received a sentence from a federal judge. The charges stated that I knowingly and willfully refused to report for the military service and training act. Had I reported, would I not have been a part of the military according to the act? (Anon., 8-68)

Joining the Church to Escape the Draft?

An interesting side effect of this rumor about the reinstatement of the draft is the number of young people in some communities who are quickly joining the church. They have been told that if the draft is reinstated, any eligible persons of draft age who are not *members* of a peace church will be forced to go to the army.

We even hear of cases where young people, fearing lest they needlessly give up their liberty to do as they please, say they are waiting until New Year's before they start joining. Perhaps by then they will hear the draft is not coming back after all. What a shame if they had joined the church only to discover they wouldn't have had to!

We find it difficult to imagine what kind of upbuilding church members these young people are going to be, who are joining merely to escape the draft. It would surely be in place for church leaders everywhere—bishops, ministers, and even parents—to cry out against this hypocrisy.

We are thankful for the religious liberty we enjoy, so that those who are sincerely conscientious objectors do not need to kill their fellow men. However, if we knowingly shelter insincere persons among us, someday we will surely have to give an account for it.

We have heard from reliable sources that before too long a worldwide inquest and thorough investigation is going to be made into this matter, among other matters. It is not a false rumor. The Bible calls it the Great Judgment Day.   ("Staff Notes," E. Stoll, 1-79)

14

The Amish Sense of Humor

Edwin B. Wallace
'99

It seems only appropriate now to take time for some relief from the preceding serious subject matter. My Amish friends would certainly take me to task if the reader came away feeling the Amish are a pious, somber people who never laugh or have a good time. The pages of *Family Life* contain many delightful stories, most of which are drawn from personal observation and experiences. In them one can share both the humor and the joy of life's happier moments.

Out of the Mouth of Babes

I was teaching the children the Lord's Prayer, one line each evening at bedtime. One night I had to smother a laugh when our four-year-old volunteered, "Give us this day our jelly bread."

("Some Mothers Write," E. K., Lancaster, Pa., 4-77)

One morning our three-year-old son was feverish. I gave him a cold tablet.

Big sister came along and asked, "Is that a cold tablet you're giving him?"

The little tot said, "No, it's a warm tablet."

(Mrs. W. M., Wis., 1-70)

Around Christmastime last year, Daddy was reading to our three-year-old after breakfast one morning. He was reading the poem that tells about the shepherds bringing a lamb, the wise men bringing gifts, etc. Then he came to the last two lines, "And what shall I give Him? I'll give Him my—"

Before he had a chance to say "heart," our three-year-old said "oatmeal!"

(Mrs. R. L. Y., 12-77)

My sister, the mother of five small boys, was asked by one of them what she wants for Christmas. "Five good boys," she answered.

She must have been a little taken aback when another exclaimed,

"Why, then we'd have ten!"
                    ("Across the Window Sill," E. K., Lancaster, Pa., 12-74)

Little James went to church on his fifth birthday. At dinner he told his parents, "Today the preacher said, 'James is five.' "
The Bible text was chosen from the book of James, chapter 5.
                                        (Mrs. E. B., Pa., 1-77)

One morning at the breakfast table, I complained of gas in my stomach.
Later, when we arrived at Grandpa's, our five-year-old was excitedly telling grandma, "Momma don't feel good and had kerosene in her stomach!"   (Mo., 1-77)

Our three-year-old Kathy was at her grandmother's one day, and grandmother said she wanted to bake some shoofly pies.
[Referring to sticky strips hanging to catch flies,] Kathy asked, surprised, "Are you going to put the strings in, too?"   (Pa., 1-77)

My six-year-old asked, "When was I born?"
"On April 28, 1961," I answered.
"Oh, right on my birthday," she exclaimed.
                                   (Mrs. E. S. B., Ont., 11-68)

This fall while I was planting some tulip bulbs, my little three-year-old granddaughter was watching me. She asked, "Mommy, do you cover them up with dirt so nobody will steal them?"
—*A Grandmother*   (2-75)

"Why are you wiping the dust off the leaves of the rubber plant?" our three-year-old asked.
"So the plant can breathe," I answered.
The next morning the little girl energetically scrubbed the dirty washbowl. Surprised, I asked, "Why are you washing the washbowl?"
"So it can breathe," she answered.
                        ("Some Mothers Write," M. Z. M., Pa., 2-77)

At the dinner table, our five-year-old began pouring his glass of water on his helping of fish. I asked him what he was doing, and he said he wanted to see if the fish will awake again.   (Pa., 2-77)

Childish Ways

The Leaf Collection

My son had just started his leaf collection last spring, and spent hours in the woods collecting, labeling, and pressing them. The latter consisted of sticking them in old books, under newspapers, in drawers and, unknown to me, in our Bible and in our New Testament. Since we had an old Bible we used for everyday, I wasn't aware of this until the day church services were held at our house.

Our whole congregation was gathered in the shed. We had a very inspiring sermon by Uncle Mose from Northfield District. Then he gave a few final comments, glanced at the clock, and announced that it was time to read the text from the New Testament.

He picked up the book, opened it, and immediately a large oak leaf fell to the floor. A whimsical grin spread over his face, and as he turned the pages some more leaves came fluttering down. I glanced up just in time to see a maple leaf land at Uncle Mose's feet. For a moment I couldn't believe my eyes, until I realized Johnny's leaf collection was being discovered. Uncle Mose regained his composure, found the correct text, and read the chapter while the stem of one leaf stuck out of the side of the book.

("Tadpoles in the Bathtub," 8/9-88)

Bantam Rooster

Back when I was four or five,
(Or maybe I was six),
We had a bantam rooster
That got me in a fix.

When I was heading for the barn,
He'd stand and bar my way.
I guess he thought he owned that barn,
And all the cows and hay.

He's long been dead, with all his hens,
(And surely he had oodles).
I wonder how he met his end?
I hope he flavored noodles.

(Janice Etter, 2-88)

A Handicapped Husband

My husband's handicap is that he is absentminded, unbelievably absentminded. He's constantly losing things.

He takes the flashlight to the barn, and it's never seen again. He uses a Vice-Grip wrench in the pigpen and leaves it lie to fetch a bolt from the shop. When he returns, the pigs have claimed the wrench and buried it in the manure.

In the house it's the same story. He starts a fire in the kitchen stove and leaves the plastic pail with corncobs on top of the stove.

At the table, the children and I have learned to expect anything when we ask Dad to pass a dish for us. The first problem is to get him to hear us. We often have to ask him three or four times to do a simple thing, like pass the bread. At last he will look up, truly sorry for having kept us waiting, and quickly pass the *milk*.

When our oldest daughter started going to school, she was so used to repeating everything she said that the teacher thought she stuttered.

Who wants to say things four times in the presence of company? One of the boys tried that one time. He sat right next to Dad, and so undertook to get his attention by tugging on his shirtsleeve. "You gave me too many beans. You gave me too many beans. You gave me too many beans." Finally, he did succeed in getting Dad's attention, but all that soaked in was the word "beans." Dad smiled lovingly, nodded his head and, to the little boy's dismay, dished out some *more* beans! (2-79)

Confession

When the handicapped husband found out how many people were condemning his wife for not being more loyal to him, it proved to be a time for confession. "I am horrified to know that people are criticizing my wife," he writes. "She is a patient, loving, kind person who has never done me a bad turn in her life. She does her best to look after me every waking hour. So in conclusion, let me say two things. The first thing—please don't blame my wife, for she didn't write that article at all. I wrote it *myself*, as it seemed to me the way my wife could feel many times. And the second thing—alas, I have forgotten what it was!" ("Staff Notes," 4-79)

A Handicapped Wife

One day I went to the shop for my hammer. Our washhouse and shop are built together. My wife had turned the water on to fill the kettle so she would have an early start at washing the next morning. By the looks of things, it must have been full and running over a good half hour.

I opened the door to the kitchen and was greeted with the smell of popcorn and the sound of five happy children gathered around the table for a winter picnic. I looked at my wife and just opened my mouth to say something when she cried, "Oh no, the water!" and she was out the door.

A little later I needed another item in the house. Two-year-old Samuel was standing at the door, holding his empty plate and calling, "Mom, when will the popcorn be ready?"

Above his voice, Rachel screamed, "Something is burning and it's getting smoky in here!"

All this time my wife had been in the washhouse, sweeping down the water, but now she sped past me into the house, muttering, "Could I have possibly left the popcorn on the stove all this time?"

One day my wife went to the neighbor's to get apples. When she came home, she complained about old Bess, our horse, getting retarded. She simply refused to turn the corners no matter how hard my wife pulled on the lines. When I put the horse into the barn, I noticed that she didn't have the bit in her mouth!

The list could go on and on, but I've written enough so you are aware that there are others who are "handicapped" people. My advice would be to accept your lot in life and enjoy it. After all, it is a very interesting one! ("Letter," M., Ont., 4-79)

Tourists

A Typo

Mistakes do happen. Sometimes the result is humorous, sometimes startling and dangerous. Only one letter misplaced, or a word left out, can change the meaning.

One of the best examples of this we have ever seen appeared in the nationally distributed newspaper *Travel*, in the April 1968 issue. In the article "Ohio's Amish Country," there was supposed to be the statement, "They do not bear arms, will not take *oaths*, and believe that the end of the world is imminent."

The typesetter got one letter wrong, and hundreds of readers learned a new fact about the Amish: "They will not take *baths*"!

So if you read something in a Pathway paper you find hard to believe, check with us before you stop your subscription.   (6-68)

Local Entertainment

Isn't it true that all of us know what it feels like to do "something dumb"? Maybe that is why it makes us feel good every now and then to learn that others also make goofs. A while ago a reader in Lancaster County couldn't resist sending us two humorous incidents provided for the local residents by the area's tourists. Here is the first story as it was sent to us:

"This area is advertised across the United States as the place to go to see the Amish on the road and in the fields with horses. This spring a lady wanted to take a picture of an Amishman when he was plowing. She wanted him to stand next to her husband, beside his team of horses. The Amishman refused to do it, so she went to the state police office to report it. She wanted them to report him to his boss, or have him arrested, because she thought he was working for the state of Pennsylvania! She did not realize he was his own boss!

"The policeman on duty said he could hardly keep from laughing because she was so serious about this. He could not get her to understand that this is the way we live, and that we are not being paid by the state to farm and live the way we do so the tourists can come and watch us."

The next story was taken from a newspaper clipping entitled

"Tourist Tells Shocking Story About Amish." The clipping predicted, "Local farmers will get a charge out of this story. A woman from New York was hoping to get some pictures of the Amish. She stopped by the side of the road, along with her son, and walked up to an electric fence [powered by a battery]. You can guess the rest. She reported the incident to the local chamber of commerce. Hopefully, the people there told her the fence was actually intended for straying livestock, and not straying tourists! ("Staff Notes," 3-90)

15
Odds and Ends

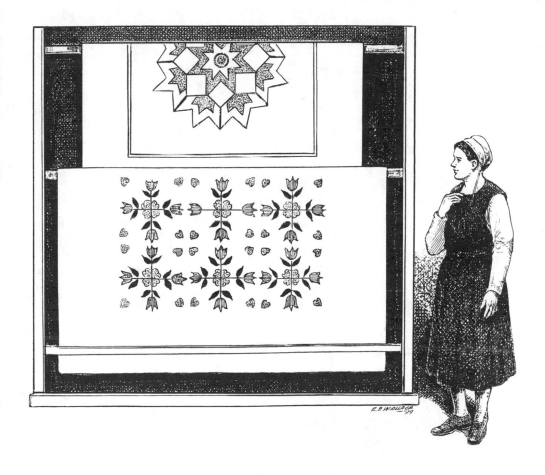

As with any compilation, there are always items that just don't seem to fit anywhere, but which you simply can't throw out. Luckily, someone invented the wonderful category of "Miscellaneous," which fits this chapter. Here are everything from home remedies and recipes, to entries that are properly under the title of "Believe It or Not!"

Recipes

Washing Hens

When doing hens for canning, I have found it easy to wash them in the wringer washing machine. Fill the tub with warm water. Add a little soap, three or four hand towels, and four or five chickens, depending on size. (Remove feet before washing.) Let them wash several minutes. I can set my motor to run very slowly, otherwise it might break the unlaid eggs.

("Homemaker's Page," Millersburg, Ohio, 10-82)

Simple Apple Butter

4 gallons of apples (unpeeled and cut in quarters)
1 gallon of corn syrup
6 lbs. of sugar
Put apples in a heavy kettle or canner with tight-fitting lid. Pour syrup and sugar over apples and let set overnight to form juice. Bring to a slow boil and cook for three hours. Don't open lid or stir during the entire cooking period. Put through strainer, and it's ready to eat.

(Mrs. Thomas Peachey, 1-78)

Aggression Cookies

There are many ways to keep children out from underfoot on those rainy days or when you are busy. Older children can help you make Aggression Cookies.

3 cups oatmeal

1 ½ cups brown sugar

1 ½ cups flour

3 sticks butter

1 ½ tsp. baking powder

Let your children dump all the ingredients in a bowl. In this recipe, the fiercer the pounding, the better the cookies, so they can squeeze, mush, pound, pinch, slap, and hit the dough to their heart's content. Roll into small balls and bake on ungreased cookie sheet for 10 minutes at 350 degrees F.

("More Mother Hints," Mrs. Andy Miller, Smicksburg, Pa., 5-83)

Bacon Dandelion

Fry dandelions in butter until crisp (will turn black but add butter). Add salt. When done (all black), put eggs on top, cover, put back on stove until eggs are done.   (Leola, Pa., 5-73)

Remedies

General-Purpose Home Remedy

Boil one gallon dandelion flowers and one gallon hot water for five minutes. Let stand for three days (best kept in a crock jar). Strain. Boil the peelings of two lemons and one orange with the dandelion water for fifteen minutes. Let stand until lukewarm. Slice in the two lemons and the orange. Add two teaspoons of yeast and three pounds of sugar, and let stand for six days. Bottle. (The Bylers like it best with less sugar.)   (Ben E. Byler, Selinsgrove, Pa., 9-70)

Against Car Sickness

To avoid car sickness, pin a fair-sized piece of brown paper from a paper bag over your breast. My mother, sister, and I all do this and have no trouble with getting sick anymore while traveling.

(C. B., Ont., 5-76)

For Sleep

If some nights sleep doesn't come, I don't count sheep, I talk to my Shepherd.   (Mrs. P. W. Jr., Pa., 4-70)

Marking Clothing

A mother from Ontario has advised that instead of making children's stockings and other things with the child's initial, mark them with the child's age. When a garment is passed down, it will stay with the child nearest that age, and they will be able to find their belongings without confusion. This works as long as the younger child does not outgrow the older one.

("Across the Windowsill," Aunt Becky, 12-72)

Outside

It's Garden Time!

Try these directions for your spring garden.

First, plant five rows of peas: preparedness, promptness, perseverance, politeness, and prayer.

Next to them plant three rows of squash: squash gossip, squash criticism, squash indifference.

Now how about five rows of lettuce? Let us be faithful. Let us be unselfish. Let us be loyal. Let us be truthful. Let us love one another.

And no garden is complete without turnips: Turn up for church. Turn up with a smile. And turn up with determination.

Do this and you will have the best garden you ever had.   (5-78)

The Purple Martin—Nature's Insect Controller

Did you know that a purple martin bird can eat up to two thousand mosquitoes in a day? They also feed on flies, gnats, beetles, moths, and all manner of flying insects. Because of this amazing capacity to consume objectionable insects, the purple martin can make any neighborhood more pleasant.   (4-73)

How We Relate

Old Order Mennonites

Some time ago a man came to our house who said he grew up among the Amish and Mennonites in Iowa. When he learned that we are Old Order Mennonites, he asked which we are most like, the Amish or Mennonites? I told him right away we are more like the Amish. Later, as I thought over it, I had to wonder why. It has been over three hundred years since we parted from the Amish, but only a hundred years since we parted from the more-liberal Mennonites. Yet I feel we are more like the Amish.   ("Letter," M. B., Pa., 3-73)

The "English" and the Amish

The term "English people" is commonly used in many areas of the United States and Canada to mean that the people are not Amish or Mennonite. It is not intended to disparage or belittle anyone. It is simply more convenient to say "English" than it is to say "non-Amish," etc.   ("Editor's Note," 5-72)

Circle Letters

A circle letter is started when ten or a dozen people living at different addresses make up a group, and the pack of letters goes round and round the circle, each member taking out his old letter and adding a new one every time the envelope comes to his mailbox. Some kinds of circle letters the Amish write:

1. Family letters—brothers and sisters, or cousins, living in different places.

2. Wheelchair writers—from these letters the shut-in gathers courage and faith, for they tell of others suffering in the same way and overcoming the same temptations.

3. Teachers—from this experience of teachers writing to each other, the idea for an Amish teachers' magazine emerged. In the autumn of 1957, the *Blackboard Bulletin* was first published, consisting of articles by and for teachers.

4. I-W's and wives of those serving in camps as conscientious objectors (COs).

5. Organic farmers.

6. Amish bakers.

7. Amish bishops.

8. Teenage girls.

9. Andy Mast Circle Letter—consisting of fourteen Amish with the same name, from Ohio to Ontario, aged twenty to eighty.

"Circles of friendship—that's what circle letters are."

(J. Stoll, 7-69)

The Most-Common Names

Have you ever wondered what Amish names are the most common last names and first names? Recently we took a survey of the names of subscribers listed in the Pathway files. We found the following results: Miller is by far the most common last name, having 1,389; next is Yoder, 955; then Beiler/Byler, 417; Stoltzfus, 383; Bontrager, 335; and Hostetler/Hochstetler, 300.

To determine the most common first names, we took the three most common last names and counted how often each first name appeared. The top five first names are listed here:

Miller		Yoder		Beiler/Byler	
1. John	76	1. John	52	1. John	34
2. Eli	57	2. Eli	35	2. Jacob	23
3. Dan	55	3. Dan	33	3. Dan	21
4. Levi	44	4. Henry	29	4. Andy	20
5. Andy	38	5. David	28	5. Crist	18
Joe	38				

(6-71)

It's a Fact: Unusual Amish Happenings

For many years papers have carried a short but popular feature, "Ripley's Believe It or Not," which describes remarkable yet true happenings. A much-talked-about volume of a similar nature is *The Guinness Book of World Records*, which includes intentional and unintentional records set by people all over the world.

Within Amish history there have been many unusual and unique happenings. They are gathered together here as a sort of Amish "Believe It or Not" and arranged in specific categories.

Births

The first two children of John I. and Susie (Schmucker) Schwartz of Adams County, Indiana, were born in the same year, one on the first day and the other on the last day. William was born January 1, 1973, and Leah on December 31, 1973.

When Bennie A. Fisher and Annie Kinsinger of Somerset County,

Pennsylvania, married on November 15, 1923, they never imagined there would be a gap of nearly 22 years between the births of their first two children. Noah was born August 22, 1924, and John on July 1, 1946. Two more children were born to them in 1948 and 1950, when Mrs. Fisher was 45 and 47 years old.

Burials

While most Amish bury their dead in family plots within community cemeteries, the Swiss Amish residing in Adams and Allen Counties, Indiana, have never done so. Each row of burials in their large cemeteries is according to whether the deceased is a child, youth, or adult. Also, the graves are not marked with a gravestone. Instead, plain wooden markers without inscriptions are used. A booklet is kept where each burial is recorded. If someone wants to know where a particular person is buried, the booklet is consulted.

Grandchildren

John J. and Lydia (Shetler) Miller of Danville, Ohio, in 1986 had 99 grandchildren on his mother's 99th birthday. Several days later their 100th grandchild was born, making an even 50 grandsons and 50 granddaughters.

Henry Raber of Daviess County, Indiana, on July 12, 1985, welcomed his 70th grandchild, Vera Sue Raber, on his 70th birthday.

Marriages

Eli J. Troyer (b. Sept. 4, 1904), a retired farmer and minister near LaGrange, Indiana, has the distinction of being able to reverse his age at his first marriage to form his age at his second marriage. He was 18 when he married Anna Christner on November 30, 1922, and 81 when he married Emma (Schwartz) Eicher on November 28, 1985.

Some Amish couples have been married for 70 years and a few for even longer. Jacob J. Borkholder (1864-1963) of Bremen, Indiana, was married to Anna Schlabach (1862-1963) for a record 75 years.

Daniel J. Yoder (1863-1932) of Custer County, Oklahoma, was married almost as long to his fourth wife as he was to all three of his other wives:

1. Lucy Lehman (1866-1889)—4 years, 3 months
2. Rebecca Schrock (1869-1899)—8 years, 3 months
3. Elizabeth Miller (1873-1908)—6 years, 3 months
4. Miriam (Hershberger) Mullet (1873-1942)—18 years, 3 months

Migration

Jacob K. Miller was born in Somerset County, Pennsylvania, in 1852. At the age of thirteen he moved with his parents to Arthur, Illinois—550 miles. In 1873, he married Elizabeth Yoder and moved in 1879 to Needy, Oregon—2,000 miles. Within Oregon he moved to Hubbard and later to McMinnville—50 miles. In 1903 he left Oregon for Geauga County, Ohio—2,200 miles. Several years later he returned to Oregon—2,200 miles. In 1913 he moved 650 miles to Salinas, California, and in 1914 across the nation 2,550 miles to Norfolk, Virginia, where he rented a house for three months before moving 200 miles to Dover, Delaware. In 1918 he was scared out of Delaware by World War I and moved 1,700 miles to Glendive, Montana. From there he again moved to Oregon—900 miles. Then in 1921, he moved for the last time—2,600 miles back to Dover, Delaware. Altogether, Jacob K. Miller, or "Oregon Jake" as he was nicknamed, had migrated a total of 15,600 miles and had lived in eight states.

Ordinations

Since the Amish use the casting of lots to ordain ministers, no one knows who the new minister will be until the ordination service is held. On October 16, 1982, Allen Brenneman was ordained a minister in the Southeast District of the Ashland, Ohio, community. The following day his twin brother, Alvin Brenneman, was ordained in the Northeast District.

Aaron Esh of Lancaster County, who died at the age of 100, was the oldest ordained Amishman.

When 97-year-old David (D. K.) Borntrager died on March 29, 1988, at Haven, Kansas, he had been an Amish minister longer than anyone on record. He was a minister 73 years, 5 months, and 4 days, having been ordained on October 25, 1914. He had given *Zeugnis* (testimony) four weeks before his death and had preached his last

Anfang (opening sermon) on January 6, 1985.

The 99-year-old John L. Schwartz of Nappanee, Indiana, was ordained a minister on May 7, 1916, and a bishop in 1933. He has served in the Amish ministry longer than anyone on record—74 years, of which 17 were as a minister and 57 as a bishop. In 1989 he was regularly taking his turn to preach the opening sermon.

Quilting

The average quilt requires 250-350 yards of thread. Intricate patterns require more. Some Amish women have used 1,000 or more yards of thread in a single quilt. Such quilts were made for non-Amish customers. The record is held by "The Shetlers" of Glasgow, Kentucky, who stated in the January 17, 1990, issue of *The Budget* that they used 1,270 yards of thread for a "big ocean wave" quilt. Their record is closely followed by 1,250 yards in a flower garden quilt by Nancy Beachy of Arthur, Illinois, who also did another plain-marked quilt using 1,000 yards.

Travel

The traveling-est Amishman was Jonathan B. Fisher (1878-1953) of Lancaster County, Pennsylvania. Besides taking many trips within the United States, he traveled extensively abroad. In 1908 he made his first trip to Europe and published an account of it three years later, entitled "A Trip to Europe and Facts Gleaned Along the Way." On March 4, 1913, he married Sarah Farmwald. On February 17, 1934, (traveling alone) he boarded the vessel *California* at New York City and began a trip around the world, which he described in a book, *Around the World by Water and Facts Gleaned Along the Way*, published in 1937. In 1950 he toured Mexico and in 1952 went again to Europe. On the latter trip, he accompanied a shipment of cattle for relief purposes, which he had helped to solicit through his weekly column "Lancaster Co. Briefs" in the national Amish newspaper, *The Budget*.

More than a half million miles were traveled by Eli J. Bontrager (1868-1958), an Amish bishop who resided in Indiana, North Dakota, Wisconsin, Mississippi, and Florida. Besides the thousands of miles he traveled when migrating, he made many trips on church-related matters, including visiting Amish young men in Civilian Public Service (CPS) camps during World War II. In his retirement years, he often traveled to Mississippi and Florida from his home near Shipshewana, Indiana. In his autobiography, *My Life Story*, he states, "I have traveled more than 466,000 miles by railroad and nearly 60,000 by bus and car. I have traveled on all the larger railroads in the USA and Canada, except two, and have traveled on about 40 of the larger lines and many of the smaller roads."

Twins

With 21.1 twins per 1,000 births, the Amish residing in Adams-Allen and Elkhart-LaGrange Counties, Indiana, are said to have the highest twinning rate in the world (Berne, Indiana, *Tri-Weekly News*, Sept. 26, 1979). Four sets of twins have been born to several Amish families.

Widowhood

Lizzie Miller (1876-1965) of LaGrange County, Indiana, was a widow much longer than she was married to her three husbands:
1. Samuel C. Miller (1868-1898)—2 years, 9 months
2. Jacob Troyer (1872-1907)—4 years, 6 months
3. John E. Christner (1861-1939)—about 21 years
She was married for a total of 28 years and a widow for 41.

Hymns

The hymn "O Gott Vater, wir loben dich," first included in the third edition of the *Ausbund* in 1622, is the second song sung at every Amish church service except funerals. It has four 7-line stanzas, for a total of 28 lines, which take 20-25 minutes to be sung.

The *Ausbund*, the hymnal that most Amish use for congregational singing, is the oldest hymnal in continuous use in the world. Its first printing was in 1564, and its latest in 1987, with some 47 printings between those dates. It is still in print.

Long Lives

The oldest Amish couple resided near Bremen, Indiana. Jacob J. Borkholder (b. May 6, 1864) married Anna Schlabach (b. Oct. 28, 1862) on November 10, 1887. She was 100 years old when she died March 23, 1963. He died five weeks later on May 7, just one day after his 99th birthday.

The oldest Amish person was Salina Stoltzfus, who died on January 27, 1981, in Lancaster County, Pennsylvania, at the age of 108. She was born September 25, 1872, the daughter of Benjamin and Jemima (Beiler) King. She married Enos F. Stoltzfus on December 16, 1897.

The story is told that at age 100, Salina was to undergo an operation and was rather concerned because of her advanced age. The doctor, with tongue in cheek, assured her she need not worry because he had never lost a patient her age. The truth of the matter was, of course, that he had never operated on anyone that old.

Another story is told of an Amish minister from Canada who visited Salina when she was well past 100. He asked her if she took a lot of vitamins. She replied, "No, I never was one to take many vitamins. I have coffee soup each morning for breakfast."

Salina's sister Sarah (Mrs. Daniel F. Zook) was yet alive in 1989 and celebrated her 105th birthday on August 15th. [She died in Franklin County, Pennsylvania, on February 19, 1991, at the age of 106.]

("Yesterdays and Years," D. Luthy, 6-90)

The Blue-Gate Legend

The blue-gate legend is simply that an Amishman announces he has a marriageable daughter by painting his front gate blue. That the blue-gate legend is currently found in Lancaster County tourism is evidenced by a note card sold in many tourist shops. One of the twelve "Pennsylvania Dutch Neighborly Greetings" being distributed in 1980 by Conestoga Crafts of Gettysburg, Pennsylvania, shows an Amish girl and boy standing on opposite sides of a gate painted bright blue. The note card's caption reads:

When a Dutch girl feels fer courtin'
(At least they say it's true),
Her Pop chust takes a can of paint
And makes the front gate blue!

No one knows when the "blue gate" legend began. The two oldest known references to it both appeared in print in 1937. In a completely false article, "Der Bell Don't Make Bump," in the February 1937 issue of the magazine *Esquire*, the "blue gate" was first mentioned.

The other 1937 account was much more detailed. It appeared in Berenice Steinfeldt's 31-page tourist booklet *The Amish of Lancaster County,* which went through numerous reprintings:

"The sign of a blue painted gate grew to be the advertising sign of an Amish daughter ready to marry. The Amish are quick to deny the truth of this story. The legend of this "Amish blue gate" really started about thirty years ago. At that time a certain Amish bishop lived along the Lincoln Highway, east of Lancaster.

"He was a leading member of the church, and as such received visitors from different parts. To simplify directions, visitors were told to ask the conductor of the trolley car that ran out that way to leave them off at the "blue gate," the chief distinguishing mark of the bishop's home. It was the only one so painted. The only reason the bishop's gate was blue was he happened to like the color."

In 1960, the sociologist Elmer Lewis Smith stated his opinion of the "blue gate" legend in his book *The Amish Today:* "Probably the most simple method of dealing with this myth is to state directly that not more than one or two blue gates exist in all of Lancaster County."

Following is a letter sent by a Lancaster Amishman, dated December 12, 1980:

> The gate was probably blue so the dirt would not show so much, since it was handled much more than the rest of the fence. You see, this was back when people had picket fences around their yards and gardens, and whitewashed them every spring. Yes, some Amish did paint their gates blue, and our Bishop Benj. F. Beiler had a blue gate probably longer than most people. When people came from the West and didn't know where to go, they were told to take the Coatesville trolley and get off at the blue gate, which of course was the bishop's.

> So there is some truth in the story after all, but it has nothing to do with a marriageable daughter. Still, the legend continues. It likely will last as long as commercialism—the selling of the Amish to the gullible public.   (D. Luthy, 5-81)

Even today, there is an Amish roadside stand, apparently at this same farm on Route 30 in Lancaster, for the sign reads "Blue Gate Farm." There is no blue gate now, just a metal fence. The stand is a favorite among locals and visitors for its delicious baked goods.

Discover
Discover what invigorates you physically,
Restores you spiritually,
Balances you mentally,
And relaxes you emotionally.

16
Amish Parables
Lessons from Life

As I read through several hundred issues of *Family Life*, I especially enjoyed those stories in which people related a personal incident, and then went on to reflect upon it in larger terms, finding an important message in something simple. These Amish writers were able to reflect on some daily event and then take it to a higher level.

I was reminded of stories about Zen monks in Japan who suddenly reached enlightenment while going about an everyday task, like raking leaves. Similarly, while going about their daily chores, these Amish also found lessons for their own lives. In a sense, daily life and religion come together here in the most natural way. Perhaps these stories best summarize "what it means to be Amish." They form a fitting conclusion to this book. Not unlike the parables in the Bible, these Amish parables from everyday life are meaningful for every one of us.

The Luxuries of Life

Elam Stoltzfus was reading an article a newspaper reporter had written about the Amish. "These devout people live in a simple, austere fashion, denying themselves most of the luxuries of life." Elam looked about himself at his plain clothes, the simple furniture, the bare floor, and the unadorned walls of his house. It was true; they really didn't have many luxuries—no car to speed to town with, no electricity, and none of the hundreds of labor-saving appliances and handy gadgets that went with it, nothing automatic, no buttons to push, no carpets on the floor—

His thoughts were interrupted by his son. "Daddy, what is this picture about?" six-year-old Cephas asked.

The boy held in his hands the *Martyrs Mirror*, a book almost too big for him to handle. He had it open to a picture that had aroused his curiosity. It showed a man who seemed to be half-sitting, half-lying on a heap of straw in a poorly lighted room. One end of a heavy chain was fastened to the man's leg, and the other end was fastened to a ring in the wall. Several toads hopped at the man's feet, a snake crawled nearby, and most terrifying of all was that the man had a coat of some sort draped over his head.

It was the account of George Wanger, found on page 1081 in the *Martyrs Mirror*. It told how George, an Anabaptist, had been imprisoned for his faith. He was held in prison for a year in all; part of the time he was kept in the dungeon room shown in the picture. Rats, scorpions, toads, and snakes were so bad in this dungeon that he had to keep a coat thrown over his head to prevent the vermin from running over his head. The church authorities questioned and tortured him relentlessly in an effort to persuade him to recant. Twice he was tortured so cruelly that marks remained three months afterwards.

After much suffering, George was executed for his faith. The executioner, before beheading George, offered him one last chance to recant. He promised him a large sum of money, as well as offering to bear the guilt himself if George did wrong in recanting. But George had only one last request: "Please loosen the chains on my hands a bit, so I can lift them in a prayer of thanks to God before I die."

After little Cephas carried the large book back to its place on the shelf, Elam found himself comparing his own life with that of George Wanger. He thought of the freedom of worship he enjoyed, a warm house, clean clothes, good food on the table, the privilege of being at home with his family. How easy his life was compared with that of George Wanger. Yes, what luxuries he enjoyed! The newspaperman had been terribly mistaken, but perhaps he had never read the account of George Wanger.   ("Views and Values," E. Stoll, 4-78)

Are We Helping?

The bishop has often compared our churches to a herd of horses grazing in a pasture. It is a beautiful picture to see them all grazing together contentedly. Everything seems to be going fine. But then there are always those who try to reach across the fence and get something they shouldn't have. These have to be brought back into the group. If they aren't, they will soon break down the fence, and then there is trouble. Not only will they slip out of the field, but they open the way for the rest to get out as well. (2-81)

The Greedy Heifer

One evening when I was helping my husband do the chores, I decided to feed the heifers so he would be done with his work sooner. First, I gave them a good helping of silage. On top of that, I heaped their feed supplement, which they liked even more. After I had fed them all and they were eating contentedly, I walked past them with another shovelful of silage to feed the dry cows. As I walked past, a young heifer tried to snatch a mouthful off the shovel, ignoring all the feed she had before herself.

"You silly, greedy heifer," I couldn't help but think. It was disgusting, really. She had all the feed in front of her that she could possibly eat, and yet she was trying to snatch away some of the other cows' silage.

Later, after thinking it over, I had to wonder how often we are in the eyes of God like that greedy heifer. We are blessed with plenty to eat, warm houses, good homes, family and friends, and all the material things we will ever be able to use and more. Yet we look about and lament when we see others who appear to have more than we do.

Are we in the habit of counting our many blessings and appreciating all we have, or are we often wishing for and wanting what others have? ("Pathway Pen Points," Lancaster, Pa., 4-83)

Sprinkling Cans

It was getting dry. The lettuce, celery, and cabbage seedlings we had transplanted needed to be watered for them to survive. Each morning I took the sprinkling can, filled it with water, and carried it to the garden. Each day I wished for rain, not only to be relieved of carrying water, but because the rest of the garden was suffering, too.

Then one morning the sky was overcast. At noon there were a few raindrops on the window. The clouds turned a shade darker. We waited hopefully.

Then the rain fell. Big drops fell to the ground and bounced like thousands of miniature marbles. I thought of our garden. It was being watered far beyond what I had been able to do in the past week or two. Not only was the whole garden being watered, but the yard, the pasture fields, the cornfields, the trees—acres and acres of crops for miles around would revive and yield better because of this rain. Gallons, no, tons of water were falling. My mind was too small to compare it with the two or three gallons I had been carrying each day.

"Just think how small and meager my little sprinkling can is compared to a shower like this."

My friend thought a moment, then said, "But your sprinkling can kept the plants alive until this shower came. They would have died if you hadn't watered them."

Her statement, so simply stated, became a sermon that stuck in my mind long after we had both returned to our work. The more I thought about it, the more I realized that there were other "sprinkling cans" in our life.

The help we give our fellowmen and neighbors is small when we compare it with what God does for us. And yet the smallness of things we can do for each other does not give us the right to sit back and do nothing. Even though our "sprinkling cans" seem hopelessly small, our concerns and prayers and admonishments and good example must not cease as long as there is still hope. Oh, for more sprinkling cans—small vessels of love and peace, of goodwill and patience and hope!   (8/9-81)

A Deed of Kindness

It was around Christmas, and our family had just retired for the night. We were awakened out of our sleep by the sound of seemingly heavenly music outside the house. We got up, and after coming to our senses, realized it was the community's young folks caroling for us. I was with the young folks at the time and began to question why they hadn't included me. I felt very sorry for myself.

After they left as quietly as they had come, one of us opened the door to peer out into the night, stumbling over a large tub and containers. What was it? Upon investigating, we discovered them filled with ground meat. We had suffered a fire loss, and so the youths had assembled at one of the neighbors to work up a beef for us. We felt unworthy of such a gift, but filled with gratitude at the thoughtfulness.

Needless to say, I was very ashamed over the first feelings I had toward the young folks.

Sometimes it takes a jolt like this, a deed of genuine kindness, to waken us to our real sense of values and make us appreciate our blessings more. ("Pathway Pen Points," Wis., 10-90)

Two Common Green Bowls

The last of the two bowls is gone. I knocked it against the side of the cupboard, breaking it in two jagged halves. I stood with the pieces in my hand, thinking back to the day I had gotten it and its identical partner.

At the time, I was sixteen, the age when pretty things meant so much to me. I was working for Dave Beilers, people who were known to be slightly "different" from most people. For one thing, they were old-fashioned. Anna Beiler clung to her mother's ways.

In those days, when a family needed soup plates or serving dishes or cups, the thing to do was to write Mr. Baker. A few days later, his panel truck would slowly drive in the lane, carefully avoiding the bumps. Inside the truck, piled high on shelves and stored in boxes underneath , would be all the dishes the average housewife needed.

I longed to run out to the "store on wheels," but I didn't. I was the hired girl, so I decided to wait for an invitation. I didn't have to wait long. Little Fannie Beiler came to the garden, where I was working, and said, "Mother said you may come look at the dishes, too." I wasn't slow in going. And my, what pretty dishes he had!

Later that afternoon, I went into the house to get the lettuce seeds for the late-summer lettuce. Anna was putting her new dishes away. "Here, I got these for you," she said.

I spun around expectantly. Had she bought something pretty after all? I couldn't believe my eyes. Anna was holding out two ordinary, common green bowls, the kind my mother used for everyday in the kitchen. What did I want with *bowls*? I held them in my hands and looked at them. I was seeing all the pretty, fancy dishes I had wanted so desperately. I fared better at other places I worked.

The day came when I had a kitchen of my own. Now the dishes were no longer stored away in boxes; they were put into the cupboard to be used. Then I realized I didn't have many practical dishes intended to be used every day. "At least I've got my Anna bowls," I thought, putting them where they would be handy.

To my surprise, I learned to love those bowls. I knew they were just the right size to beat up a couple of eggs or to hold a quart of applesauce. I rarely got them out of the cupboard without remembering who had given them to me. At the same time, the pretty dishes I had were stored away in boxes, and I didn't remember who had given many of them!

The first bowl met its end when it was knocked over the edge of the kitchen table, and now, almost ten years later, I broke the other one, too. I know these bowls are no longer available. It's not that I need the bowl as much as I need the lesson it would never fail to remind me of—that the things we would like to have are not always the things we need.   (M., Ohio, 4-76)

Fixing Up the House

Barbara Mast had company again. Barbara looked up from her work one day to see her parents drive in the lane with the double buggy. "Who would they have along?" she wondered. "I wonder if it might be Uncle Amos and Aunt Mary."

A few moments later the buggy was close enough for Barbara to see that she had guessed right. Uncle Amos was one of her favorite relatives, and so was plump, jolly Aunt Mary. It was interesting to hear about the old times when Amos and her dad were young boys and lived with their parents on a farm.

Later, at the dinner table, Barbara said, "Let's see. David and his wife are living with you and doing the farming, aren't they?"

"Yes, they are now, but they aren't staying," Uncle Amos said, a trace of a frown crossing his face. "We're not sure what we'll do yet. All the other children have farms of their own, and I had depended on David to stay with us."

"It's not David's choice to move away," Aunt Mary said quickly, glancing at her husband as if wondering how much she should tell. Then, being Aunt Mary, she added, "I guess maybe they would stay if we remodeled the house and fixed it up the way Laura wants it."

"But you did remodel the house not so very long ago, didn't you?" Mom asked.

"There's nothing wrong with the house, but it is old-fashioned when you compare it to the house she lived in before she was married. Laura's used to having a furnace and a long worktable and lots of cupboards. And I always think I can't blame her. She was brought up with these things in the house, and it's hard to adjust to doing without them."

"Wouldn't these young people learn a thing or two if they had to start up the way we did?" Amos said, looking at Barbara's dad. "When we started housekeeping, we didn't have a drain in the house. Mary carried every drop of water she used into the house and back out. She really thought she had something when I put in a little sink with a drain. And the day we installed the kitchen pump, she thought she really was living in luxury."

Barbara's head nodded in agreement. "Isn't it something how soon a luxury becomes a necessity? All it takes is one generation."

"It doesn't take that long," Amos said. "I can easily remember when bathrooms in Amish homes were few and far between. And now, how many homes do you find without bathrooms?"

"We didn't have one when we first moved here," Barbara said. "And I remember the time we didn't have one at home. I know it's nice to have a bathroom, but I could do without one if I had to."

"All right," Uncle Amos said, looking directly at Barbara. "You say you could get along without a bathroom if you had to, but could your girls when they grow up and get married? I've often said it and I'll say it again: what you give a daughter as a luxury becomes a necessity in a matter of years."

"Then the young people get criticized for wanting such nice homes and new furniture when they start up," Barbara's mother said, her voice sounding concerned. "It's not all the young people's fault."

"I've often said the same thing," Aunt Mary said. "Just like David's Laura. She's a nice girl, and we think a lot of her. It's just that so many things we look at as being luxuries have become necessities to her."   (Anon., 7-78)

Learning to Know Yourself

A few months ago we were in Fort Wayne, Indiana, to visit a couple of hospital patients. Then we stopped at a big clothing store. As we were walking around in there, I saw an elderly Amishman come walking toward me. "Now who is this old man?" I thought, and then I realized I was looking into a big glass mirror. I didn't know myself right away!

This started me to thinking that I should learn to know myself better, so this would not happen again. But then I had to think of how the Word of God is like a mirror, and how much more important it is that we learn to know ourselves in a spiritual sense, and see ourselves as we look in God's Word.

("Pathway Pen Points," Abe Lehman, Middlebury, Ind., 10-86)

The World's Bible

My dad orders his checks with a Bible verse printed on them. A few years ago he ordered several tons of coal and sent a check along with the neighbor man who was going to haul it home for us. The man at the coal mine looked at the check and remarked, "It should be all right. It has a Bible verse printed on it."

We do not have Bible verses printed on us, but our plain clothes should be worn as a testimony to what we believe. Our words, actions, and dealings must correspond with our plain clothes, or it will not benefit us at all to wear them. How sad that the world is sometimes deceived by the deeds of the plain people. I have heard that a Christian is the only Bible some people read. Let us strive to be more careful so that nothing is "read" in us that is contrary to God's Word.

("Pathway Pen Points," Pa., 3-82)

The Better Plan

As a young married couple, my husband and I lived on a farm with Grandfather, who was a widower and the deacon of our church. One Sunday we discovered fresh car tracks beside our gas tank, close by the barn. We decided to keep an eye open during the nights and try to catch the thieves.

Sure enough, several nights later I awoke to hear a motor take off.

I went to the window and saw the car drive away, the tank obviously filled with *our* gas. We were upset about it because we had a hard time making ends meet the way it was. We kept planning and thinking what we would do when they came again. We thought of draining the tank and putting in water. We even mentioned shooting into the air to frighten the thieves, or shooting into their tires to keep them from making a getaway.

Grandpa didn't like this idea. He said, "I will see if I can put a stop to it." He took a chain and fastened the hose to the spigot and locked it with a dial lock. He put a note on the tank that read, "If you need gas, come to the house, and we will give you some. That way you won't need to steal it." He signed his full name.

The next night at about 2:30, we again heard a car motor. We watched breathlessly. The thieves weren't there long. Then the motor started again, and they raced down the lane with their lights off until they reached the road. To this day they have not been back.

At first I thought the thieves got off much too easily. But as the years go by, I have often compared our attitude with Grandpa's. I am sure that with our being Amish, they have more respect for our people than if we had used other methods. I also feel Grandpa's way as nearer to what Jesus would have done.

("Pathway Pen Points," Mrs. A. Y. M., Ohio, 10-82)

In School and Church

Sun Valley was an ordinary school with ordinary problems. There were days when nothing seemed to go right, and everybody seemed to be in some kind of mischief. But teacher Fannie stuck to her rules, and things were soon straightened out again. Her pupils knew that she would punish disobedience as fairly as she knew how, and they came to love and respect her.

Let's take a look at some of the incidents at Sun Valley School and then at some of the incidents that took place in the church services in the district most of the pupils attended.

In School

Heads are bent and pencils busily moving across papers. A car passes on the road outside. Suddenly heads go up, and necks are stretched as all eyes follow as long as the car can be seen.

In Church

The house is nearly filled with people. Some heads are bent. Others are turned toward the preacher. A buggy rattles past, and all heads turn toward the south. The preacher's voice goes on, but all eyes must watch the buggy disappear over the hill.

In School

Poor little Betty in the second grade had such a problem. About two in the afternoon, she would lay her head on her desk and sleep soundly for as long as her teacher would permit her.

In Church

The room is warm, and soon a head begins to nod, then drops low. Soon another head and then another finds a resting place on arms that have been propped on knees. It seems to the minister that nobody is interested in his message, so he loses some of his earnestness, and more heads drop.

In School

Fannie had the flu, and a substitute teacher had to be found quickly. Edna Mast agreed to help out. She followed Fannie's schedule until noon, when it was time to bow heads for a silent grace before being dismissed to eat. For some reason she skipped that part, and all the children went without praying. This happened all four days she taught. Later this incident was discussed at a quilting, and everybody agreed they were disappointed that Edna omitted such an important part.

In Church

As soon as the final note of the last song dies down, boys popped up from their seats with their eyes on the door. Once on the outside, they raced for the basement, where a table with lunch was ready. Not bothering to remove their hats, the ones that reached the table first began gulping down their food. The ones who were a bit too late crowded around, watching for the first opening when somebody left the table. Table waiters scurried around, trying to keep the table filled with food. Upstairs, mothers and fathers discussed the recent horse sale, double-knit [clothing], high prices, and other important matters.   ("Views and Values," Ohio, 7-81)

Heaven's Yardstick

The men of the community were building a new schoolhouse half a mile up the road. Since it was so near to home, William Yoder had told his wife, Mandy, not to pack his lunch; he would come home to eat and go back again.

As they began eating, Mandy said, "Well, how did it go at the school?"

William sighed. He dished out some potatoes for the two boys on either side of him, five-year-old Roy and three-year-old Elam. "It's going all right, I guess," he said. "It's just that I feel so dumb all the time. You know I'm no carpenter, and so often I don't know what to do or how to do it. I have to be asking all the time, and then it takes me longer than the others, especially longer than somebody like Ben Weaver and John Troyer. Either one of them can get four times as much done as I can."

After the meal was finished, William announced, "I sort of think I'll cultivate corn this afternoon."

"You mean you're not going back to the schoolhouse?" his wife asked.

"Oh, I don't think so. The little bit I get done won't make that much difference anyhow."

So that afternoon William Yoder didn't show up at the school frolic. Back in the house, Mandy felt sorry for her husband. Suddenly, she happened to think of something. She went to the calendar. Why, tomorrow was William's birthday. The least she could do was bake a cake for him. When the two boys, Roy and Elam, heard what she was doing and why, they wanted to make something for Daddy's birthday, too.

"We want to color some pictures for Daddy," Elam said. "We haven't colored for a long time."

Mandy agreed that they could each color three pictures.

"Happy Birthday, Daddy!"

Their faces glowing, their eyes shining, Roy and Elam brought the pages they had colored. They had awakened earlier than usual this morning. As William paged through the pictures, Roy said, "You can tell which three are Elam's pictures. Do you know how?"

"How?"

"Well, look. He didn't stay inside the lines nearly as well as I did. His aren't as nice."

It was clear that he had tried hard, extraordinarily hard, but still Elam crossed over the line in many places.

"Oh, you shouldn't say they aren't as nice," William corrected. "They are real good for Elam. You see, he's not as old as you are. You both did the best you could, so to me Elam's pictures are the same."

To him, Elam's pictures did mean just as much as Roy's. Elam had probably worked harder than Roy had, even though a stranger would never guess it by looking at the finished product.

As William finished his chores that morning, a thought came to him that had never come to him before. Was it possible that the heavenly Father felt the same way about his children as an earthly father did? Was it possible that the heavenly Father also measured the worth of his children by their love and devotion, and not by the greatness of their deeds, or the extent of their accomplishments? Was it possible that the heavenly Father was just as pleased with the bungling and slow work William Yoder did on the schoolhouse as he was with the expert craftsmanship and skill of Ben Weaver and John Troyer?

Quickly William finished his chores. The corn could wait for another day. He hurried to the house to tell his wife of his change of plans. She would be surprised that he was going to the schoolhouse, but he knew she would approve. Somehow, going to do his part, however weak and awkward and imperfect, doing it with cheer and willingness. Wasn't that as good a way as any to celebrate his twenty-seventh birthday?

What William Yoder discovered on the day of his birthday, many more of us should perhaps also discover. The true measure of a man is not how many talents he possesses, but how well he uses those talents, whether they are great or small.

Once a teacher explained to her class how the heart pumps blood through the body, how it has various compartments and valves. Then she asked Betty, an eighth-grade girl, to draw a diagram on the blackboard illustrating the parts of the heart. Betty did so. Then she asked Daniel, another pupil, to come forward and do the same thing.

Daniel, however, was unwilling: "You know I can't draw as good as Betty can."

"I'm not asking you to draw as good as Betty can," the teacher said firmly. "I'm asking you to draw as good as *you* can."

Which, to sum it all up, brings us back to what William Yoder discovered on his birthday: God does not measure us as much by our accomplishments as by our faithfulness in doing what we can. William learned a real lesson by the imperfect picture his little boy Elam colored. The flaws of the picture did not destroy the beauty of the love and effort that colored it.

In the same way, some of us are like little Elam, awkward and clumsy and inexperienced. We try to stay inside the lines, but we do not always succeed. How comforting to know that the heavenly Father sees our intentions and willingness, and thus can find acceptable the work of our hands and hearts. We can rest in the knowledge that, because of heaven's unusual yardstick, a person doing less may actually be doing more.   ("Views and Values," E. Stoll, 4-76)

What Do You Think?

Parents are humans, which leaves them subject to mistakes. There are no two sets of parents quite alike, which means there are no two children quite alike. So there cannot be one single set of rules or "letter of the law" to go by in raising children. Parents will usually be remembered by their children for the strong correction points they received. Two of my boys would remember me in two different ways.

For example, my one boy, when I started him on his first day of plowing, didn't think it made much difference where he dropped the plow at the end of the field, two feet away from the furrow or right in the furrow. It had to be explained over and over that if he didn't keep the ends fairly straight, it would cause extra driving to finish the field.

The next boy, a few years later, thought the plow had to be dropped exactly fourteen inches from the other furrow! It only had to be off very little, and he would turn around and try all over again, until it had to be explained over and over to him that he was doing a lot of extra driving and that it doesn't have to be exactly straight. Plus, if he is careful, he can straighten it out with the next furrow.

Now if either of the boys heard me admonishing the other boy, he would have thought, "Dad contradicts himself."

—*A Hard-learning Pupil*   (2-77)

When Parents Learn to Listen

Dear Young Parents:

Your God-given ministry to your children is going to take a good bit of your time. A story comes to mind of a young man who had a small son. The young father was always very busy. His small son often tagged along behind him and, as small children are, he was full of questions. The father often didn't take time to give him satisfactory answers to his many questions. His impatient answer often was "Don't ask so many questions. Don't you see that I am busy now?"

One Sunday afternoon, when the father was still out in the barn, hustling with his many chores, the mother of the small boy took her son on her lap. As was her custom, she opened a Bible storybook, showed him the pictures, and as best as she could, explained the stories and answered his many questions.

She came to a drawing of Jesus ascending to heaven. The boy listened with interest as she explained how the time will come someday when Jesus will come again, and how they will all want to go along to that beautiful place.

After a pause, the small boy looked up into her face and in all innocence remarked, "Dad probably won't go along, will he? He will probably be too busy."

With a tear in her eyes, the young mother thought, "Don't small children say things pretty blunt sometimes?"

("The Scriptures Have the Answers," 3-84)

Good Cows and Bad

A difficulty we experienced the first few days of pasturing was that some of the cows, when they came back to the barn, didn't know where their own stalls were. As we have water bowls and homemade comfort stalls, we rarely turn them out during the winter. The first few times the cows were brought in from the fields, the dog and the boys chased all eighteen of them into the barn at one time. About half of them meekly headed for the proper stalls, but the other half stalked around, looking for trouble and adventure.

We tried several ways of bringing order to the cow barn. The unsuccessful way was the method the boys used a few nights when by themselves they put the cows in. As they shooed that last cow into the barn, they quickly closed the door so none would run back out again. Then they surveyed the scene and at once spotted the cows that were wandering around and furthest from their stalls. The chase began.

The boys soon learned to pick out one cow at a time and pursue her right and left, up and down the alleyways, until that cow was properly parked in her own stall. Then they snapped her fast and set out after the next one. Eventually they would get all the cows tied up, but the cows ended up nervous and scared. Even those cows that had gone to their right stalls finished up running in circles.

With a little supervision, the boys learned to use the *positive approach*. They entered the stable and paid no attention to the cows that were wandering around. Instead, they quietly walked down the line of stalls and fastened the animals that were in the right place. With the well-behaved cows all tied up, the half-dozen wanderers usually presented no serious problem and fitted in with the same ease that the last pieces of a jigsaw puzzle fit into leftover spaces.

I got to wondering if there might be a lesson in handling cows that would also apply to people. Do we older ones—parents of families, teachers at school, or ministers in the church—perhaps make the same mistake our boys made? We have a sharp eye for the mischief-makers, the unruly, the disobedient. If someone is out of his place, we notice it at once.

Now there is nothing wrong with rebuking and discipline. No, not at all. The danger is in getting out of balance, or of punishing in anger, just as our boys were aching to crack those mean old cows across the tail with their sticks.

Perhaps we would accomplish more and get along better with the younger generation if we would occasionally show our approval when they are trying to do what is right by encouraging them and helping them. At least it would be a good place to start from.

("Fireside Chats," J. Stoll, 7-69)

I Didn't Have Time

We tend to find time to do those things we really want to get done. Too often the excuse "I meant to, but I didn't have time," is just that, an excuse.

Actually, when we stop to think, it doesn't make sense to blame our failures on a lack of time, because everyone has exactly the same amount of time. No one has more time in a day or any less. Each of us is given twenty-four hours every day.

What we really mean is that we used our time for other things considered more important. How different our excuses would sound if we made a rule to never say, "I didn't have time." Perhaps we would find the time if we knew we would have to tell the neighbor, "I meant to help you with that new building, but I decided my own work was more important." Or if we told the shut-in we didn't visit, "We talked of coming to visit you Friday evening, but decided we had things at home we would rather do." Or if we told the teacher, "We plan to visit school sometime, just as soon as we have nothing more important to do!"

Of course, we wouldn't want to say any of these rude and blunt things, which would only hurt other people's feelings. But perhaps we should stop and consider whether by our actions we are not saying some of these things to our friends and acquaintances without realizing it.   ("Views and Values," E. Stoll, 1-79)

Why Charlie Ran Away

"Mom, I'm invited to a taffy pulling at Dan Miller's on Wednesday evening. The young people aren't all invited. There would be too many for a taffy pulling. Rhoda has just invited a few of her special friends."

Something had shot through me. So Rhoda considered our daughter one of her "special friends."

"It's all planned," Alta said cheerfully. "Susan and Ralph will stop in for me."

Susan and Ralph. The band around my heart seemed to be getting tighter. They were Samuel Mast's children and among the "fastest" young people in our community. They tended to separate themselves from the rest of the group and form a little circle of their own.

[This was the day after a young people's gathering, so] I asked, "What kind of games did you play last night?"

Right away I sensed that Alta wasn't eager to tell me. "Just good, clean games," she answered. "I know you don't believe me. You don't trust me. As soon as I'm out of your sight, you're afraid I'll do something I'm not supposed to. I'm not a little girl anymore."

"No, you're not," I answered. "It's just that we're afraid of the company you're in with when you go with Susan and Ralph and their friends." I paused and then asked, "Did you play cards last night?"

"I didn't," Alta said quickly. "It's the boys that play cards mostly. I haven't played once, Mom. Not once."

"That doesn't mean you never will if you're around others who do," I said. "Sometime the others will want to play and will need you for a fourth player. Do you think you'll be able to say no and be different?"

"But the others won't ask me," Alta said. "They know I don't play cards, and they respect me for it."

"Their influence will rub off on you," I said.

"Maybe my influence will rub off on them," Alta said.

I sighed. I prayed silently that God would open her eyes to the truth before it was too late.

Days passed and it was cornhusking time. I swung my none-too-limber legs across the side of the wagon and climbed aboard. "All right. Let's go," I said to Alta, who was driving the horses. It was then that I noticed Babe, our Belgian colt. "Do you think Babe is safe? She's such a high-stepper."

"Of course. She's safe when she's with Charlie," Alta said. "She can't run off without taking Charlie with her, and Charlie won't [run wild]." Alta spoke with confidence. Yet as we left the bumpy lane and entered the cornfield, the team broke into a trot.

"Hold them in," I said. "Don't let them get away from you."

The horses went faster. "Mom, help me," Alta cried, and the tone in her voice made me jump to my feet immediately. When I saw the horses in action, I knew they were running away. They were going at a full gallop.

I grabbed the lines, and we both held on, using all our strength. "Whoa, Charlie! Whoa, Charlie!" Alta kept repeating. A bangboard flew off, and still the horses ran.

"Let's guide them up the hill. Maybe we can stop them there," Alta said. Gradually they slowed down and then came to a halt.

"I can't believe it," Alta kept saying. "I never dreamed Charlie would do anything like this."

"We'll wait till Dad comes," I said, my own voice unsteady. He came hurrying toward us.

"Dad, I can't believe it," Alta burst out. "I wouldn't have thought it of Charlie, would you?"

"No, I wouldn't have," her dad said slowly. "But even our faithful old Charlie is influenced by evil companions."

My heart jumped. How like Will! With a few well-chosen words, he was getting a point across better than I could with a long and unpleasant argument. I knew by the sober look on Alta's face that she knew what Dad was talking about.

Will took Charlie and his wild companion for a few trips around the cornfield. The team got a good lesson in stopping when he said "Whoa!" and plenty of exercise.

"It doesn't seem fair that Charlie is getting the same punishment Babe is," Alta said. "After all, it was *her* idea to run away."

"But the fact remains, Charlie ran away, too," I said carefully. "And he ruined a good reputation by doing it."

How I hoped Charlie's running away would be a lesson for Alta. If only she could realize that she, too, would be influenced by her companions, just as Charlie had been influenced by Babe, a much faster and more high-spirited horse.

My heart pounded against my ribs and tears came to my eyes. What if Alta got away from us? What if she were lured away from what we had tried so hard to teach her, and ended up out in the world, living a life of sin and selfishness? Would it be her fault or mine?

Suddenly, I was glad Charlie had run away. Even if Alta would not take the lesson to heart and learn from it, her mother had.   (8/9-93)

Free Rein

One day in late fall, snow fell and caught me unprepared for winter. Hoping to save a little time, I took a different way home, one with which I was not too familiar, yet I anticipated no problem. Old Dobbin obligingly trotted on, but I was not far until I began to have doubts that this road was leading me home. By now the only thing I was certain of was that I was not going where I wished to go.

A sudden inspiration came to me, and I urged my horse onward. I turned around and headed back the way I had come. Only this time I left it all to good old Dobbin. I knew I was too confused to decide for myself, and I believed that my horse wanted to get home every bit as much as I did. It was exactly the opposite of what seemed right to me, but I knew my hope was in trusting my horse and God, who had given him the homing instinct. We had not gone far before the faint outlines began to look familiar. My horse had found the way.

Is it not the same in our lives? We think we know, only to find ourselves on the wrong track. Our only way back is to turn around, let loose of the reins, and trust Another to lead the way, even when it is not what we might choose for ourselves. We know He guides the way and knows our every need.

—*A Teacher*   (Ind., 5-86)

The Shrinking Hills

I well remember when I was a small fellow, sitting between my parents on the front seat of the surrey when we were going to Uncle Andy's. There were several large hills to cross, and they looked especially big to my young eyes. As we crested the first one, I looked all the way to the bottom and up the next, and it appeared huge!

"Dad, do you think our horse can pull this buggy up that big hill?" I asked.

Dad chuckled a little and said, "Let's wait and see."

We descended the first hill and, as we started up the second one, it seemed to gradually shrink until it was only about a third of its original size. Mom then explained to me that hills always look bigger when we are at the top of another one and look at them from a distance.

"When we really come to a hill, it isn't as big as it seemed to be," she said.

Many times since then, I have thought about this and compared it with problems in life. We see these big mountains up ahead and worry about them. But if we just take a step at a time, with the strength from God, it is usually not nearly as hard to climb the "hills" as we had expected it to be.   (Mo., 4-92)

Footprints

Last winter the ground was covered with a heavy snowfall. One day a man visited our farm to inquire about buying logs from our woods. He walked to the woods, on a hill several fields away from the farm buildings. Later that evening I pointed out the footprints to the children. We admired the way they wound their way up the hill and disappeared into the woods.

Several weeks later it got warmer, and gradually the snow melted from the fields. One day I glanced toward the woods. There on the bare hillside were the footprints again, white and plain on the green and brown earth. The packed snow had not melted as fast as the rest, and we had a perfect set of footprints winding up the hill.

Each thought, action, and deed we do is a footprint. As they wind in and out through life, there are others about us who may look at them and notice the pattern they make.

Even after our life on earth is past, our footprints may remain. Perhaps the path we trod is one our children choose to follow. Or maybe it has influenced a neighbor who was looking for a guide to chart his course.

Where are our footprints leading? Do we follow the old paths established by the church leaders long ago? Or do we take our own

way and thus lead others further away from that simple godly life?
("Pathway Pen Points," Beth Witmer, Goshen, Ind., 1-88)

Bearing Crosses

This is an old story that has been told and retold. I have heard ministers relate it countless times in their sermons, and yet each time I find it as absorbing as it was before. The story comes in assorted versions.

Two men were traveling down the road, each carrying a heavy cross on his back. They carried their crosses cheerfully and willingly, for they did not seem too heavy at first. But as time passed, mile after mile, the men began to tire. The crosses pressed down heavier and heavier upon their weary backs.

At last the one man had an idea. The thought came to him that he could saw off a small piece from the end of his cross and make it lighter to carry.

"Why, a person wouldn't even notice that my cross is shorter than before. Just look at it," the man told himself. "But it's surprising how much lighter the cross is to carry."

The two men traveled on. After a while, the man who had sawed a piece from his cross began to wonder whether he couldn't saw off a little more and make his cross lighter. So he sawed off another piece. Again his cross felt much lighter, and the man felt better.

Since carrying the shorter cross was so much easier, the man started to think about his companion, still struggling with his cross, as heavy as ever.

"I say, friend, why don't you cut off a piece from your cross and make it lighter to carry?"

The weary man with the heavy cross paused just long enough to reply, "I believe I'll be given the strength to carry the cross as it is. When I reach my journey's end, all these hardships will then seem as nothing."

The man with the shortened cross shook his head and chuckled to himself, "Some people sure are stuck in their ways." Pretty soon he stopped again at the side of the road and sawed off another piece.

By this time he had only an abbreviated cross left, light and convenient to carry. The man now walked on with the shortened cross.

As he rounded a sharp bend, he came suddenly upon the bank of a swift and narrow river, whose waters churned over the sharp rocks between the two high banks. The man was just in time to see in the distance his former companion on the other side, before he disappeared behind some trees.

He looked up and down for a bridge, but could not see one anywhere. Then his eyes noticed a sign by the roadside, which he had overlooked at first. It read, "Your Cross Is Your Bridge."

His hand shook as he lifted the cross into place and dropped it across the chasm, but it did not reach the opposite cliff. Instead, it brushed on past and fell, twirling and spinning dizzily into the depth below. His shortened cross had been easier to carry, but now it let him down in the hour when he needed it the most. He stood there in despair, weeping tears of regret and remorse while his companion traveled on to his destination.

It's just a story, and it never really happened literally. Yet in a spiritual sense, we know it is happening all the time. We live in an age when along life's road we hear the sound of sawing as people, and even whole churches, stop and saw away at their crosses. Instead of making emotion-packed altar calls for instant commitment, Jesus advised people to count the cost first.

Let's not make the mistake of imagining, however, that all the sounds of sawing crosses along the roadside are coming from the popular, worldly churches. The same spirit of seeking an easier way than the Bible teaches is among us as plain people.

It's too hard to do a lot of the things the way we know is right and the way we should. Let each of us think of the things and conditions that fit our own church and community, and then ask ourselves if we want to choose the right way or the easy way. The way we decide may make a tremendous difference when we come to that place in the road where we read the sign that says, "Your Cross Is Your Bridge."

("Views and Values," E. Stoll, 1-73)

No Longer Time

Seventeen-year-old Sam stood before his father, his eyes stormy with anger and rebellion. "And you turned my horse out to pasture?

You knew I needed him!"

Dan put both buckets of feed down and stood facing his son. "Yes, I did, and you know why. I told you I don't want you to go to that party this evening. You had better stay at home. You know what all goes on at those parties. It's not good." And then as an afterthought, he added, "And what would you do if the end of the world should come at such a time?"

Sam turned away and walked toward the implement shed. He seethed inwardly. He knew there was no use arguing with his father. Yet this was one time Sam was going to have his own way. He would talk to the neighbors and go with a buddy.

From beneath his buggy seat, he pulled out a package of strong drink. Then, with the package in hand, he walked with determination out the lane and down the road. "Nobody, but nobody, is going to stop me from going tonight," he seethed.

The thought was hardly through his mind when suddenly the ground shook beneath his feet as a mighty blast echoed through the air. He stopped in his tracks. He looked up. His face paled at what he saw. His limbs began to shake, and his eyes bulged with terror. He tried to drop the package he held in his hands, but he couldn't. It just stuck to his fingers.

With a weak cry, he sank to the ground. He had known this day was coming sometime, yet he had not thought it would come so soon. Gone was his dream of having a few years yet of a good time, and then he would come to the church, be baptized, and settle down.

Suddenly the party which he had hoped to attend no longer seemed important. Instead, he found himself wishing for another chance to do better, show submission to his parents and God, be converted, and join the church.

But there was no longer time. *Time* was no longer! (7-81)

Postscript

FAMILY LIFE is still being published, and perhaps a compilation from the second 25 years will someday be of equal interest. Putting these excerpts together has been an enriching experience for me. I would like to make a few closing comments.

I wanted the most frequently quoted writers to provide brief biographical sketches of themselves, to help readers get to know them a little as individuals. I also asked for one of them to write a Postscript.

In response, I was respectfully informed, "We feel we will be getting enough publicity by having our names appear frequently in the book. There is no need to draw further attention to ourselves, or to in any way blow our own horns or that of Pathway."

In our modern world, where so many people seem to be promoting someone or something, often loudly and boastfully, this typical Amish attitude is refreshing. In a quiet manner, I was being told that it is not the *writers* who are significant; instead, if the ideas have value, it is the *words* that are important.

With so many negative stories and ideas bombarding us every day, I hope these writings will have some positive meaning for us. We can learn things from people who are different from ourselves. We can respect differences and even enjoy them. Sometimes in arguing our own point of view, we become closed to considering a different perspective. "Judge not, that you be not judged" is often quoted by the Amish (Matt. 7:1). We can understand and even respect other ideas without necessarily agreeing with them or accepting them as our own.

When we learn about a culture or way of thinking different from our own, we also can come to learn and understand *ourselves* better. We may like some of what we see; other aspects we may not. Indeed, each person's complex web of experiences results in the unique individuals that we are. This is something we must learn to recognize, not deny.

Each culture is an expression of the growth of a society, religion, way of life, set of values. Each person in that society is an individual expression of the development, acceptance, or denial of those elements through personal experiences in that person's life and relationships.

In the Amish world, it is not the individual so much as the group that is important. Neither their world nor ours is perfect. Far from it. Yet the Amish believe we should focus not so much on visible things, but rather on the coming world, God's kingdom. Thus these writers would not want to be praised for their writings or given any special attention.

Recognition should instead go to the faith and the God who has inspired them. Among the Amish, it is certainly appropriate to give credit to the writer, but to give the glory to God. May it be so.

—*Brad Igou*

Recommended Reading

SOME information in print about the Amish is not accurate. The following books will help you learn more about the Amish:

General Overviews

Hostetler, John A. *Amish Society.* 4th ed. Baltimore: Johns Hopkins, 1993. Definitive academic work on the Amish, giving a general sociological analysis of Amish society across the United States.

Kraybill, Donald. *The Riddle of Amish Culture.* Johns Hopkins, 1989. Dealing with Lancaster Amish, it answers many difficult questions about why the Amish do what they do. Available in a condensed version: *Puzzles of Amish Life.* Intercourse, Pa.: Good Books, 1990.

Kreps, George M., et al. *A Quiet Moment in Time: A Contemporary View of Amish Society.* Mechanicsburg, Pa.: Carlisle Printing, 1997. This readable book is one of the finest overviews of the Amish today, covering subject areas clearly and concisely.

Good, Merle and Phyllis. *20 Most Asked Questions About the Amish and Mennonites.* Good Books, 1995. Answers some of the most-common questions about these groups.

Längin, Bernd G. *Plain and Amish: An Alternative to Modern Pessimism.* Herald Press, 1994. Presents the Amish of Allen County, Indiana, and their origins. Photos by author, who spent time with them.

Nolt, Steven. *A History of the Amish.* Good Books, 1992. Enjoyable, well-written, thorough look at Amish history, from European beginnings 450 years ago, divisions, and change in America.

Schreiber, William I. *Our Amish Neighbors.* Univ. of Chicago Press, 1962; College of Wooster, Ohio: William I. Schreiber, 1992. Based on careful research. Interesting reading. Shows appreciation for Ohio Amish life.

Specific Topics

Butterfield, Jim. *Driving the Amish.* Herald Press, 1997. Visits with Ohio Amish reveal their daily life. Stunning photography by Doyle Yoder.

Committee of Amish Women, compilers. Deluxe ed. *Amish Cooking.* Herald Press, 1992. Choice recipes lovingly shared.

Fisher, Sara, and Rachel Stahl. *The Amish School.* Good Books, 1986. Readable account of the theory and daily operation of the one-room school. An Amish schoolteacher is coauthor.

Kraybill, Donald, ed. *The Amish and the State.* Johns Hopkins, 1993. Writers detail legal problems the Amish have had with governments over their religious beliefs on health, education, taxes, etc.

_____ and Steven Nolt. *Amish Enterprise: From Plows to Profits.* Johns Hopkins, 1995. How limited farmland and population growth led to an array of Amish businesses in Lancaster County; Amish society coping.

_____ and Marc Olshan, eds. *The Amish Struggle with Modernity.* Hanover, N.H.: Univ. Press of New England, 1994. Writers focus on such areas as education, tourism, telephones, farm vs. factory, and women's roles.

Raber, Ben J. *Almanac.* Baltic, Ohio: Raber's Book Store, annual. Lists church Sundays, Scripture references, hymns, ordained ministry, and Amish districts.

Roth, John D., trans. and ed. *Letters of the Amish Division: A Sourcebook.* Goshen, Ind.: Mennonite Historical Society, 1993. Documents and interprets events beginning in 1693 that led to separation between the Amish and the rest of the Anabaptists or Mennonites.

Scott, Stephen. *The Amish Wedding.* Good Books, 1988. A detailed look at weddings, funerals, baptisms, and other activities of Old Order groups. All of Scott's books are highly recommended.

_____. *Plain Buggies: Amish, Mennonite, and Brethren Horse-Drawn Transportation.* Good Books, 1981. Fascinating details, with many photos of a wide variety of rigs.

_____. *Why Do They Dress That Way?* Good Books, 1986. The title says it all. A thorough look at plain clothing, dispelling many of the myths and misconceptions behind what is worn.

_____ and Kenneth Pellman. *Living Without Electricity.* Good Books, 1990. Explains ingenious ways the Amish operate all kinds of things without the use of electrical power.

Stoltzfus, Louise. *Amish Women: Lives and Stories.* Good Books, 1994. Interviews with several Amish women. Gives a personal glimpse into their lives as individual members of the Amish community.

Picture Books

Bowen, Keith, illustrator, with Donald Kraybill. *Among the Amish.* Philadelphia: Courage Books, 1998. Gorgeous collection of original drawings and commentary, showing the Lancaster Amish.

Niemeyer, Lucian, photos, with Donald Kraybill. *Old Order Amish.* Johns Hopkins, 1996 reprint. Excellent book combining superb photographs of the Lancaster Amish with insightful text.

Fiction True to Amish Life

Bender, Carrie. Fiction series: Miriam's Journal, Whispering Brook, Dora's Diary. Herald Press, 1993-2000. Author lives among Lancaster Amish.

Borntrager, Mary Christner. Fiction about Ohio Amish by author raised in Amish family: Ellie's People Series. Herald Press, 1988-97.

Wojtasik, Ted. *No Strange Fire*. Herald Press, 1996. Novel by author who lived with the Amish in Big Valley, Pennsylvania.

Yoder, Joseph W. *Rosanna of the Amish*. 3d ed. Herald Press, 1995. Classic true story by son of Irish orphan raised Amish in central Pennsylvania.

Children's Fiction, True to Amish Life

Ammon, Richard. *Growing Up Amish*. New York: Macmillan Children's Book Group, 1989. For older readers. Delightful book on a year in the life of an Amish girl: about school, church, chores at home on the farm.

Bellafiore, Sharyn. *Amos and Abraham*. Good Books, 1994. Two boys, Amish and Hasidic Jew, learn about their differences and what they have in common on a visit to Lancaster.

De Angeli, Marguerite. *Henner's Lydia*. Herald Press, 1998 reissue of classic 1936 book about an Amish girl's farm life; illustrated by author.

Stoltzfus, John R. *A Day on the Farm with Samuel: The Life of an Amish Boy*. Riverdale, N.J.: J & M Publishing, 1995. With simple text and illustrations, a delightful book for young readers.

The Compiler

BRAD IGOU first became interested in the Amish of Lancaster County as a tour guide and came to know some Amish personally. He spent three months living with an Amish family as he studied for his sociology-anthropology major at Ithaca (N.Y.) College. Brad helped with farmwork, attended church services, visited one-room schools, and prepared papers for college.

After graduating with highest honors from Ithaca in 1973, Brad spent three years in Costa Rica. As a Peace Corps volunteer, he developed agriculture in rural areas of Guanacaste.

Later Brad was an English teacher in Japan for eight years. He lived in Kyoto with a Japanese family, taught at a private Episcopal girls high school, directed a local English language center, and wrote articles on Japanese culture, art, and religion for the English-language publication *Kansai Time Out*.

Back home in Lancaster, Brad was employed by Amish Country Tours and started reading and compiling writings from the Amish periodical *Family Life*. He has become vice president and co-owner of the Amish Experience, a center interpreting Amish culture to visitors. Brad was deeply involved in writing and producing *Jacob's Choice*, presented at the Amish Experience Theatre. This multimedia story tells of an Amish boy's decision to join the church and explores Anabaptist history, nonresistance, and adult baptism.

In July 1993, Brad presented a paper "Traditional Family Functions and the Amish" at the international conference on Amish society, at Elizabethtown College. He continues to compile information on the Amish and contributes monthly articles to a local visitors guide, *Amish Country News*.

Brad Igou also enjoys art exhibits, theater, film, and music. In 1998 Brad began serving as president of the Lancaster Community Concert Association. He was born in Hanover, Pennsylvania, and baptized in the Lutheran Church.